OXFORD
UNIVERSITY PRESS

fourth edition

English File

Intermediate Student's Book B

Units 6–10

WITH ONLINE PRACTICE

Christina Latham-Koenig
Clive Oxenden
Jerry Lambert

Paul Seligson and Clive Oxenden
are the original co-authors of
English File 1 and *English File 2*

Contents

English File

fourth edition

Welcome to **English File fourth edition**. This is how to use the Student's Book, Online Practice, and the Workbook in and out of class.

Student's Book and Workbook

The **Student's Book** contains all the language and skills you need to improve your English, with Grammar, Vocabulary, Pronunciation, and skills work in every File. There is an extra Culture and Reading section to help you deepen your knowledge of cultural topics and wider world events.

Use your Student's Book in class with your teacher.

The **Workbook** contains Grammar, Vocabulary, and Pronunciation practice for every lesson.

Use your Workbook for homework or for self-study to practise language and to check your progress.

Go to **englishfileonline.com** and use the code on your Access Card to log into the Online Practice.

ACTIVITIES   AUDIO   VIDEO   RESOURCES

LOOK AGAIN

- Review the language from every lesson.
- Watch the videos and listen to all the class audio as many times as you like.

PRACTICE

- Improve your skills with extra Reading, Writing, Listening and Speaking practice.
- Use the interactive video to practise Practical English.

CHECK YOUR PROGRESS

- Test yourself on the language from the File and get instant feedback.
- Try an extra Challenge.

SOUND BANK

- Use the Sound Bank videos to practise and improve your pronunciation of English sounds.

Online Practice

Look again at Student's Book language you want to review or that you missed in class, do extra **Practice** activities, and **Check your progress** on what you've learnt so far.

Use the Online Practice to learn outside the classroom and get instant feedback on your progress.

englishfileonline.com

Where was the film made?

I think it was shot in New York.

G passive (all tenses) **V** cinema **P** regular and irregular past participles

1 READING

a Look at the definition of an *extra* and the photos in the article. In pairs, can you think of three negative things about being an extra?

> **extra** /'ekstrə/ *n.* a person who is employed to play a very small part in a film, usually as a member of a crowd

b Read the article. Are your ideas mentioned?

c Read the article again. Complete the paragraph headings with words from the list.

**expensive   miming   ordinary
patient   real   secrets   weather**

The world of extras

Without extras, most film and TV scenes would be empty and unrealistic. But while we're obsessed with movie stars, we never hear much about the extras, because, of course, that's their job – not to be noticed. So what is the world of extras really like?

1 They have to be _____.

Days on set can be very long, sometimes lasting more than 15 hours. A lot of that time is spent just sitting around, waiting to be used in a scene, or repeating a single shot a dozen times. Extras usually spend their 'waiting time' reading or playing cards. 'There are days you get to the set and you wait and wait, but you aren't used,' says Amy Rogers, a regular extra in TV shows, including *Homeland*.

2 They need to be good at _____.

Extras often need to make a scene appear alive and busy, while at the same time remaining totally silent so as not to interfere with the actors' dialogue. This means they have to pretend to have a conversation without actually making any noise. Also, dance scenes are often filmed in silence and the music is added in later. When a crowd scene was being filmed for the movie *Jersey Girl*, the extras had to pretend to clap and cheer. But it was all done in silence, and when they clapped, their hands never touched.

On the set of Bollywood film *Nayak*

3 They have to put up with all kinds of _____.

Sometimes, when a winter scene is being filmed, and all the extras are wearing thick jackets and hats and gloves, it's actually 30 degrees and the snow is fake. You can tell whether it's really cold if you can see the breath coming out of people's mouths. Also, when scenes are being filmed inside during the summer, the air conditioning has to be turned off because of the noise.

4 They have to be able to keep _____.

Phones aren't allowed on set, and photos are strictly forbidden. While the film *Insurgent* was being made, one extra took a photo of the set and posted it online. Since then, she has never been employed as an extra again.

On the set of *Ripper Street*

d Work in pairs. Can you answer these questions from memory? Then quickly look back at the article to check.

1 What do extras often do while they're waiting?
2 What did the extras have to do in the crowd scene in *Jersey Girls*?
3 How do you know if the snow is real or not in winter scenes?
4 What did an extra do during the filming of *Insurgent*, and what happened as a result?
5 Why are a lot of British films made in Eastern Europe?
6 Why are inflatable extras popular nowadays?
7 What happens when extras watch TV?

e Do you know anybody who's been an extra? What in? Why do you think some people enjoy being extras? Would you like to be one? Why (not)?

5 They are extremely _____.

Although extras aren't individually very well paid, a film with a lot of extras needs a big production budget, especially in Britain. The cost of extras is one of the reasons why epics such as *Ben-Hur* are largely a thing of the past. *Gandhi* was the last one – the funeral scene alone needed 300,000 extras. This is why now a lot of British films are being shot in countries where extras are paid less, for example, in Eastern Europe.

6 Sometimes they are not _____.

Nowadays, where possible, crowds are digitized. In *Gladiator*, they used 2,000 live actors to create a digital crowd of about 35,000 people. For some of the crowd scenes, in addition to the real-life extras and the digital ones, they also used cut-outs made of cardboard. But digital extras can look fake, and cardboard extras can look very two-dimensional, particularly if the camera moves. The latest thing is inflatable extras, which look more real. They can be deflated, stored – a crowd of 10,000 can fit into one large truck – and reused.

'Inflatable crowd' dolls

7 They can't watch films like _____ people.

Once you know how a movie has been filmed, it's hard to just watch it like any other person. 'I can't watch TV any more without looking at the extras to see who's doing it right and who's doing it wrong,' said one extra.

2 GRAMMAR passive (all tenses)

a Look at six extracts from the text. What tense or form of the passive are the verbs?

1 You wait and wait, but you aren't used.
2 When a crowd scene was being filmed,…
3 But it was all done in silence…
4 Sometimes, when a winter scene is being filmed,…
5 …the air conditioning has to be turned off…
6 Since then, she has never been employed…

b **G** p.142 Grammar Bank 6A

3 PRONUNCIATION regular and irregular past participles

a Look at the sound groups and the past participles. Tick (✓) the groups where the sounds of the pink letters are all the same. If they aren't the same, circle the word that is different.

1 **d** filmed used recorded owned
2 **t** finished directed released booked
3 bought caught worn drawn
4 **ɒ** shot gone lost done
5 **əʊ** forgotten spoken stolen known
6 **e** spent said meant read
7 **eɪ** made paid taken fallen
8 **ʌ** won put sung drunk
9 built written driven given

b **6.2** Listen and check. What are the sounds in the circled participles? Practise saying the groups of words.

c **6.3** Listen and change the sentences into the present or past passive.

1 ») *They shot the film in Poland. The film…*

(*The film was shot in Poland.*

4 VOCABULARY cinema

a Look at some extracts from the text in **1**. What do you think the highlighted words mean?

1 A lot of that time is spent just sitting around, waiting to be used in a **scene**.
2 Phones aren't allowed **on set**.
3 This is why now a lot of British films are being **shot** in Eastern Europe.
4 The cost of extras is one of the reasons why **epics** such as *Ben-Hur* are largely a thing of the past.

b **V** p.159 **Vocabulary Bank** Cinema

c Explain the difference between these pairs of words and phrases.

1 *a plot* and *a script*
2 *a horror film* and *a thriller*
3 *a musical* and *a soundtrack*
4 *the cast* and *the stars*
5 *a dubbed film* and *a film with subtitles*
6 *the set of a film* and *the film was set in…*
7 *a critic* and *a review*

5 LISTENING

a Read about the film *Schindler's List*. Have you seen it? If yes, did you like it? If no, would you like to see it? What other Spielberg films have you seen and enjoyed?

Schindler's List is a 1993 historical epic directed by Steven Spielberg. The film is based on the true story of Oskar Schindler, a Czech businessman, who saved the lives of more than a thousand Polish-Jewish refugees during the Second World War. The film was shot in black and white. It stars Liam Neeson, Ralph Fiennes, and Ben Kingsley. It is often listed among the greatest films ever made, and it won seven Oscars, including Best Picture and Best Director.

b 🔊 **6.7** Look at the photos of Dagmara Walkowicz and Spielberg. Where were they and what do you think Dagmara was doing in the black-and-white photo? Listen to Part 1 of an interview with Dagmara and check.

c Listen again and mark the sentences **T** (true) or **F** (false). Correct the **F** sentences.

1 When the film company came to Krakow, Dagmara was working as a teacher.
2 She got a job doing translations for them.
3 There was a party at the hotel to celebrate Spielberg's birthday.
4 Spielberg's interpreter was late.
5 Dagmara was very nervous, so she drank a bottle of champagne to give herself courage.
6 Spielberg was very pleased with the way she did her job.

> 🔍 **Making notes**
> When we make notes, we only write down key words, e.g. we write *film set every day* **NOT** ~~She had to go to the film set every day~~.

d ◆ 6.8 Now listen to three extracts from Part 2 of the interview. Complete the gaps with the key words.

1 I had to go to the ▢▢▢▢ and Spielberg's ▢▢ to the Polish ▢▢ , and also to the ▢▢ .
2 It was ▢▢ ▢▢ , and I often felt as if I was a ▢▢ ▢▢ .
3 The ▢▢ was when we had to ▢▢ a ▢▢ ▢▢ and ▢▢ because Spielberg thought it ▢▢ exactly ▢▢ .

e ◆ 6.9 You're now going to listen to the whole of Part 2. Read the questions. Then listen and write down some of the key words.

1 How many times were some scenes repeated? How did that make Dagmara feel?
2 Why did Spielberg start shouting at her? What happened after that?
3 In general, how did Spielberg treat her? What example does she give?
4 What scenes was she going to appear in as an extra? Why did she not appear in the final version of the film?
5 Did she ever work with Spielberg again?
6 What offer did Spielberg make to Dagmara? Does she regret not accepting it?

f Compare your key words with a partner. Then listen again and try to add more.

g Now, with a partner, answer the questions in **e**. Use your key words.

h Would you like to have done Dagmara's job? Do you think she made the right decision in the end?

6 SPEAKING

a Read the cinema interview. Think about your answers and reasons.

THE
★★ **CINEMA** ★★
INTERVIEW

1 **Can you think of a film you've seen which…?**
★ was incredibly funny
★ made you feel good
★ had a very sad ending
★ you've seen several times
★ sent you to sleep
★ had a memorable soundtrack

2 **Do you prefer…?**
★ seeing films at home or in the cinema
★ seeing a American films
         b other foreign films
         c films from your country
★ seeing foreign films dubbed or with subtitles

3 **Tell me about a really good film you've seen in the last year.**
★ What kind of film is it?
★ Is it based on a book or on a real event?
★ Where and when is it set?
★ Who stars in it? Who is it directed by?
★ Does it have a good plot?
★ Does it have a good soundtrack?
★ Why do you like it?

b In pairs, interview each other. Ask for and give as much information as you can. Do you have similar tastes?

7 WRITING

Ⓦ p.119 Writing A film review
Write a description of a film you would recommend.

She can't be his mother.

She is his mother. She looks very young for her age.

G modals of deduction: *might, can't, must*   **V** the body   **P** diphthongs

1 READING & SPEAKING

a Do you have a profile photo or photos that you use on social media? Show any that you can to your partner. Why did you choose them? How often do you change them?

b Read the article about choosing profile photos. Tick (✓) two true statements.

1 The writer only likes certain types of profile photos.
2 The writer jokes about why people choose common types of photos.
3 The article is funny because the writer is rude about common types of profile photos.

What your profile photo says about you

Choosing a profile photo is a serious business. It will be the first thing old school friends, jealous exes, and even potential bosses see when they search for you online. Your image depends entirely on your choice of photo. Here are the most common types of profile photo on social media. Is yours one of them? And if so, what does it say about you?

The portrait
A clear, close-up photo.

What it says about you You are quite boring. If it's a selfie, you are quite annoying.

The childhood photo
A cute picture of you as a baby.

What it says about you You are the type of person who thinks that everything used to be better than it is now. You still listen to the same music, wear the same clothes, and love the same things you did at school, and you'll probably never change.

The pet
Your pet looking adorable.

What it says about you It depends on what kind of animal it is. Cat: You are a woman without a boyfriend. Dog: You are a man without a girlfriend. Snake: You are a teenage boy or death metal fan.

The wedding photo
Man, woman, dress, suit – you know, the usual.

What it says about you You want everyone to think that you are a grown-up. You don't go out and have a good time any more. No, you are married! Also, you don't feel you exist as an individual any more, and don't have any friends of your own.

The family photo
A photo of your children / baby.

What it says about you The main thing you have accomplished in your adult life is having children. You used to be fun and fabulous and have a lot of friends, but now all you talk about is nappies and children's TV.

The popular culture reference
A picture of a cartoon character, a movie poster, a book cover, a musical act, a celebrity, etc.

What it says about you You have no personality of your own. Your identity depends on your entertainment choices – television, music, sci-fi, literary, or other. You own at least two T-shirts with stupid slogans on them.

The party photo
You, often with other people, enjoying yourself at a party.

What it says about you You are young and stupid, and will be fired from at least one job for something you posted on Facebook. One day, you might regret this picture and replace it with a wedding picture, and then photos of your children.

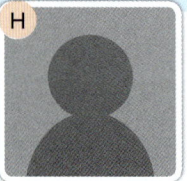

No photo at all
An icon, not a photo.

What it says about you You are technologically incompetent and don't know what a jpeg is; or you think you're too busy to find a photo; or you think not having a photo is 'cool'. Having no profile photo is annoying for everybody else. Get a photo.

Adapted from a website

c Now read a positive interpretation of each type of profile photo and match it to A–H.

1. ☐ You adore animals – in fact, in many ways, you prefer them to people.
2. ☐ You are a normal person and are happy with your appearance.
3. ☐ You're a dedicated parent and your children always come first.
4. ☐ You're a very private person. You prefer to talk to people face to face rather than use social media.
5. ☐ You're very up to date – you know everything about the latest films, TV, and books.
6. ☐ Your friends and your social life are what matter most to you.
7. ☐ The day you got married was the happiest day of your life.
8. ☐ You had a wonderful childhood.

d Talk to a partner.

- Is your profile photo type included? If yes, do you agree with any of the positive or negative interpretations of your profile photo(s)? If not, what is your interpretation of your photo?
- Can you think of any friends or family members whose photos fit with the interpretations in the article?

2 GRAMMAR modals of deduction

a 🔊 6.10 Listen to two people talking about a photo. Complete the sentences.

A I love your profile picture. How old are you in the photo?

B I ¹_____ be about five or six. Definitely not more than that.

A Where are you?

B Do you know, I can't remember. It ²_____ be the south of France. My grandmother had a house near Montpellier, so we sometimes spent the summer there.

A It ³_____ be the south of France – not in summer. You're wearing boots and a sweater! And it doesn't look like a Mediterranean beach.

B No, you're right. It ⁴_____ be Scotland, then. We sometimes went there.

b Look at the highlighted modal verbs and answer the questions.

1. Which modal verbs mean *it's possible*? *might*, _____
2. Which modal verb means *it's very probable*? _____
3. Which modal verb means *it's impossible*? _____

c 🅖 p.143 **Grammar Bank 6B**

d Look at the photos of four people. Make four deductions about each person, one with *must*, one with *might / could / may*, and one with *can't* + the phrases in the list. You can use the phrases more than once.

- be American
  be Asian
  be English
  be Mexican
  be Spanish

- be a criminal
  be a millionaire
  be a model
  be a politician
  be a sportsperson

- have a degree
  have a fashion business
  have a good job
  have a grandchild
  have an Olympic medal

- be in his / her 20s
  be in his / her 30s
  be in his / her 50s
  be in his / her 80s

(I think) he might be English.

True, but he could be American, too.

e 🅒 **Communication** Judging by appearances **p.107** Find out who the four people are. Were you surprised?

3 VOCABULARY the body

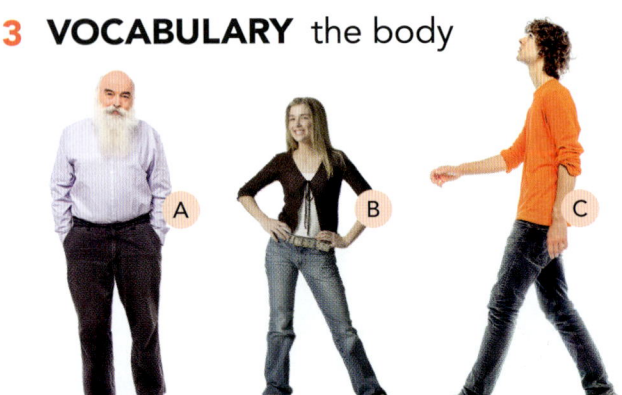

a Look at the three photos. What do the people look like?

Who…?

1 ▭ is tall and thin
2 ▭ has straight blonde hair
3 ▭ is bald and slightly overweight
4 ▭ has dark curly hair
5 ▭ has a beard
6 ▭ is quite short and slim

b **V** p.160 **Vocabulary Bank** The body

c ◐6.16 Listen and follow the instructions.

4 PRONUNCIATION diphthongs

> 🔍 **Diphthongs**
> Diphthongs are a combination of two short vowel sounds, e.g. the /e/ sound and the /ə/ sound said together make the longer /eə/ sound.

a ◐6.17 Read the information box. Then listen and repeat the words and sounds below.

1 aɪ	2 eɪ	3 əʊ	4 aʊ	5 eə

b Write the words from the list in the correct columns.

bite eyes face hair mouth nose shoulders
smile stare taste throw toes

c ◐6.18 Listen and check. Then practise saying the phrases below.

f**ai**r h**ai**r   narr**ow** sh**ou**lders   a w**i**de m**ou**th
br**ow**n **eye**s   a R**o**man n**o**se   a r**ou**nd f**a**ce

---

d Do the quiz with a partner. Answer with *your / their* + a part of the body.

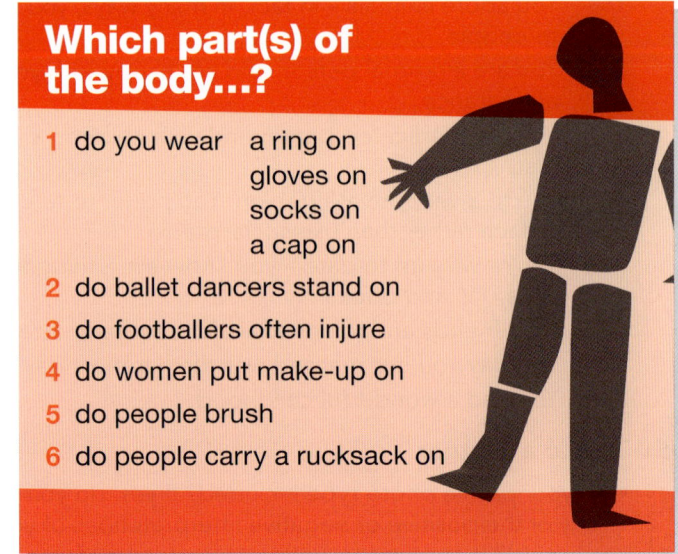

Which part(s) of the body…?

1 do you wear   a ring on
                gloves on
                socks on
                a cap on
2 do ballet dancers stand on
3 do footballers often injure
4 do women put make-up on
5 do people brush
6 do people carry a rucksack on

5 READING & LISTENING

a Read the definition of *charisma*. Can you name any public figures who you think have charisma?

> **charisma** /kəˈrɪzmə/ *n.* the powerful personal quality that some people have which attracts and impresses other people

b Look at the photo on p.63. One of the men is a journalist and one is a charisma coach. Who do you think is who? Why?

c Read the beginning of the journalist's article and check your answer to **b**. Answer the questions.

1 What experience does Danish Sheikh have?
2 Is he successful?
3 What did he do yesterday? Why?
4 What problems does Colin have?

d With a partner, tick (✓) any of the things in the list that you think a person with charisma does.

A person with charisma…

1 ▭ shows other people what he / she is like
2 ▭ makes other people feel important
3 ▭ talks a lot about himself / herself
4 ▭ never says anything about himself / herself
5 ▭ is self-confident
6 ▭ stands with his / her feet apart and arms wide
7 ▭ makes eye contact, but doesn't stare
8 ▭ uses a lot of hand gestures
9 ▭ speaks very slowly
10 ▭ listens to people carefully

e ◐6.19 Listen to Colin talking about what he learns. Check your answers to **d**.

Can you learn how to be charismatic?

Colin Drury and Danish Sheikh

In the 21st century, *charisma* is the quality that people in all fields of life, from business to politics, would most like to have. But can you learn it? The man I have just met thinks so. His name is Danish Sheikh, and he is a charisma coach. He has worked with Microsoft, Yahoo, and the BBC, and he thinks he can turn anyone into George Clooney. He charges £150 an hour, and plenty of people are paying. And for two days, I'm going to be his student.

Yesterday, he followed me everywhere and watched how I behaved with people – in shops, in the hairdresser's, and in work meetings. His impressions of me are not good – for example, I can't make conversation, I have negative body language, and I don't smile enough. I also seem bored when I'm talking to people.

'But don't worry!' Sheikh says, cheerfully. 'We're going to fix all this.'

f Listen again. What does Colin say about…?
1 talking about yourself
2 remembering a past success
3 how to enter a room
4 what happens if you aren't really listening

g 🔊 6.20 At the end of the two days, Colin has a practical test. Listen and summarize.
1 In the pub, Colin has to…
2 Sheikh helps him by…
3 In the end, Colin thinks that charisma is about…

h Look at these 'body' phrases from the listening. Can you demonstrate them?

> stand with your feet apart
> have your chin up and your shoulders back
> make eye contact   use hand gestures
> cross your arms   shake hands   give a thumbs up

i Do you think it's possible to teach people to have charisma? Would you ever do a course like this? Why (not)?

6 ▶ VIDEO LISTENING

a Watch Part 1 of *A day with a personal stylist* and pause when Sam has tried on four outfits. Which do you like best?

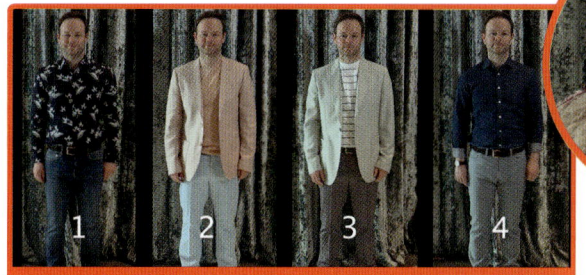

b Watch the rest of Part 1. Which outfit did Sam like best? Why?

c Put the events in the correct order. Then watch Part 1 again and check.

☐ Sam goes shopping with Elin.
☐ Elin asks Sam questions about his lifestyle.
☐ Sam tries on four outfits.
☐ Sam meets Elin at the Fashion Lounge.
☐ Sam fills in a questionnaire.

d Watch Part 2 and complete Elin's golden rules for dressing well.
1 Look at _____ before you go shopping.
2 Stay _____ when you go shopping.
3 It doesn't matter _____ you've got – you can look good.
4 Everyone should have _____ in their wardrobe.

e Do you agree with Elin's rules?

 Go online to watch the video and review the lesson

GRAMMAR

Circle a, b, or c.

1 Elliot served, but the ball _____ into the net.
   a went   b was going   c had gone
2 The athlete fell when she _____ towards the finishing line.
   a run   b was running   c had run
3 I didn't realize that you two _____ before.
   a didn't meet   b weren't meeting
   c hadn't met
4 A I can't find my glasses anywhere.
   B _____ them when you left home this morning?
   a Did you wear   b Were you wearing
   c Had you worn
5 _____ walk to work, or do you drive?
   a Do you use to   b Do you usually
   c Use you to
6 When I was a child, I _____ like vegetables.
   a don't used to   b didn't used to
   c didn't use to
7 _____ do any sport at university?
   a Did you use to   b Use you to
   c Did you used to
8 Lots of famous films _____ in San Francisco.
   a have shot   b have been shot
   c has been shot
9 He hates _____ about his private life.
   a asking   b being asking   c being asked
10 Why _____ in New Zealand?
   a is the film being made   b is the film making   c is making the film
11 Many people believe that Columbus _____ America.
   a didn't really discover   b wasn't really discovered   c weren't really discovered
12 A I've just rung the doorbell, but there's no answer.
   B They _____ in the garden. Have a look.
   a can't be   b might be   c can be
13 I'm 29 and he's a bit older than me, so he _ in his thirties now.
   a must be   b may be   c can't be
14 A Ann and Simon have broken up!
   B That _____ true! I saw them together just now.
   a mustn't be   b might be   c can't be
15 A Does your sister know Liam?
   B She _____ him. I'm not sure.
   a can't know   b may know   c can know

VOCABULARY

a Write the parts of the body that you use to do these actions.

1 smile _____   3 smell _____   5 bite _____
2 stare _____   4 clap _____

b Circle the correct word or phrase.

1 Arsenal *won / beat* Chelsea 2–0.
2 Can you book a tennis *course / court* on Friday?
3 Sports players are very careful not to *get injured / get fit*.
4 Real Madrid *scored / kicked* a goal just before half-time.
5 I *do / go* swimming every morning during the week.

c Complete the words.

1 Luke is a very cl_____ friend. I've known him all my life.
2 My wife and I have a lot in c_____.
3 Gina and I lost t_____ after we both changed jobs.
4 We g_____ to know each other very quickly.
5 Linda is getting married next month. Her f_____ is Italian.

d Write words beginning with *s* for the definitions.

1 _____ the music of a film
2 _____ the translation of the dialogue of a film on screen
3 _____ _____ images often created by a computer
4 _____ the most important actor in a film
5 _____ a part of a film which happens in one place

e Complete the sentences with one word.

1 I love working _____ at the gym. I go every evening.
2 The player was sent _____ for insulting the referee.
3 My sister and her boyfriend have split _____.
4 Did you know Jane is going _____ with Jessie's brother?
5 Is there anything good _____ TV tonight?

PRONUNCIATION

a Practise the words and sounds.

Vowel sounds   Consonant sounds

bird   phone   egg   owl   television   zebra   dog   tie

b p.166–7 Sound Bank Say more words for each sound.

c What sound in **a** do the pink letters have in these words?

1 book**ed**   2 cr**ow**d   3 **eye**s   4 sh**ou**lders   5 w**or**ld

d Underline the stressed syllable.

1 re|fe|ree   3 spec|ta|tors   5 co|lleague
2 re|view   4 di|rec|tor

CAN YOU understand this text?

a Read the article once. What does the article say is the best exercise for all body types?

What is the best sport for your body type?

Just because someone has dreamt of playing football from childhood does not mean it is the best sport for him or her. Finding the sport your body is best suited to can make a big difference to how much you enjoy it and how good at it you are.

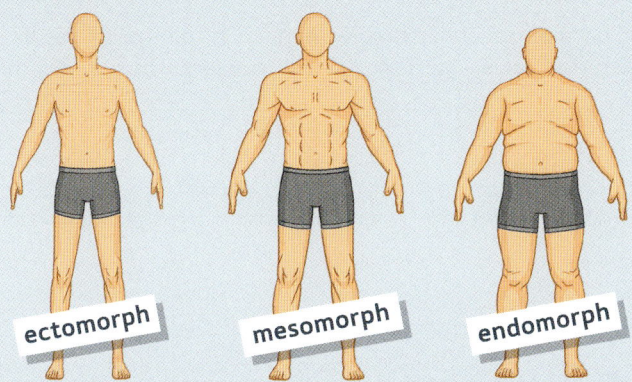

ectomorph   mesomorph   endomorph

A person with an **ectomorph** body type is tall and slim with little fat or muscle. This person has narrow shoulders, chest, and hips, and thin arms and legs. Ectomorphs have difficulty putting on weight because of a fast metabolism. ¹ __ . What suits ectomorphs is endurance sports. Marathon running, swimming, and football are excellent choices for them. ² __ , basketball may also be a great option. Ectomorphs also generally do well in gymnastics.

Mesomorph body types are the stereotypical image of an athlete. ³ __ . Mesomorphs can put on or lose weight easily and build muscle quickly. ⁴ __ . Possibilities range from weightlifting and boxing to athletic sprinting and cycling for shorter distances.

A person who is an **endomorph** naturally carries more body fat. ⁵ __ . They are often short, with a high waist, and well developed upper arms and thighs. While it may seem that an endomorph will not be very athletic, they can be very good at power sports because of their larger mass. ⁶ __ , but strength activities like wrestling, discus-throwing, or power-lifting can be a great fit.

A few extra considerations

It is important to note that the three body types are extremes. No one is 100% ectomorph or completely endomorph. ⁷ __ . Another key point is that diet and environment also contribute to athletic ability and genetics plays a large part. And the most important thing is to choose a sport you enjoy. The best exercise of all is the one that you will do!

Adapted from a fitness website

b Read the article again. Complete the gaps with A–G.

A A person with this body type has more choice of sports
B For the same reason, it takes them longer to build muscle
C Their arms and legs are muscular and they have broad shoulders and narrow hips
D Everyone is a bit of a mix
E If a person with this body type is very tall
F It is difficult for them to lose weight, but they gain muscle rapidly
G This body type is not suited for agility and speed

▶ CAN YOU understand these people?

🔊 6.21 Watch or listen and choose a, b, or c.

1	2	3	4	5
Philomena	Rachel	Aileen	Coleen	Miranda

1 Philomena enjoys ____.
a watching tennis   b doing gymnastics
c watching diving
2 Rachel says that most people she knows who have been out with someone they met online ____.
a are still with the other person
b married the person they met
c broke up with the person they met
3 Aileen kept a tissue with answers to the exam in ____.
a her pocket   b the bathroom   c her backpack
4 Coleen ____.
a prefers the *Lord of the Rings* films to the books
b loves the books and the films
c prefers the books to the films
5 Miranda chose a picture for her profile photo because ____.
a she liked how she looked in it
b it was taken in Las Vegas
c it was taken on her wedding anniversary

CAN YOU say this in English?

Tick (✓) the box if you can do these things.

Can you…?

1 ▢ tell an anecdote about something that happened to you using the past simple, past continuous, and past perfect

2 ▢ talk about three past and three present habits of yours

3 ▢ describe a film, saying where it was set, what it is based on, who it was directed by, and what you thought of it

4 ▢ make deductions about a photo on a friend's phone using *might be*, *must be*, and *can't be*

🔵 **Go online** to watch the video, review Files 5 & 6, and check your progress

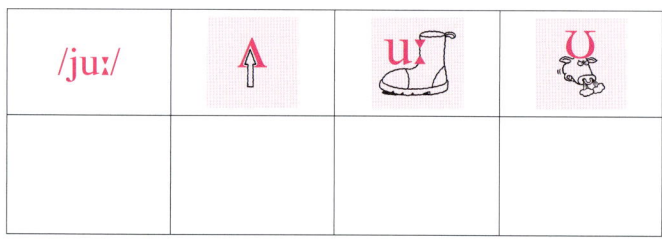

What will you do if you don't pass your exams?

I'll probably retake them.

G first conditional and future time clauses + *when*, *until*, etc.   **V** education   **P** the letter *u*

1 VOCABULARY education

a Answer as many of questions 1–8 as you can in two minutes. How many did you get right?

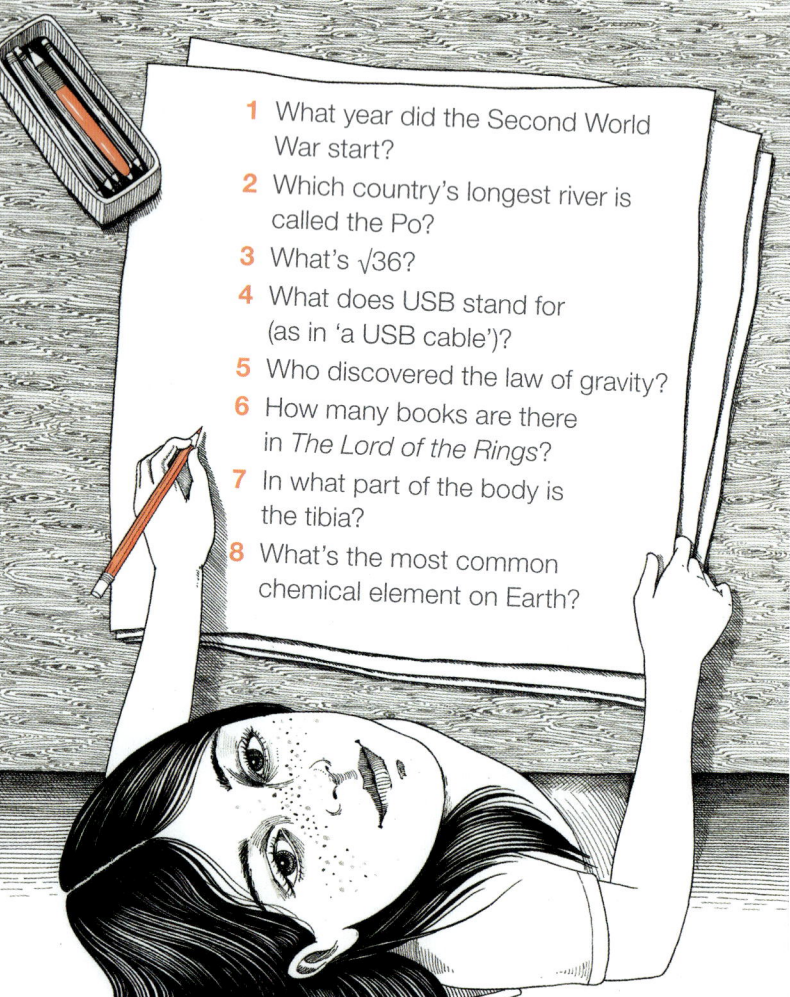

1 What year did the Second World War start?
2 Which country's longest river is called the Po?
3 What's √36?
4 What does USB stand for (as in 'a USB cable')?
5 Who discovered the law of gravity?
6 How many books are there in *The Lord of the Rings*?
7 In what part of the body is the tibia?
8 What's the most common chemical element on Earth?

b Complete the school subjects.

bio_____
chem_____
geo_____
his_____
infor_____ tech_____ (IT)
liter_____
mat_____
phy_____

c ◑ 7.1 Match the questions in **a** to the subjects in **b**. Then listen and check. Under<u>line</u> the stressed syllable(s).

d **V** p.161 **Vocabulary Bank** Education

2 PRONUNCIATION the letter *u*

> 🔍 **The letter *u***
> The letter *u* is usually pronounced /juː/, e.g. *uniform*, or /ʌ/, e.g. *lunch*, and sometimes /uː/, e.g. *blue*, or /ʊ/, e.g. *put*.

a Put the words from the list in the correct column.

education   full   lunch   music   pupil   put   result
rude   rules   student   study   subject   true   university

/juː/	ʌ	uː	ʊ

b ◑ 7.5 Listen and check. Practise saying the words.

c ◑ 7.6 Listen and write four sentences.

3 SPEAKING

Interview your partner using the questionnaire. Ask for more information.

What kind of secondary school did (do) you go to?

YOUR EDUCATION

Your school
- What kind of secondary school / you go to? / it a mixed school or single-sex?
- / you like it?
- How many students / there in each class? Do you think it / the right number?
- What time / your school day start and finish?

Subjects and homework
- Which subjects / you good and bad at?
- Which / your favourite subject?
- How often / you do PE or play sports?
- How much homework / you usually get? / you think it / too much?

Rules and discipline
- / you have to wear a uniform? / you like it? Why (not)?
- / your teachers too strict, or not strict enough? Why? What kind of punishments / they use?
- / pupils behave well, or / they misbehave?

4 LISTENING

a Read the description of a BBC programme and answer the questions.

1. Why is the Asian education system considered superior?
2. What experiment is a British school setting up?
3. What do you think the result will be?

b ⏴7.7 Listen to Week 1. Why are these times and numbers a shock for the students?

7.00 a.m.	30 minutes a day	50
11.30 a.m.	5.00 p.m.	7.00 p.m.	12 hours

c ⏴7.8 Listen to Weeks 2 and 3. Tick (✓) the things which are true about the Chinese teachers in the experiment.

1. They teach very quickly.
2. They make students copy from the board.
3. They let students do experiments on their own.
4. They're not surprised by the students' attitude to learning.
5. They try punishing students to make them pay attention.
6. They have problems with disciplining the British students.
7. They expel several students from the class.
8. When they see their method isn't working, they change their approach.
9. They make the children do t'ai chi.
10. They make a good impression on the parents.

d ⏴7.9 Listen to Week 4 and complete the numbers in the chart. What did the British and Chinese teachers learn?

Test results	Students with British teachers	Students with Chinese teachers
maths	_____%	_____%
science	_____%	_____%
Mandarin	_____%	_____%

e Answer the questions in small groups.

1. What do you think is good or bad about the Chinese system?
2. Would secondary school students in your country be shocked by the Chinese education system? Why (not)?
3. Would you prefer to study in a British school or a Chinese one? Where would you prefer to work as a teacher?

Chinese v British –
which education system is better?

According to the latest studies, Asian countries have better education systems than most Western countries, and in some subjects, Asian students are three years ahead of Western students of the same age.

In this unique experiment, five teachers from China come to a British school for four weeks to teach maths, science, and Mandarin to half of the Year 9 students, aged 13 and 14. The rest of the students in Year 9 will have their normal British teachers. After four weeks, the two groups will take tests to see which teaching style gets better results.

So, can British schools learn from the highly successful Chinese education system? Will the 12-hour days and strict discipline produce better results? Week 1 of the experiment is a shock for the students...

5 GRAMMAR first conditional and future time clauses + *when*, *until*, etc.

a In pairs, answer the questions.

1 When was the last time you did an exam? Did you pass or fail?
2 What's the next exam you are going to do? How do you feel about it?
3 What do you usually do the night before an exam?
4 How do you usually feel just before you do an exam?
5 Have you ever failed an important exam you thought you had passed (or vice versa)?

b ◗ 7.10 Listen to Olivia, who is waiting for her A level results, and answer the questions.

1 Does she think she's passed?
2 When and how will she get her exam results?
3 How will she celebrate if she gets good results?
4 What does she want to do if she gets good results?
5 What will she do if she doesn't get the results that she needs?

> 🔍 **Exam results**
> Exam results can be given as *marks* (usually out of 10 or 100), or as *grades* (A, B, C, etc.). A level marks are given as grades. The top grade is A* (A star), which is better than an A.

c ◗ 7.11 Listen to Olivia after she got her results. What grades did she get? What's she going to do?

d ◗ 7.12 Can you remember what Olivia said? Try to complete the sentences. Then listen and check.

1 They won't give me a place **unless** _____ at least two A*s and an A.
2 **As soon as** _____, I'll go to school and pick up the envelope.
3 I don't want to plan any celebrations **until** _____ the results.
4 **If** I don't get into Cambridge, _____.
5 **When** _____ a bit more positive, I'll try to get a place at another university.

e ⒢ p.144 **Grammar Bank 7A**

f Ask and answer with a partner. Make full sentences.

What will you do...?
• as soon as you get home
• if you don't get a good mark in your next test
• when this course finishes
• if it rains at the weekend

6 READING & SPEAKING

a In pairs, answer the questions that match your situation.

> **Are you at university now?**
> What are you studying? Are you enjoying it? Is there anything you don't like? What are you planning to do when you graduate?

> **Have you been to university?**
> **Yes** What did you study? Did you enjoy it? Was there anything you didn't enjoy?
> **No** Are you happy you didn't go? What are you doing now?

> **Do you want to go to university?**
> **Yes** What would you like to study? Why? Do you think you'll enjoy it?
> **No** Why not? What would you like to do instead?

b Look at the question on a UK student website. What do you think *Is it really worth...?* means?

c Now read the comments and mark them ✓ (= yes, it's worth it), ✗ (= no, it isn't worth it), or **S** (= it's sometimes worth it).

d Which of the comments do you think are true about university education in your country?

e Look at the photos of Jack Turner and Emily-Fleur Sizmur. Which of them do you think is happier?

Jack Turner, 23, has a degree and is unemployed.

Emily-Fleur Sizmur didn't go to university and runs her own business.

f ⒞ **Communication** University or not? **A p.108 B p.112** Ask and answer about Jack and Emily-Fleur.

g In your opinion, who made a better decision about university, Emily-Fleur or Jack? Why?

The UK student site

| Home | Forum | Schools | University | Careers |

Is it really worth going to uni?

Comments

1. It depends what you want to do. Some degrees are worth it, like medicine or dentistry. But I think media studies, and things like that, are a waste of time.

2. Uni gives you the time and space to find out what you really want to do in life. And it has a lot of social benefits, like friends, clubs – that sort of thing.

3. There are so many better alternatives out there, in my opinion. I got a place at uni to do accountancy, but I chose to do an apprenticeship. All my friends are now at uni and in debt. I'm 20 and I'm earning money and learning on the job.

4. It still amazes me how everyone thinks that uni is the only solution to their future. Trust me, it isn't. Some people are just not made for uni.

5. I'm a software engineer at a global tech company. A degree is preferred, but not essential. The recruitment team always say if they have two people, and one is self-taught and has experience, and the other has just finished uni with no experience, they'll choose the first. But often they ask for a degree AND experience.

7 SPEAKING

a In small groups, each choose a different topic from the list. Decide if you agree or disagree and write down at least three reasons.

School

- School doesn't prepare students for life. They should be taught practical things, like childcare, and how to cook healthy food.
- Physical education should be optional, and boys and girls should be taught PE separately.
- Primary pupils shouldn't get any homework, and secondary students not more than one hour a night during the week.
- Schools should spend most of the time on maths, science, and IT, and less on arts subjects like history and literature.

University

- University courses are too long. They should be a maximum of two years.
- University students shouldn't be allowed to have jobs during term-time.
- Students should choose to study a subject they love, not necessarily one that will get them a good job.
- University students should live independently, not with their parents.

b Explain to the rest of your group what you think about your topic. The others in the group should listen. At the end, they can vote for whether they agree or disagree with you, and say why.

> 🔍 **Organizing and presenting your opinions**
>
> *The topic I've chosen is…*
>
> *I completely agree / partly agree / completely disagree that…*
>
> *First of all, (I think that…)*
>
> *My second point is that…*
>
> *Another important point is that…*
>
> *Finally,…*

> I like living with my parents.

> I don't. If I could afford it, I'd move out.

1 READING & SPEAKING

a With a partner, look at the photos and answer the questions.

  1 Where do you think these young people are living? Which do you think is the most comfortable place to live? Why?

  2 Which place would you prefer to live in? Why?

  3 Where do you live? How comfortable is it? Who do you live with? Do you get on well? Do you argue about anything? What?

b Look at the title of the article. With a partner, think of one advantage and one disadvantage of living with your parents when you're an adult.

c Read the article. Were your ideas in the list?

Things you know if you still live with your parents

In the UK, 25% of young adults aged 20–34 still live at home with their parents. This has gone up by 20% in the last 20 years. So what are the pros and cons?

The downside

- It doesn't ¹_____ how old you are, you'll always be a child to them. They'll tell you to put a coat on every time you leave the house.
- It's really ²_____ when you meet new people to admit you're still sleeping in your childhood bedroom.
- You have to ³_____ them know all your movements and text them to say you're going to be home late.
- 99% of the time after a night out, your parents will be ⁴_____, waiting for you – even if it's 4.00 a.m.

- Every day of your life, you ⁵_____,'You treat this house like a hotel.'
- You become the household IT technician. If anything goes ⁶_____ in the house to do with phones, broadband, or TV, you're called to the rescue.

But on the other hand...

- At weekends, you wake up with the smell of bacon and eggs.
- The fridge and cupboards always have something in them, and generally a lot better than you could ⁷_____.

- There's nothing better than home-cooked food, and you've ⁸_____ that you'll never be able to cook as well as your parents.
- You've also realized that your mum has magical laundry powers that ⁹_____ all the stains from your washing and make it super clean.
- You had no idea how much ¹⁰_____ cost. In fact, you didn't even know until recently that you had to pay for water!

So, despite how much you complain about still living with your parents, you know perfectly well that they've allowed you to save money, you have somewhere (nice) to live for far less than the cost of renting elsewhere, and they fill your stomachs with good food. And for that, you're eternally grateful.

Adapted from Metro

d Read the article again and choose the correct word to complete the gaps.

1 matter / mind
2 embarrassing / embarrassed
3 leave / let
4 wake / awake
5 hear / listen

6 bad / wrong
7 afford / pay
8 realized / known
9 remove / retire
10 notes / bills

e Cover the text and, in pairs, try to remember all the pros and cons of living with your parents.

f Talk to a partner.

- What percentage of young people aged 20–34 do you think live with their parents in your country?
- Are the pros and cons similar in your country?
- Which two advantages and two disadvantages do you think are the most important?
- How do you think parents feel about having their adult children living at home?

2 GRAMMAR second conditional, choosing between conditionals

a Read some comments posted in response to the article in **1**. Do they want to leave their parents' home? Why (not)?

Vivienne@Montreal, Canada

I know there's a good side, but all I want is somewhere that's my own, where I can do what I want, where I can have my own furniture and pictures, where no one can tell me what to do. If I had the money, I'd move out immediately.

Marco@Naples, Italy

I'm perfectly happy living with my parents. If I lived on my own, I'd have to pay rent and do the housework and the cooking. Here, somebody else cooks and cleans, I have a nice room... Why would I want to leave? Even if I could afford it, I wouldn't move out. Not until I get married...

Andrea@Melbourne, Australia

It isn't that my parents aren't good to me – they are. If they weren't, I wouldn't live with them. But I'm 29 and I just don't feel independent.

Carlos@Valencia, Spain

I'd love to move out. I get on well with my parents, but I think I'd get on with them even better if I didn't live at home. My mum drives me mad – it isn't her fault, but she does. And I'd really like to have a dog, but my mum is allergic to them.

b Now answer the questions with a partner.

1 In the highlighted phrases, what tense is the verb after *if*?
2 What form is the other verb?
3 Do the phrases refer to a) a situation that will probably happen soon, or b) a situation they are imagining?

c **G** p.145 Grammar Bank 7B

d **C** **Communication** Guess the sentence **A** p.108 **B** p.113 Practise first and second conditionals.

3 PRONUNCIATION & SPEAKING sentence stress

a ◆7.16 Listen and repeat the sentences. Copy the rhythm.

1 If I **lived** on my **own**, I'd **have** to **pay rent**.
2 If we **get** a **mortgage**, we'll **buy** the **house**.
3 Would you **leave home** if you **got** a **job**?
4 I **won't move out** if I **can't afford** it.
5 If it were **my flat**, I'd be **happy** to **do** the **cleaning**.

b Choose six sentence beginnings and complete them so they are true for you.

If I…

could live anywhere in my town or city, I'd…
have some free time this weekend, I'll…
won a 'dream holiday' in a competition, I…
could choose any car I liked, I…
get a new phone this year, I…
could choose my ideal job, I…
don't have time to do the homework tonight, I…
was asked to work abroad for a year, I…
couldn't use the internet for a week, I…
feel like going out tonight, I…

c Work with a partner. **A**, say your first sentence. Try to get the correct rhythm. **B**, ask for more information. Then **B**, say your first sentence.

If I could live anywhere in my city, I'd live in the old part.

Why the old part?

4 VOCABULARY houses

a With a partner, write three more words in each column.

living room	kitchen	bedroom
table	washing machine	lamp

b **Ⓥ p.162 Vocabulary Bank** Houses

c Answer the questions with a partner.

What's the difference between...?

1 *the outskirts* and *a suburb*
2 *a village* and *a town*
3 *a roof* and *a ceiling*
4 *a balcony* and *a terrace*
5 *a chimney* and *a fireplace*
6 *the ground floor* and *the first floor*
7 *wood* and *wooden*

5 PRONUNCIATION the letter c

a With a partner, practise saying the words in groups 1–5.

1 carpet   castle   location
cosy   country   balcony   cooker
cupboard   cushion   curtains
2 city   cinema   decide
centre   entrance   ceiling   terrace
cycle   agency   icy
3 spacious   special   musician
4 occasion   accommodation   accuse
5 accent   success   accident

b Complete the pronunciation rules with /s/, /ʃ/, /k/, or /ks/.

1 *c* before *a, o,* or *u* is pronounced ____.
2 *c* before *i, e,* or *y* is pronounced ____.
3 *ci* before a vowel is pronounced ____.
4 *cc* before *a, o,* or *u* is pronounced ____.
5 *cc* before *e* or *i* is pronounced ____.

c **◑ 7.20** Now listen to the words in **a** and check your answers to **b**.

6 LISTENING

a Look at the pictures of George Frideric Handel and Jimi Hendrix. What do you know about them?

b Look at the poster and read the information about a London museum. Check your answers to **a**. Which bedroom do you like best? Why?

c You're going to listen to an audio guide to the *Handel & Hendrix in London* museum. Before you listen, look at extracts 1–8. Who do you think each extract is about, Handel or Hendrix? Write **Han** or **Hen**.

1	However, after becoming a British citizen five years later, he decided to continue renting the house.
2	He moved in briefly in July, before returning to the United States for an extensive tour.
3	There was a basement containing the kitchens, and on the ground floor, there was a room at the front for receiving visitors.
4	In the largest room, he kept his instruments (a harpsichord and a little house organ), and he occasionally rehearsed there.
5	He bought curtains and cushions from the nearby John Lewis department store, as well as ornaments from Portobello Road market and elsewhere.
6	In January the following year, he gave a series of press and media interviews and photo shoots in the flat.
7	Over the years, his flat was used as an office, until it was taken over in 2000 by the Handel House Trust.
8	He was buried in Westminster Abbey, and more than 3,000 people attended his funeral.

Glossary

Surrey a county in the south-east of England
the *Messiah* Handel's most famous choral work
Westminster Abbey one of London's great churches
the Royal Albert Hall a concert hall in south-west London

d **◑ 7.21** Listen and check.

Handel & Hendrix in London

Two successful and innovative musicians left their countries and came to live in London, the city where music was happening. One came in the early 18th century, when London was the centre for opera, and one came in the swinging 1960s, when the Beatles and the Rolling Stones were revolutionizing pop music. Where did they choose to live? In the same building, 23–25 Brook Street…

Buy your tickets now

NOW OPEN

Hendrix Flat

Find out more about Hendrix's flat

Read more ›

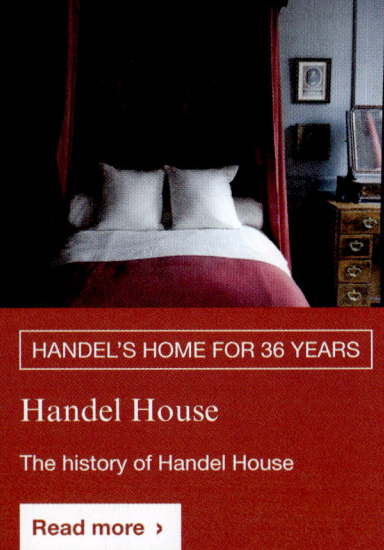

HANDEL'S HOME FOR 36 YEARS

Handel House

The history of Handel House

Read more ›

---

e Listen again and answer the questions.

1 Who lived in 25 Brook Street before Handel?
2 Why was he not allowed to buy the house?
3 What did Handel use the rooms on the first floor for?
4 What rooms were there on the second floor?
5 Who lived in the attic?
6 How long did Hendrix's career last?
7 Who was Kathy Etchingham?
8 When did Hendrix leave the flat?
9 Where did he die?
10 What was the flat used for before it became a museum?

f 🔊 **7.22** Read some extracts from the listening and try to complete the missing words. What do they mean? Then listen and check.

1 Handel decided to s_____ permanently in England…
2 After living in Surrey for some years, he m_____ to London…
3 He was the first o_____ of the house…
4 The flat on the u_____ floors of 23 Brook Street was found by…
5 He spent some time d_____ the flat to his own taste.
6 The whole house is now a museum and a concert v_____…

g Have you ever visited a house where a famous person lived? Where was it? What was it like? What do you especially remember about it?

7 SPEAKING & WRITING

a Think for a few minutes about what your dream home would be like and make brief notes. Use **p.162 Vocabulary Bank Houses** to help you.

• Where would it be?
• What kind of house or flat would it be?
• How many rooms would it have?
• What special features would it have?
• What would the decoration be like?

b In groups, describe your dream homes. Give as much detail as possible. Whose do you like best?

c Ⓦ **p.120 Writing** Describing a house or flat Write a description of your house or flat.

Go online to review the lesson

Practical English Boys' night out

making suggestions

1 ▶ ROB AND PAUL CATCH UP

a 🔊7.23 Watch or listen to Rob and Paul. What does Paul think of Jenny?

b Watch or listen again and mark the sentences **T** (true) or **F** (false). Correct the **F** sentences.

1 Rob used to play pool when he was younger.
2 Rob has a lot of free time.
3 Rob had fair hair the last time Paul saw him.
4 Paul thinks Rob has changed a lot.
5 Jenny's parents gave Rob the shirt he's wearing.
6 Rob doesn't want to keep Jenny waiting.

2 ▶ MAKING SUGGESTIONS

a 🔊7.24 Watch or listen to Paul, Rob, and Jenny talking about what to do after dinner. What do Paul and Rob decide to do? What excuse does Jenny give? What does she do in the end?

b Watch or listen again. Answer with **P**aul, **R**ob, or **J**enny.

Who suggests…?

1 ☐ going dancing
2 ☐ doing some exercise
3 ☐ going to a club
4 ☐ going to an art gallery
5 ☐ staying at home
6 ☐ going to a gig
7 ☐ meeting Kerri

c 🔊7.25 Look at some extracts from the conversation. Can you remember any of the missing words? Watch or listen and check.

1	Paul	What shall we _____ now?
	Rob	What do you want to do?
	Paul	Well…I haven't been on a dance floor for weeks now. I've got to move my body. _____ go dancing!
2	Jenny	I'm going running in the morning. Why _____ you join me?
	Paul	No thanks. I'm not very _____ on running. But I've read about this place called Deep Space, where they play great music. We _____ go there.
3	Jenny	_____ about going to the late show at MOMA?
	Paul	MOMA? What's that?
4	Jenny	_____ about staying in and watching a movie on TV?
	Paul	I'm in New York. I can watch TV anywhere.
5	Paul	I didn't think so. So _____ we go there?
	Rob	_____ not?
6	Rob	We _____ meet her outside and go together.
	Paul	That's a great _____!

d Look at the highlighted expressions for making and responding to suggestions. Which expression is the most emphatic, *What about…?*, *Let's…*, or *We could…?*

e ◐ **7.26** Watch or listen and repeat the highlighted phrases. Copy the rhythm and intonation.

f Practise the conversations in **c** with a partner.

g In small groups, practise making suggestions and responding.

You are going to have an end-of-term class party. You need to decide…
• when to have it.
• where to have it.
• what time to have it.
• what food and drink to have.

3 ▶ THE MORNING AFTER THE NIGHT BEFORE

a ◐ **7.27** Watch or listen to Rob and Jenny talking on the phone. What's the problem?

b Watch or listen again and complete the sentences with 1–3 words.
1 Rob says that he's feeling _____.
2 Kerri invited Rob and Paul to _____.
3 Rob says that he can't make _____.
4 Jenny is upset because it's an _____.
5 Rob promises that _____ again.
6 Rob also says that Paul _____ that afternoon.
7 Jenny tells Don that Rob is such _____.

c Look at the **Social English** phrases. Can you remember any of the missing words?

> 💬 **Social English**
> 1 **Jenny** Where are you, _____?
> 2 **Rob** That's _____ I'm calling. I'm not going to make it.
> 3 **Rob** It won't _____ again.
> 4 **Rob** He's _____ to Boston this afternoon.
> 5 **Jenny** I mean, it's not _____ I don't like Paul, but…
> 6 **Don** I wanted to have a _____ with him before the meeting.
> 7 **Jenny** He's _____ a professional.

d ◐ **7.28** Watch or listen and complete the phrases. Then watch or listen again and repeat.

e Complete conversations A–G with **Social English** phrases 1–7. Then practise them with a partner.

A	Your mum's ▨ darling! She's just mended my jeans!	That's so typical. She's always trying to be useful.
B	Have we got anything for supper tonight?	No, nothing. ▨ I'm ordering takeaway.
C	Is your brother around? I need to ▨.	I think he's in his room. Shall I call him?
D	You don't like my new shirt, do you?	▨ I don't like it, it's just that the colour doesn't suit you.
E	That's the third time this week you've come home late.	▨, I promise. This week's been really busy.
F	Is Jason coming tonight?	No, he can't. ▨ Manchester really early tomorrow morning.
G	Aren't you going to finish your vegetables?	They're cold. And ▨, I don't like cabbage.

CAN YOU…?
▨ use different ways of making suggestions
▨ respond to suggestions
▨ apologize and make an excuse

🔄 **Go online** to watch the video, review the lesson, and check your progress

8A The right job for you

> What would you like to do after university?

> I'd like to be an accountant. I enjoy working with numbers.

1 VOCABULARY work

a Look at the picture story. Match sentences A–I to pictures 1–9.

- A ☐ She decided to **set up** an online business selling birthday cakes.
- B ☐ Her business is **doing very well**. Clare is a success!
- C ☐ She was **unemployed**, and had to **look for a job**.
- D ☐ They had an argument, and Clare **was sacked**.
- E ☐ 1 Clare **worked for** a marketing company.
- F ☐ She **applied for** a lot of jobs, and sent in CVs.
- G ☐ She had a **good salary**, but she didn't like **her boss**.
- H ☐ She had some interviews, but didn't **get the jobs**.
- I ☐ She had to work very long hours and **do overtime**.

b 🔊 **8.1** Listen and check. Then cover the sentences and look at the pictures. Tell the story from memory.

c **V** p.163 **Vocabulary Bank** Work

> 🔍 **Words with different meanings**
>
> Sometimes the same word can have two completely different meanings, e.g.
>
> She has a **degree** in economics.
> (= a university qualification)
>
> It was only four **degrees** this morning.
> (= temperature)

d With a partner, explain the difference in meaning between the pairs of sentences.

1 a He's **running** a business.
   b He's **running** a marathon.
2 a Marion **was fired** last week.
   b When the man **fired** the gun, everyone screamed.
3 a I **work** in a shop.
   b My laptop **doesn't work**.
4 a There's a **market** for this product.
   b There's a **market** where you can buy vegetables.
5 a Steve has set up a **company**.
   b Steve is very **good company**.

2 PRONUNCIATION & SPEAKING word stress

a Under<u>line</u> the stressed syllable in each word. Use the phonetics to help you.

1 ap|ply /əˈplaɪ/
2 sa|la|ry /ˈsæləri/
3 re|dun|dant /rɪˈdʌndənt/
4 ex|pe|ri|ence /ɪkˈspɪəriəns/
5 o|ver|time /ˈəʊvətaɪm/
6 per|ma|nent /ˈpɜːmənənt/
7 qua|li|fi|ca|tions /ˌkwɒlɪfɪˈkeɪʃnz/
8 re|sign /rɪˈzaɪn/
9 re|spon|si|ble /rɪˈspɒnsəbl/
10 tem|pora|ry /ˈtemprəri/

b 🔊 **8.5** Listen and check. Practise saying the words.

c Think of someone you know who has a job. Prepare answers to the questions below.

- What does he / she do?
- What qualifications does he / she have?
- Is his / her job…?
  full time or part time
  temporary or permanent
- Where does he / she work (in an office, at home, etc.)?
- What hours does he / she work?
- Does he / she have to do overtime?
- Does he / she get a good salary?
- Does he / she like the job? Why (not)?
- Would you like to do his / her job? Why (not)?

d Work in pairs. **A**, interview **B** about his or her person's job. Ask more questions if you can. Then swap.

I'm going to tell you about my cousin. Her name's Corinne.

What does she do?

3 GRAMMAR choosing between gerunds and infinitives

a Complete the questionnaire by putting the verbs in the correct form: the gerund (e.g. *working*) or *to* + infinitive (e.g. *to work*).

Match your personality to the job

1 I'd like *to work* as part of a team. *work*
2 I enjoy _____ people with their problems. *help*
3 I don't mind _____ a very large salary. *not earn*
4 I'm good at _____ to people. *listen*

5 I'm good at _____ quick decisions. *make*
6 _____ risks doesn't worry me. *take*
7 I'm happy _____ by myself. *work*
8 I'm not afraid of _____ large amounts of money. *manage*

9 I'm good at _____ myself. *express*
10 I always try _____ my instincts. *follow*
11 It's important for me _____ creative. *be*
12 I enjoy _____. *improvise*

13 _____ complex calculations is not difficult for me. *do*
14 I enjoy _____ logical problems. *solve*
15 I find it easy _____ theoretical principles. *understand*
16 I am able _____ space and distance. *calculate*

b Read the questionnaire and tick (✓) **ONLY** the sentences that you strongly agree with. Discuss your answers with a partner.

c **C** **Communication** Match your personality to the job **p.108** Find out the results. Do you agree?

d Look at the sentences in the questionnaire. Complete the rules with the gerund or *to* + infinitive.

1 After some verbs, e.g. *enjoy* and *don't mind*, use _____.
2 After some verbs, e.g. *would like*, use _____.
3 After adjectives, use _____.
4 After prepositions, use _____.
5 As the subject of a phrase or sentence, use _____.

e **G** p.146 Grammar Bank 8A

f Write something for **FIVE** of the things in the list.

- something you are **planning to do** in the summer
- a country **you'd like to visit** in the future
- somebody you **wouldn't like to go** on holiday with
- a job **you'd love to do**
- a job you **hate doing** in the house
- somebody you find very **easy to talk** to
- something you're **afraid of doing**
- a sport, activity, or hobby you **love doing**
- something you **enjoy doing** on Sunday mornings
- something you **must do** or **buy** urgently

g Work in groups. Tell the others about what you have written and answer any questions they have.

I'd love to be an architect.

Why?

Because I think it would be great to…

4 WRITING

W p.121 **Writing** A covering email
Write an email to send with your CV to apply for a job.

5 READING

a Read the first part of an article about the TV programme *Dragons' Den*. Answer the questions.

1 Who are the 'Dragons'?
2 Where do the contestants meet them?
3 How does the programme work?
4 Is there a similar TV programme in your country?

b Look at the photos and read about three products that were presented on the show. Answer the questions and say why.

Which product do you think…?
1 the Dragons invested in and has been successful
2 the Dragons didn't invest in and has been a failure
3 the Dragons didn't invest in, but has been very successful

In the DRAGONS' DEN

Dragons' Den is a UK TV series, with similar versions in many different countries, which has been on TV every year since the original show in 2005. In the UK programme, contestants have three minutes to present their ideas for a product or service to five very successful business people. These people are nicknamed 'the Dragons', and the intimidating room where they meet the contestants is 'the Den'. The Dragons, who are multi-millionaires, are prepared to invest money in any business that they believe might be a success. In return, they take a share in the profits. The contestants are usually young entrepreneurs, product designers, or people with a new idea for a product or a service. They have three minutes to make their pitch, then the Dragons ask them questions about it and its possible market. Finally, the Dragons say if they are prepared to invest or not. If they are not convinced by the presentation, they say the dreaded words, 'I'm out'. So far, the Dragons have agreed to invest in more than 250 businesses.

From left to right: Duncan Bannatyne, Nick Jenkins, Deborah Meaden, Kelly Hoppen, Peter Jones

Glossary
den the hidden home of some types of wild animal
entrepreneur a person who makes money by starting or running businesses
make a pitch present something you're trying to sell

Tingatang

Gill and Clare, from Leeds, in the north of England, designed Tingatang, a range of silver jewellery for men and women to show that they're single, in the same way that a wedding ring shows that you're married. The pair asked the Dragons to invest £500,000 in their business.

Slappie watches

David, from Birmingham, asked the Dragons for £50,000 in exchange for 25% of his watch company, Slappie. The watches, which cost under £20, are on straps of many different colours, and the watch faces are also available in different designs. The straps and watch faces can be bought separately and are interchangeable, so you can create your own watch.

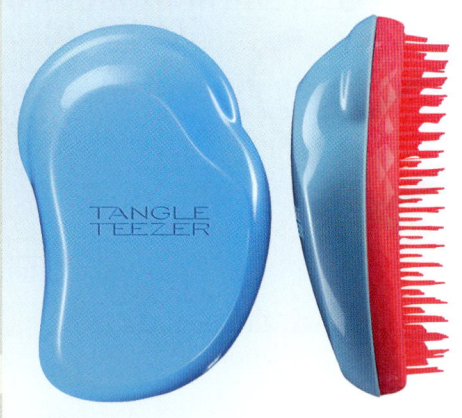

Tangle Teezer

Shaun, a hairdresser from London, set up a company to produce brightly-coloured plastic hairbrushes which were especially good at untangling hair. He demonstrated the brushes on the show and asked for an £80,000 investment in exchange for 15% of his company.

c **G Communication** Dragons' Den **A** p.109 **B** p.113 **C** p.114
Work in groups of three. Find out what happened.

d Which (if any) of the three products would you be interested / definitely not interested in buying? Why? Do you think they are, or could be, successful in your country? Why (not)?

6 LISTENING

a Look at the photo of two more *Dragons' Den* contestants and their product. Do you think they were successful?

Jake and Joe asked for £60,000 in exchange for 20% of their online photo-framing business Frame Again.

b 🔊 8.9 Listen to Part 1 of an interview with Joe about his experience. Mark the sentences **T** (true) or **F** (false).

1 Joe and Jake applied to be on *Dragons' Den* together.
2 They prepared their pitch very quickly.
3 The show was filmed in Manchester.
4 They didn't do any preparation the night before.
5 They only slept for a few hours the night before the programme.
6 They were the third contestants on that programme.
7 Other contestants waited for up to 12 hours for their turn.
8 They met one of the Dragons while they were waiting to go on.

c Listen again. Correct the **F** sentences.

d 🔊 8.10 Listen to Part 2. What was different about Joe and Jake's experience compared to other contestants?

e Listen again and make notes. What does Joe say about…?

1 smiling at Deborah Meaden
2 Jake's first words
3 'I'm out.'
4 Peter's appearance
5 Jessops
6 the job offer

f 🔊 8.11 Listen to the end of the interview. What did Joe and Jake decide to do? Why? Did they think it was the right decision?

7 SPEAKING

a 🔊 8.12 Listen to Joe and Jake giving their *Dragons' Den* pitch for Frame Again. Number the questions 1–5 in the order they answer them.

> A ☐ How much will it cost?
>
> B ☐ What is the product? Give a detailed description.
>
> C ☐ Who are you? What's the name of your product?
>
> D ☐ Do you have an advertising slogan for the product?
>
> E ☐ Who is the product for?

b Work with a partner. Imagine you are going to appear on the programme. Choose one of the products below, or invent your own, and think about your answers to the questions in **a**.

> an app   a chair   a dessert   a drink
> a gadget   a lamp   a pen   a phone
> a sandwich

c Present your product to the class together. Spend a few minutes preparing your pitch. Take turns to give the information. Use the language from the **Presenting a product** box.

> 🔍 **Presenting a product**
>
> *Good morning. I'm _____, and this is _____, and we're here to tell you about our new product…*
>
> *It's a…, and it's called…*
>
> *This product is for…*
>
> *We think it will be very popular because…*
>
> *It will cost…*
>
> *Our slogan is…*

d You also have money to invest in one of the products your classmates present. Listen to their presentations and decide which one to vote for.

Go online to review the lesson

G reported speech: sentences and questions **V** shopping, making nouns from verbs **P** the letters *ai*

1 READING & SPEAKING

a Look at these phrases. Who usually says them? Mark them **C** (customer) or **SA** (sales assistant).

1 ⬚ Do you need any help?
2 ⬚ What size are you?
3 ⬚ Do you have this in blue?
4 ⬚ Have a nice day!
5 ⬚ No, thanks, I'm just looking.
6 ⬚ Are you looking for anything in particular?
7 ⬚ It's a bit big – have you got a smaller size?
8 ⬚ Can I try these on?
9 ⬚ Shall I put your receipt in the bag?
10 ⬚ The changing rooms are over there.

b Read the article. Did the writer find the sales assistants helpful? Why (not)?

c Read the article again. Underline the questions that the second sales assistant asks. Which questions do you think aren't appropriate in this situation?

d Think of some shops that you go to frequently. Are the sales assistants helpful or unhelpful? In what way?

2 GRAMMAR reported speech

a Cover the article and look at the sentences. Can you remember what the second sales assistant asked and what the customer said?

1 He asked me if I needed any help. I said that I was just looking.

Do you need any help?) (*I'm just looking.*

2 He asked me where I worked. I said I worked in an office round the corner.
3 He asked me if I liked football. I said it was OK.
4 He asked me if I was going to watch the England match. I said that I wasn't.
5 He asked me what I was doing after work. I told him I was having dinner with a friend.

b **G** p.147 Grammar Bank 8B

c 🔊 8.15 Listen. Change the conversations into reported speech.

1 ») *'Where do you live?'* (*He asked her where she lived.*

») *'I live in the city centre.'*
(*She said that she lived in the city centre.*

When 'happy to help' becomes a problem

Jonathan Haynes

It's my lunch break. I work near King's Cross, a major London train station, and I've gone to the shopping mall there to buy a new wallet. It's a very simple shopping trip. At least, I think it's simple, but five minutes later, I'm not so sure.

As I enter the shop, a sales assistant at the far end shouts at me:

'Hi, how are you doing today? Do you need any help?'

I answer:

'I'm fine. I'm just looking, thanks.'

That should be the end of the conversation, and I go to look at the wallets.

'Hello, do you need any help?'

Here is another sales assistant, who I will call SA2.

Me: 'I'm fine, thanks. I'm just looking.'

I don't know why he needed to ask me this, as I'm certain he heard me tell his colleague.

SA2: 'Are you going anywhere nice?'

This seems a strange question. I expected, 'Are you looking for anything in particular today?' As I don't answer, he repeats the question.

SA2: **'Are you going anywhere nice?'**

I remember that I'm in a shop in a train station and I now understand his question.

Me: **'No. I work near here. I just came in to look for a new wallet.'**

SA2: **'Where do you work?'**

Me: **'Oh, er, I work in an office round the corner.'**

I try to look at wallets, and hope he goes away.

SA2: **'Do you like football?'**

It's a simple question, but I know that if I say yes, he will ask me questions about 'your team'. I'm not sure how this helps me to buy a wallet.

Me: **'Er, it's OK.'**

SA2: **'Are you going to watch the England match?'**

I want him to stop.

Me: **'No, I'm not.'**

I walk to another part of the shop. The sales assistant follows me.

SA2: **'What are you doing after work?'**

Me: **'I'm having dinner with a friend.'**

SA2: **'Are you doing anything for the rest of the day?'**

Me: **'Um, thank you for your help!'**

I run away without a wallet. His never-ending questions lost him the sale. Shopping didn't use to be like this. In the USA, perhaps, but not in the UK. It is a big improvement that sales assistants nowadays acknowledge your existence and are sometimes actually helpful. But there's a difference between being helpful and trying to pretend you're a shopper's best friend.

Adapted from The Guardian

3 VOCABULARY & SPEAKING shopping

a In pairs, explain the difference between…

1 *a basket* and *a trolley.*
2 *a credit card* and *a debit card.*
3 *a receipt* and *a refund.*
4 *a discount* and *a bargain.*
5 *a chain store* and *a department store.*
6 *a library* and *a bookshop.*
7 *put on a shirt* and *try on a shirt.*
8 *It fits you* and *It suits you.*

b Look at the questions together and answer them. Ask for and give as many details as you can.

---

1 **How often do you shop…? What do you buy?**
- ○ in street markets
- ○ in supermarkets
- ○ in shopping centres or malls
- ○ online

---

2 **What's your favourite shop or website to buy…?**
- ○ clothes
- ○ shoes
- ○ books and music
- ○ presents
- ○ food

---

3 **What…? Why?**
- ○ do you enjoy buying
- ○ do you hate buying
- ○ would you never buy online

---

4 **Do you prefer shopping for clothes…?**
- ○ by yourself or with somebody
- ○ at the beginning of the season or in the sales
- ○ in small shops or in department stores

---

5 **What do you think are the advantages and disadvantages of buying these things online?**
- ○ clothes
- ○ groceries
- ○ electronic items
- ○ books

---

6 **Do you ever look at things in shops and then buy them online? Why do you think people do this?**

4 READING

a Read the introduction to the article. Why is good customer service more important than it used to be?

b Read the five stories. In pairs, try to guess how the last sentence of each story ends.

c **ⓒ Communication** Going the extra mile p.109 Read and check. Were you correct?

d Read the stories again. In which stories…?
1. ▢▢▢ does someone get what they wanted to buy without paying
2. ▢▢ does someone get something in the post
3. ▢ is someone hungry
4. ▢▢ is the problem solved on the same day

e Which example A–E do you think…?
- is the funniest
- cost the company most money
- took the company most time
- was the most difficult to organize
- is the best customer service

5 PRONUNCIATION the letters *ai*

a 🔊 8.16 Listen and underline the stressed syllable. Then write the words in the correct column.

airline	bargain	certain	claim	complain
contain	email	explain	paid	repair
waiter				

(train)	(chair)	(computer)

b 🔊 8.17 Listen and check. Then answer the questions.
1. How is *ai* usually pronounced a) when it's stressed, b) when it's unstressed? Which word is an exception?
2. How is *air* usually pronounced?
3. Is *said* pronounced /seɪd/ or /sed/?

Going the extra mile ➤

In the age of social media, a story about a good (or bad) customer service experience is not limited to you and your friends. The best stories can go viral on social networks very quickly, bringing good or bad publicity to companies overnight. Here are five heart-warming true stories that reached millions of people because of the power of the internet.

A ➤ Nordstrom

One day, a member of the security staff in a Nordstrom department store noticed a woman crawling around on her hands and knees in the clothes department. She said she was looking for a diamond that had fallen out of her wedding ring while she was trying on clothes earlier that day. The man got down on the floor and searched with her. Then he asked a group of cleaners to help, and they searched, too. Finally, they looked through _____!

B ➤ Morton's, The Steakhouse

Peter Shankman was boarding a flight to Newark Airport, near New York. It was dinnertime, and he knew he would be starving when the plane arrived. There's a Morton's near the airport, one of Peter's favourite restaurants, so he tweeted, 'Hey, @Morton's – can you meet me at Newark Airport with a steak when I land in two hours? Thanks. ☺'. He was joking, but amazingly, when he got off the plane, in the Arrivals area there was _____.

C ➤ Ritz-Carlton Hotels

Chris Hurn's family spent their holiday at the Ritz-Carlton Hotel in Florida. Unfortunately, when they got home, they realized that they had left Chris's young son's favourite toy, Joshie the giraffe, at the hotel. The child was very upset, so Chris told him that Joshie was staying at the hotel for a bit of extra holiday. That evening, the hotel phoned to say that they had found Joshie. Chris thanked them and explained that he'd told his son that Joshie was having an extra holiday. Two days later, a parcel arrived. In it was Joshie, a present of a Frisbee and a football, and a photograph of _____.

D ➤ Trader Joe's

At Christmas a few years ago, in Pennsylvania, USA, it snowed so hard that an 89-year-old man couldn't leave his home. His daughter was worried that he didn't have enough food. She called several stores and asked if they would deliver food to her father's home, but they all said no. Eventually, she spoke to someone at a store called Trader Joe's. They also told her that they didn't deliver – normally. But because she was so worried, they said that they would make an exception. The employee then wished her a Merry Christmas. Half an hour later, the food arrived at her father's house, with _____!

E ➤ Apple

A man bought the latest iPad online, but when his wife saw it, she thought it was too expensive, so he immediately sent it back to Apple. He put a Post-it note on the screen that said, 'Wife said no'. Apple employees thought this was very funny, and the story reached two senior managers, who decided to do something about it. They refunded his money, but they also sent the iPad back to him with another Post-it note saying, '_____'.

6 LISTENING

a Have you ever had a problem with luggage when you were travelling, e.g. on a train or flight? What happened?

b 🔊 **8.18** You're going to listen to a story about bad customer service. First, listen to six extracts and complete the gaps with the verbs in the list.

claim   complained   contacted   dropped   offered
produced   reported   throwing

1 My God! They're _____ guitars out there!
2 They immediately _____ to United Airlines.
3 For nine months, he tried to _____ compensation.
4 Dave wrote a song about his experience, and _____ a video to go with it.
5 United Airlines _____ Dave and _____ him a payment.
6 The BBC _____ that United Airlines' share price had _____ by 10%.

c 🔊 **8.19** Now listen to the whole story. Answer the questions.

1 Why did Dave Carroll write a song?
2 Why did it have such a dramatic effect?

d Try to put the events in the correct order 1–10. Then listen again and check.

- *1* Dave and his band flew from Halifax to Chicago.
- ☐ He wrote a song about his experience.
- ☐ United Airlines contacted him and offered him money.
- ☐ They got their connecting flight to Omaha, Nebraska.
- ☐ Dave discovered that his guitar was broken.
- ☐ He complained again to United Airlines by phone and email, but they didn't help him.
- ☐ He did lots of media interviews.
- ☐ They saw the baggage handlers throwing their guitars, and complained to airline staff.
- ☐ He put a video of the song on YouTube.
- *10* United Airlines lost a lot of money.

e Have you ever experienced very good or very bad customer service? What happened?

7 VOCABULARY making nouns from verbs

a Look at some nouns from the guitar story. What verbs do they come from?

compensation   complaint   payment

b 🟢 **p.164 Vocabulary Bank** Word-building Do Part 1.

8 ▶ VIDEO LISTENING

a Have you ever complained about something in a hotel, restaurant, or shop? What happened?

b Work in pairs. What do you think are the top five things that people complain about in hotels?

c Watch Part 1 of a short programme about how to complain and check your answers to **b**.

d Now watch Part 2. Phil, a hotel guest, complains in three situations. What does he do wrong each time? How does he do it better the second time?

e 🟢 **Communication** I want to speak to the manager **A p.109 B p.113** Role-play two conversations.

9 WRITING

🟣 **p.122 Writing** An email of complaint Write an email of complaint about something you bought online.

GRAMMAR

Circle a, b, or c.

1 We'll miss the train if we ____.
 a don't hurry b won't hurry
 c didn't hurry
2 If you help me with the washing-up, ____ in five minutes.
 a we'll finish b we finish c we finished
3 I won't get into university unless ____ good grades.
 a I'll get b I get c I don't get
4 If we moved to a bigger house, we ____ a dog.
 a can have b could have c will have
5 I'd be sad if my brother and his wife ____.
 a break up b 'll break up c broke up
6 If I had a job, I ____ live with my parents.
 a won't b wouldn't c didn't
7 If I won a lot of money, ____ a big house.
 a I'd buy b I'll buy c I buy
8 Tom's really good at ____ problems.
 a solve b solving c to solve
9 ____ clothes online saves a lot of time.
 a Buying b To buy c Buy
10 I wouldn't ____ that car if I were you.
 a get b getting c to get
11 It's really important ____ the receipt.
 a keep b to keep c keeping
12 He said he ____ to his lawyer tomorrow.
 a will speak b spoke c would speak
13 I asked Sally if ____ coming to the party.
 a she is b she was c was she
14 The little girl ____ that she was lost.
 a told b said us c told us
15 Sandra asked me where ____.
 a did I work b I was work c I worked

VOCABULARY

a Complete with one word.

1 The UK school year has three _____.
2 Children under five can go to _____ school.
3 UK high schools are called _____ schools.
4 Children who _____ very badly at school may be expelled.
5 A school where you study, eat, and sleep is called a _____ school.

b Circle the correct word.

1 We live in a residential area in / on the outskirts of Cambridge.
2 The roof / ceiling in our flat is very low, so don't hit your head!
3 Close the garden gate / door or the dog might get out.
4 Our flat is in / on the fifth floor of a large block of flats.
5 On the shelf above the chimney / fireplace there are some photos.

c Complete the words.

1 I did a lot of ov_____ last week – two hours extra every day.
2 He works night sh_____ at the local factory.
3 It's only a t_____ job, from March to September.
4 I'd like to s_____ up a small business, making children's clothes.
5 Lewis loves being s_____-_____ – it means he's his own boss.

d Complete the sentences with a noun formed from the bold word.

1 I don't like shopping in supermarkets because there is too much _____. choose
2 My flatmates and I have an _____ about who does what in the house. agree
3 I'm sure the new company will be a _____. succeed
4 I made a _____ about the service in the hotel. complain
5 We went on a _____ to support the unemployed. demonstrate
6 The new staff restaurant is a great _____ on the old one. improve
7 If you want to get a job, you need good _____. qualify
8 My sister has been working as a _____ for the EU. translate
9 Some _____ say that drinking coffee may be good for us. science
10 I want an _____ for what happened yesterday. explain

PRONUNCIATION

a Practise the words and sounds.

Vowel sounds: boot, bull, chair, train
Consonant sounds: key, snake, shower, nose

b P p.166–7 Sound Bank Say more words for each sound.

c What sound in a do the pink letters have in these words?
1 ceiling 2 email 3 repair 4 roof 5 spacious

d Underline the stressed syllable.
1 se|con|dary 3 de|li|ve|ry 5 a|chieve|ment
2 un|em|ployed 4 a|pply

CAN YOU understand this text?

a Read the article once. Choose the best title.

   1 **IT'S GOOD TO...**   2 **LOOK, BUT DON'T...**
   3 **PAY LESS IF YOU DON'T...**

b Read the article again. Complete the gaps with the best word or phrase for the context.

   1 break / create / obey
   2 value / weight / cost
   3 able / interested / prepared
   4 choosing between / depending on / thinking of
   5 less / longer / shorter
   6 encourage / tell / don't allow
   7 buying / finding / losing
   8 colleagues / shoppers / sales assistants

▶ CAN YOU understand these people?

🔊 8.22 Watch or listen and choose a, b, or c.

  1 Philomena   2 Adina   3 Daniel   4 Scott   5 Coleen

   1 Philomena's maths teachers ____.
    a made her want to become a teacher herself
    b were very inspiring
    c weren't as good as her history teacher
   2 Adina is happy to buy ____ online.
    a anything   b most things   c food and clothes
   3 Daniel remembers being annoyed with a waiter who ____.
    a didn't want to serve his table   b complained about the tip
    c wasn't polite
   4 Scott currently ____.
    a only has a small garden   b doesn't have a garden
    c has a lot of plants in his garden
   5 At the start of her career, Coleen thought that a good salary was ____ an enjoyable job.
    a more important than   b less important than
    c as important as

CAN YOU say this in English?

Tick (✓) the box if you can do these things.

Can you...?

   1 ☐ describe the schools you went to (or have been to) and say what you liked or didn't like about them
   2 ☐ describe your ideal holiday house
   3 ☐ say a) what will you do if you don't pass your English exam at the end of the course, b) what would you do if you won a lot of money
   4 ☐ report three questions that somebody has asked you today and say what you answered

TOUCH!

IF YOU want to save money when shopping, ¹_____ the simple rule that you've probably shouted at the kids 100 times: don't touch anything! Touching anything, from a banana to a Ferrari, makes your brain automatically place more ²_____ on an item.

This has been revealed in a study from Ohio and Illinois state universities, which investigated how much people were ³_____ to pay for an item before and after touching it. The item was a cheap coffee mug, but just a few seconds of contact made people want to pay more for it than those who had looked but not touched.

The study, published in the journal *Judgment and Decision-Making*, tested 144 people and examined how much they were prepared to pay in an auction for the mug, ⁴_____ how long they had held it. The ⁵_____ people held the mug, the more they were prepared to pay, with those holding it for ten seconds valuing it at $2.44 and those who held it for 30 seconds valuing it at $3.91.

Some kinds of stores have been using these tactics for years; for example, car showrooms ⁶_____ customers to test drive new cars and pet shops give people animals to hold. But Waleed Muhanna, the author of the study, was surprised how quickly people felt that, once they had touched something, it was theirs. 'People become attached and are prepared to pay more to avoid ⁷_____ the object,' he said. He hopes that understanding how quickly they can get attached to something may help ⁸_____ to make better decisions about what to buy.

Adapted from The Times

🔵 **Go online** to watch the video, review Files 7 & 8, and check your progress

G third conditional | **V** making adjectives and adverbs | **P** sentence rhythm, weak pronunciation of *have*

You were really lucky!

Yes. If he hadn't helped me, I would have missed my train!

1 LISTENING & SPEAKING

a Answer the questions with a partner. Say what you would do and why.

What would you do if...?

1 somebody in the street asked you for money on your way home tonight
2 you were driving home at night and you saw somebody who had run out of petrol
3 you saw an old man being attacked in the street by a couple of teenagers
4 you were in a queue at a station or airport and someone asked to go in front of you because he / she was in a hurry
5 you were driving to work and you saw someone by the road, hitchhiking
6 you saw someone on a bus or train, looking really upset

b ◉9.1 Read and listen to writer Bernard Hare on a radio programme talking about something that happened to him when he was a student. Then in pairs, summarize what happened. Use the words and phrases below.

the police   a phone box   ill
the last train   hitchhike from Peterborough
the ticket inspector   upset

c ◉9.2 Decide what you think happened next. Then listen. Were you correct?

The ticket inspector

I was living in a student flat in North London when the police knocked on my door one night. I thought it was because I hadn't paid the rent for a few months, so I didn't open the door. But then I wondered if it was something to do with my mother, who I knew wasn't very well. There was no phone in the flat, and this was before the days of mobile phones, so I ran down to the nearest phone box and phoned my dad in Leeds, in the north of England. He told me that my mum was very ill in hospital and that I should go home as soon as I could.

When I got to the station, I found that I'd missed the last train to Leeds. There was a train to Peterborough, from where some local trains went to Leeds, but I would miss the connection by about 20 minutes. I decided to get the Peterborough train – I was so desperate to get home that I thought maybe I could hitchhike from Peterborough.

'Tickets, please.' I looked up and saw the ticket inspector. He could see from my eyes that I'd been crying. 'Are you OK?', he asked. 'Of course I'm OK,' I said. 'You look awful,' he continued. 'Is there anything I can do?' 'You could go away,' I said rudely.

But he didn't. He sat down and said, 'If there's a problem, I'm here to help.' The only thing I could think of was to tell him my story. When I finished, I said, 'So now you know. I'm a bit upset, and I don't feel like talking any more, OK?' 'OK,' he said, finally getting up. 'I'm sorry to hear that, son. I hope you make it home.'

I continued to look out of the window at the dark countryside. Ten minutes later, the ticket inspector came back.

d Listen to the second part of the story again and answer the questions.

1 What did the ticket inspector do for Bernard?
2 How did Bernard react?
3 What did the ticket inspector then ask Bernard to do?
4 How did this experience change him?

e 🔊 **9.3** Listen to three people who phoned in with their stories about being helped by strangers. Which one(s) happened when the people were travelling?

Story 1

Story 2

Story 3

f Listen again and match three sentences to each story.

A ☐ The problem happened at airport security.
B ☐ The problem happened when the speaker was shopping for food.
C ☐ The speaker had forgotten an important rule.
D ☐ The speaker was travelling with his / her family when something happened.
E ☐ The speaker didn't have enough money to pay for something.
F ☐ The speaker lost something that was really important for him / her.
G ☐ A week later, the man returned the items which had been taken away.
H ☐ The stranger was very scary.
I ☐ One of the strangers who helped him / her was a child.

g Which of the four stories do you think is a) the most surprising, b) the most moving? Why?

h Have you ever helped a stranger, or been helped by a stranger? What happened?

2 GRAMMAR third conditional

a Match the sentence halves about the stories in **1**.

1 ☐ If the inspector hadn't stopped the train to Leeds,…
2 ☐ If the biker hadn't found the little girl's blanket…
3 ☐ If the girl and her mother hadn't bought the groceries,…
4 ☐ If the security man had thrown the woman's paints away,…

A the man and his wife wouldn't have had anything to eat.
B she wouldn't have been able to sleep.
C Bernard would have missed his connection.
D she wouldn't have got them back.

b Now read the sentences about Bernard's story. Which one describes what happened? Which one describes an imaginary situation?

1 If the inspector hadn't stopped the train, he would have missed his connection.
2 The inspector stopped the train, so he didn't miss his connection.

c 🄖 **p.148 Grammar Bank 9A**

d Complete the sentences in your own words to make third conditional sentences.

If the dog hadn't barked,…
We wouldn't have missed the bus if…
If I had listened to my friend's advice,…
I would have won the race if…
If I hadn't got up so late,…
I would have been really annoyed if…

e Compare sentences with a partner. Check that they are all correct.

3 PRONUNCIATION sentence rhythm, weak pronunciation of *have*

a 🔊 **9.5** Listen and repeat the sentences. Copy the rhythm. How is *have* pronounced after *would*?

1 If I'd **known** you were **ill**,
  I would have **come** to **see** you.
  If I'd **known** you were **ill**, I would have **come** to **see** you.
2 If the **weather** had been **better**,
  we would have **stayed longer**.
  If the **weather** had been **better**, we would have **stayed longer**.
3 If I **hadn't stopped** to **get petrol**,
  I **wouldn't** have been **late**.
  If I **hadn't stopped** to **get petrol**, I **wouldn't** have been **late**.
4 We would have **missed** our **flight**
  if it **hadn't** been **delayed**.
  We would have **missed** our **flight** if it **hadn't** been **delayed**.

b 🔊 **9.6** Listen and write five third conditional sentences.

c 🄖 **Communication** Guess the conditional **A p.109 B p.113** Practise third conditionals.

4 READING & SPEAKING

a Do you consider yourself in general to be a lucky person? Why (not)?

> 🔍 **Topic sentences**
> In a text, paragraphs usually begin with a *topic sentence*. This sentence tells you what the paragraph is going to be about.

b You are going to read an article about luck. Read the information box about topic sentences, and sentences A–E. Then read the article and complete the paragraphs with A–E. Use the <mark>highlighted</mark> words and phrases to help you.

A But <mark>is it possible</mark> to use these techniques to win the lottery?

B A few years ago, I led <mark>a large research project</mark> about luck.

C Eventually, we uncovered <mark>four</mark> key psychological <mark>principles</mark>.

D In <mark>a second phase</mark> of the project, I wanted to discover whether it was possible to change people's luck.

E <mark>The results revealed that</mark> luck is not a magical ability, or the result of random chance.

c Read the article again. Choose a, b, or c.

1 In his first research project into luck, the author asked the volunteers to ____.
   a record what happened to them every day
   b answer questions about their jobs
   c live together for a few months

2 In one experiment, the unlucky people ____.
   a didn't count the photographs correctly
   b didn't notice something important in the newspaper
   c were not able to finish the task

3 The researchers concluded that lucky people are generally ____.
   a optimistic   b hard-working   c ambitious

4 In a second phase of the project, Wiseman asked his volunteers to ____.
   a change their jobs
   b change their attitude
   c change their lifestyle

5 Wiseman believes that ____.
   a being lucky in your personal life is more important than being lucky at work
   b winning the lottery is as important as being lucky in your personal life
   c winning the lottery is less important than being lucky in your personal life

How to improve your **luck** and win the lottery **twice** (possibly)

Richard Wiseman

A British couple have just won £1m in the EuroMillions lottery for a remarkable second time. The chances of this happening are more than 283 billion to one. They are clearly incredibly lucky – but is there anything we can all do to increase the chances of being lucky ourselves?

1 _____ I studied the lives of more than 400 people who considered themselves either very lucky or very unlucky. I asked everyone to keep diaries, complete personality tests, and take part in experiments.

2 _____ Nor are people born lucky or unlucky. Instead, lucky and unlucky people create much of their good and bad luck by the way they think and behave. For example, in one experiment, we asked our volunteers to look through a newspaper and count the number of photographs in it. However, we didn't tell them that we had placed two opportunities in the newspaper. The first was a half-page advert clearly stating, 'STOP COUNTING. THERE ARE 43 PHOTOGRAPHS IN THIS NEWSPAPER.' A second advert later on said, 'TELL THE EXPERIMENTER YOU'VE SEEN THIS AND WIN £150.' The lucky people quickly spotted these opportunities, partly because they tended to be very relaxed. In contrast, the unlucky people focused anxiously on the task of counting the photos and so tended not to see the advertisements. Without realizing it, both groups had created their own good and bad luck.

3 _____

- Lucky people create and notice opportunities by developing a relaxed attitude to life and being open to change.

- Lucky people tend to listen to their intuition and act quickly. Unlucky people tend to analyse situations too much, and are afraid to act.

- Lucky people are confident that the future will be positive, and this motivates them to try, even when they have little chance of success. Unlucky people are sure that they will fail, and so they often give up before they have begun.

- Lucky people keep going, even when they are likely to fail, and they learn from their mistakes. Unlucky people get depressed by the smallest problem, and think that the problems are their fault, even when they aren't.

4 _____ I asked a group of 200 volunteers to use the four key principles and to think and behave like a lucky person. The results were remarkable. In a few months, about two-thirds of the group became happier, healthier, and more successful in their careers.

5 _____ Unfortunately not. Lotteries are purely chance events, and nothing can really influence your chances of success. However, the good news is that being lucky in your personal life and career is far more important than winning the lottery.

Adapted from The Guardian

d Ask and answer the questions with a partner.

1 Do you agree with Richard Wiseman that people are not born lucky or unlucky, but can learn to make their own luck?

2 Can you remember a time when you were either very lucky or very unlucky? What happened?

3 Do you know anyone who you think is particularly lucky or unlucky? Why?

4 Think of a time when you were successful at something. Do you think it was because you worked hard at it, or because you were lucky and in the right place at the right time?

5 VOCABULARY making adjectives and adverbs

> A few years ago, I led a large research project about **luck**. I studied the lives of more than 400 people who considered themselves either very **lucky** or very **unlucky**.

a Look at the **bold** words in the sentences above. Which is a noun and which are adjectives? Using the word *luck*, can you make…?

1 a positive adverb
2 a negative adverb

b **V** p.164 **Vocabulary Bank** Word-building Do Part 2.

c Read the rules for the sentence game.

The sentence game

1 You must write correct sentences with the exact number of words given (contractions count as one word).

2 The sentences must make sense.

3 You must include a form of the given word (e.g. if the word is *luck*, you can use *lucky*, *luckily*, *unlucky*, etc.).

d Work in teams of three or four. Play the sentence game. You have five minutes to write the following sentences.

1 **fortune** (11 words)   4 **care** (6 words)
2 **comfort** (9 words)   5 **patience** (12 words)
3 **luck** (7 words)

e Your teacher will tell you if your sentences are correct. The team with the most correct sentences is the winner.

Go online to review the lesson

9B Digital detox

You look a bit stressed!

Yes, I have too much work and not enough time!

G quantifiers **V** electronic devices **P** linking, *ough* and *augh*

1 VOCABULARY & PRONUNCIATION
electronic devices; linking

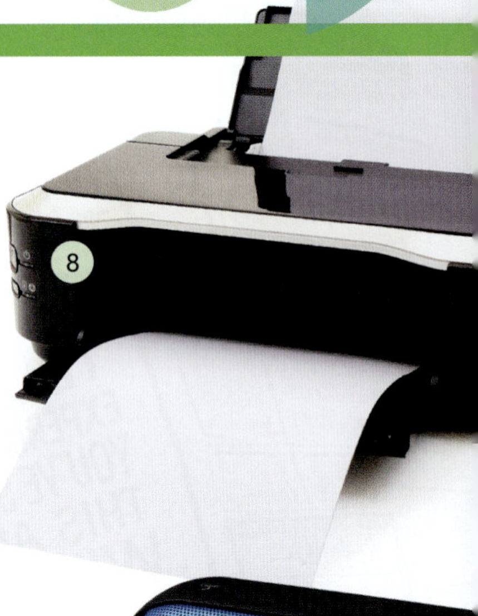

a How many devices do you have with screens? Which one do you use the most?

b Match the words and photos.

- ☐ an adaptor /əˈdæptə/
- ☐ a charger /ˈtʃɑːdʒə/
- ☐ a keyboard /ˈkiːbɔːd/
- *1* a memory stick /ˈmeməri stɪk/
- ☐ a mouse /maʊs/
- ☐ a plug /plʌɡ/
- ☐ a printer /ˈprɪntə/
- ☐ a remote control /rɪˌməʊt kənˈtrəʊl/
- ☐ a router /ˈruːtə/
- ☐ a socket /ˈsɒkɪt/
- ☐ a speaker /ˈspiːkə/
- ☐ a switch /swɪtʃ/
- ☐ a USB cable /ˌjuː es ˈbiː keɪbl/

c 9.9 Listen and check. Then cover the words and test each other.

d Match the sentences to phrasal verbs A–J.

1 ☐ I changed the heating from 20° to 18°.
2 ☐ I disconnected my printer from the computer.
3 ☐ I made the volume on the TV louder.
4 ☐ I pressed the 'off' button on the TV.
5 ☐ I programmed the alarm on my phone for 7.30.
6 ☐ I put my phone charger into a socket.
7 ☐ I pressed the 'on' button on my laptop.
8 ☐ I got the latest version of an app.
9 ☐ I put antivirus software on my computer.
10 ☐ I removed a photo I didn't like.

A I **switched** it **off**.
B I **deleted** it.
C I **updated** it.
D I **turned** it **up**.
E I **installed** it.
F I **unplugged** it.
G I **set** it.
H I **turned** it **down**.
I I **plugged** it **in**.
J I **switched** it **on**.

e 9.10 Listen and check.

f 9.11 Listen and repeat A–J. Try to link the words. Now cover A–J and look at sentences 1–10. Say A–J from memory.

> **Separable phrasal verbs**
> Remember that many phrasal verbs are separable, i.e. the object can go between the verb and particle, e.g. ***switch** the TV **on***, or after the particle, e.g. ***switch on** the TV*. However, if the object is a pronoun, it must go between the verb and particle, e.g. *switch **it** on* **NOT** ~~*switch on it*~~.

g Answer the questions with a partner. Give reasons.

1 Do you prefer to use a keyboard with or without a mouse? Do you prefer a wireless mouse?
2 Do you normally listen to music with headphones or with a speaker?
3 How many remote controls do you have? Do you think you have too many?
4 How many pins do plugs in your country have? Do you need a travel adaptor if you go abroad?
5 In your house, do you usually agree about what the temperature should be, or is someone always turning the heating or air conditioning up and down?

2 LISTENING & SPEAKING

a Do you think you're addicted to your phone? How many times an hour do you look at it? What for?

b Read the article about digital detox. Then answer the questions with a partner.

1 What does *digital detox* mean?
2 Do you think phone stacking is a good idea? Do you and your friends ever do it?
3 What does *unplug* mean in the third paragraph? Do you have periods in the day or during the week when you 'unplug'? Do you enjoy life more when you're 'unplugged'?

Less time online:
millions of Britons take digital detox

Taking a break from technology is on the rise. According to a recent study by Ofcom, the UK Office of Communications:

- More and more young people are 'phone stacking' when they go out for a coffee or a meal, putting their phones in the middle of the table and agreeing not to look at them. The first person who looks at their phone pays the bill!

- 34% of internet users have taken a break from their devices in the last 12 months. This break was usually for no more than a day, though some people took a break of a week, or even a month.

- The under-25s are most likely to 'unplug'. Feedback from these 'digital detoxers' is very positive – 33% said they got more done in their lives when they weren't online, and 21% said they enjoyed life more. Only 8% found the experience 'stressful'.

c 🔊 9.12 Australian journalist Anna Magee went on a three-day digital detox course run by the organization Time to Log Off. Listen to five things she said about the course. Are they positive or negative?

d 🔊 9.13 Now listen to her talking about it on a radio programme. On the whole, did she feel it was a positive or negative experience?

e Listen again and mark the sentences **T** (true) or **F** (false). Correct the **F** sentences.

1 A quarter of UK adults check their phones in the middle of the night.
2 When Anna arrived at the house in Dorset, she felt very nervous.
3 The activities were not exactly what she was expecting.
4 The second day of the detox was easier than the first.
5 By the third day, her ability to concentrate had improved.
6 On her train journey home, she spent the time checking her phone.
7 Since the detox, her weekends and evenings are technology-free.
8 She enjoys her friends' company more than she used to.

f Discuss the questions with a partner.

1 If you went on a digital detox course, what do you think you would miss the most? How would you feel?
2 Do you think digital detoxes are a good idea or a stupid idea? Do you think it's really necessary to take a break from technology?
3 Have you been without the internet (or phone coverage) recently? Why? Did you miss it?

3 GRAMMAR quantifiers

a With a partner, read sentences 1–6 and think about what the missing words could be. Don't write them in yet.

1 I used to have _____ _____ of different gadgets, but now I use my phone for almost everything.
2 I'd like to have a better computer, but I don't have _____ _____ to buy one right now.
3 I spend _____ _____ time online. I think I need a digital detox.
4 I have a lot of friends on Facebook, but only _____ _____ of them are close friends.
5 I never watch TV or films on my phone, because the screen isn't _____ _____.
6 I like Apple products, but I can't afford them – I think they're _____ _____.

b 🔊 9.14 Now listen and complete the sentences in **a**. Did you guess correctly?

c Ⓖ p.149 Grammar Bank 9B

d Talk to a partner. Are the sentences in **a** true for you? Say why (not).

4 PRONUNCIATION *ough* and *augh*

> 🔍 **ough and augh**
> Be careful with the letters *ough* and *augh*. There are several different pronunciations. Try to remember how to pronounce the most common words which have this combination of letters, e.g. *although*, *daughter*.

a Write the words from the list in the correct column.

although   bought   brought   caught   cough   daughter
enough   laugh   thought   through   tough

b 🔊 9.19 Listen and check. Which is the most common sound? Which four words finish with the sound /f/?

c 🔊 9.20 Listen to sentences 1–5. Practise saying them.

1 I bought a new iPhone, although I thought it was very expensive.
2 My daughter's caught a bad cold.
3 We've been through some tough times.
4 I didn't laugh! It was a cough.
5 You haven't brought enough wine!

5 READING & SPEAKING

a Work with a partner and answer the questions. Who has a more organized digital life?

- How many **photos** do you have on your phone? Are they organized into albums? How quickly could you find a photo you wanted to show someone?
- Do you have any **apps** on your phone that you never use?
- How many **email accounts** do you have? Approximately how many emails do you have in your inbox?
- How many **songs** do you have on your phone or MP3 player? How many of them do you listen to regularly?
- How many **friends** do you have on Facebook? How many of them are real friends?
- How many people in your 'contacts' have you not contacted in the last year?
- How many different **passwords** do you have? How do you remember them?
- What's the **wallpaper** on your phone or computer screen? Is it one of your photos, or did it come with the phone or device?
- How many digital **devices** do you have that you never use, e.g. old phones / cameras / MP3 players, etc.?

b Look at the title of the article and the 11 headings. Tick (✓) the areas of your digital life that you think you need to tidy up.

11 WAYS TO
TIDY UP YOUR DIGITAL LIFE

A clean, tidy room makes you feel better about your home. In the same way, a tidy phone, tablet, or computer makes you feel better about your digital life. So if your digital life is a mess, try these tips – the benefits are huge.

1 INBOX MESSAGES
Most people have too many emails in their inbox. You don't have hundreds of unopened or unanswered letters in your house, so why should you have hundreds of unopened or unanswered emails? If you can _____ an email in less than two minutes, do it right away. If it will take longer, don't leave it in your inbox – move it into a 'work in progress' folder and reply later.

2 OLD SOFTWARE OR APPS
Uninstall software or apps that you don't use. This will _____ a lot more space on your hard drive or phone.

3 PHOTOS
You wouldn't put bad photos in a physical photo album, so don't keep bad photographs (or videos) on your phone – just delete them. Having poor-quality photos just makes it more difficult to _____ a good photo when you need one.

4 MUSIC AND MOVIES
One of the best things about digital media is that you have every song and movie at your fingertips. Unfortunately, one of the worst things about digital media is that you have every song and movie at your fingertips. _____ any music or movie files that you're never going to listen to or watch again.

5 FACEBOOK FRIENDS
Having too many friends on Facebook makes it more difficult to _____ in touch with the ones you really care about. You can 'unfollow' Facebook friends without them knowing, so you won't hurt their feelings.

6 OLD CONTACT INFORMATION
_____ contact information regularly and delete contacts you no longer need. Most people don't do this often enough.

7 PASSWORDS
Use a password manager app, like 1password. This gives you as many different passwords as you need and remembers them for you. You'll never _____ a password again.

8 EMAIL MARKETING
If you get too many emails from companies and organizations, don't just delete them – unsubscribe. It should only take a few seconds. Just _____ on the 'unsubscribe' link at the bottom of the email.

9 EMAIL ACCOUNTS
Never _____ more than two email accounts (work and personal). For most people, one should be enough.

10 DESKTOP BACKGROUND OR WALLPAPER
_____ a simple background or wallpaper for your screens. This will improve your productivity and attention span more than you think.

11 OLD DIGITAL DEVICES
If you've been using technology for any length of time, you probably have a small collection of devices that you no longer use – cameras, memory sticks, MP3 players, and mobiles. If you can't give them to somebody who would use them, _____ old devices properly.

Adapted from a website

---

c Read the article and complete the gaps with a verb from the list.

> answer   choose   click   delete
> find   forget   keep   make   recycle
> set up   update

d Search the text. Find five words with the prefix *un-* to complete the tips.

Tip 1 Why should you have hundreds of un_____ or un_____ emails?

Tip 2 Un_____ software or apps that you don't use.

Tip 5 You can 'un_____' Facebook friends without them knowing…

Tip 8 Click on the 'un_____' link at the bottom of the email.

e Complete the sentences with *un-* and the words from the list.

> clear   comfortable   do   friend
> helpful   known   lock   read

1 Why do you have over 100 _____ emails?

2 If you want to _____ what you've done, press Ctrl+Z.

3 What's the difference between *to unfollow* and *to* _____ somebody on Facebook?

4 I can't _____ my phone – I've forgotten the password.

5 The IT Support person was very _____. I still can't print anything.

6 I didn't answer the phone, because it said 'caller _____'.

7 I can't set up the new router – the instructions are really _____.

8 I hate earphones – I find them really _____.

f Which of the tips in the article would be most useful for you? Choose your top three. Then discuss your choices in small groups and say why.

6 WRITING

W p.123 **Writing** An article – advantages and disadvantages Write an article about the advantages and disadvantages of smartphones.

Go online to review the lesson

Practical English Unexpected events

indirect questions

1 ▶ JENNY GETS A SURPRISE

a 🔊 **9.21** Watch or listen. How do you think Jenny and Rob feel at the end?

b Watch or listen again and mark the sentences **T** (true) or **F** (false). Correct the **F** sentences.

1 Jenny didn't expect Paul to be there.
2 Paul tells Jenny that Rob is planning to stay in New York.
3 Rob arrives with croissants for breakfast.
4 Paul lies to Jenny about Rob's plans.
5 Rob insists that he's serious about Jenny.
6 Rob says he will drive Paul to Boston.

2 ▶ INDIRECT QUESTIONS

a 🔊 **9.22** Watch or listen to Rob and Jenny talking in the office. Do they resolve their problems?

b Watch or listen again and answer the questions.

1 What reason does Rob give for Paul being in his flat?
2 How does Rob know that Paul is really leaving?
3 Why doesn't Jenny believe that Rob wants to stay in New York?
4 According to Jenny, how did Rob behave when he was with Paul?
5 What does Jenny think about their relationship?

c 🔊 **9.23** Look at some extracts from the conversation. Can you remember any of the missing words? Watch or listen and check.

1	Jenny	Could you _____ me why Paul is still in your apartment?
	Rob	Well, he couldn't get a ticket to Boston…
2	Jenny	Do you _____ if he's got one now?
	Rob	I bought it! He's leaving this evening.
3	Jenny	Look Rob, I'd _____ to know what you really want.
	Rob	What do you mean?
4	Jenny	I _____ if you really want to be here. I wonder if…
	Rob	Jenny, what is it?
5	Don	I need a word. _____ you tell me what you decided at the last meeting?
	Jenny	Right away, Don. Rob was just leaving.

d 🔊 **9.24** Watch or listen and repeat the highlighted phrases. Copy the rhythm and intonation.

e Practise the conversations in **c** with a partner.

f Read the information about indirect questions. Then make questions 1–5 more indirect by using the beginnings given.

1 Where's the station?
   Excuse me, can you tell me _____?

2 What did he say?
   I'd like to know _____.

3 Does she like me?
   I wonder _____.

4 Is your brother coming tonight?
   Do you know _____?

5 What time does the shop close?
   Could you tell me _____?

g 🌐 **Communication** Asking politely for information
A p.110 B p.114 Practise indirect questions.

3 ▶ ROB GETS SERIOUS

a 🔊 **9.25** Do you think there's going to be a happy ending? Watch or listen to Rob and Jenny and check.

b Watch or listen again and complete the sentences with no more than four words.

1 Rob is trying to convince Jenny that he _____.
2 Jenny says that she's sure that Rob wants to _____.
3 Rob says that he loves his _____.
4 Jenny and Rob are going to visit _____.
5 Rob promises not to forget _____.
6 Rob asks Jenny to _____.

c Look at the **Social English** phrases. Can you remember any of the missing words?

💬 **Social English**

1 **Jenny** It's _____ you want to go back.
2 **Rob**   Of _____ I miss London, but I love my life here.
3 **Rob**   And I won't forget the chocolates this time _____.
4 **Jenny** Well, that's a start, I _____.
5 **Rob**   _____ if I proposed to you?
6 **Jenny** Rob, _____ it. It's embarrassing.

d 🔊 **9.26** Watch or listen and complete the phrases. Then watch or listen again and repeat.

e Complete conversations A–F with **Social English** phrases 1–6. Then practise them with a partner.

A	Are you sure you want to come out with me tonight?	☐ I want to come. I'm looking forward to it.
B	Ten times one is ten, ten times two is twenty, ten times three is…	Please ☐. You're really annoying me.
C	What shall I get, spinach or cauliflower?	Actually, I don't like spinach and I don't really like cauliflower ☐. How about broccoli?
D	When's the best day for us to meet?	Tomorrow or Thursday, ☐. You decide.
E	I still can't decide which restaurant to book.	☐ we stayed at home and got a takeaway?
F	Do you think we could leave now? I'm really tired.	OK. ☐ you're really not enjoying the party.

CAN YOU…?

☐ make indirect questions, e.g. beginning with *Can you tell me…?*

☐ discuss a problem

Who is she?

She's the author who wrote *To Kill a Mockingbird*.

1 READING

a Look at the nine photos and read the introduction. How many people can you name? Go to **Communication p.110** and check. Then write their names next to 1–9 in the texts.

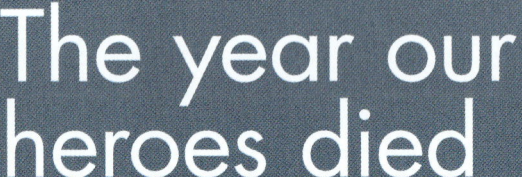

The year our heroes died

Many people think that 2016 was one of the worst years in history for deaths of influential people. They were people who entertained us and educated us, people we loved and people we hated, but all of them were icons…

b Now read about the people. Which ones did you already know most about?

1   **Died 10 January 2016 aged 69**

His death came as a shock to many, including his friends, and in the hour after his death was made public, 20,000 tweets a minute were posted about him. He had released his album *Blackstar* only two days before he died. It went on to win five Grammys in 2017.

2   **Died 14 January 2016 aged 69**

From Shakespeare to Severus Snape in the Harry Potter films, his voice was memorable in every role he played. He was 41 when he made his breakthrough film performance, playing opposite Bruce Willis in *Die Hard*. When he died, J.K. Rowling tweeted, 'There are no words to express how shocked and devastated I am to hear of his death. He was a magnificent actor & a wonderful man.'

3   **Died 19 February 2016 aged 89**

She wrote one of the United States' best-loved novels, *To Kill a Mockingbird*, which is considered a classic of modern literature and has sold more than 40 million copies worldwide. After its publication in 1960, she retreated from public life and became an object of curiosity in the modern media age. Her only other novel, *Go Set a Watchman*, was written before *To Kill a Mockingbird*, but not published until July 2014, 54 years later.

4   **Died 24 March 2016 aged 68**

A football legend who made his name as a forward with Ajax and Barcelona, he was European Footballer of the Year three times and later became a successful coach. The Dutch FA described him as the 'greatest Dutch footballer of all time and one of the world's best ever'.

5   **Died 31 March 2016 aged 65**

Born in Iraq, she was a world-famous architect, whose Aquatic Centre at the 2012 London Olympics was probably her best-known work in the UK. Her buildings were modern and futuristic, with sensuous lines, and she was the first woman to receive the Royal Institute of British Architects Gold Medal.

6   **Died 21 April 2016 aged 57**

Born in Minneapolis, USA, he was a child prodigy and a self-taught multi-instrumentalist, best known for hits including *Purple Rain*, *When Doves Cry*, and *Alphabet St.* In addition to making 39 studio albums himself, he also wrote many songs for other artists.

c Read questions 1–9 and find the answers in the texts. Write the initials of the person.

According to the texts, who…?

1 ____ was the youngest when he / she died
2 ____ changed jobs but did equally well in both
3 ____ was child, friend, and partner of famous singers
4 ____ had a connection with the Olympic Games
5 ____ changed his / her name completely, and had a famous nickname
6 ____ became famous for the first time when he / she was middle-aged
7 ____ did not want any publicity or recognition in later life
8 ____ spent time following a particular religion
9 ____ was awarded prizes for something he / she did shortly before dying

d Do you particularly admire any of these people? What other famous people do you admire?

---

7 **Died 3 June 2016 aged 74**

Born Cassius Clay and nicknamed 'The Greatest', he was widely considered to be the best heavyweight boxer of all time. He was famous for his comments both before and after matches almost as much as for his boxing skills. He also became a prominent civil rights figure, who campaigned for black equality and refused to fight in the Vietnam War.

8 **Died 7 November 2016 aged 82**

A Canadian singer-songwriter, poet, and novelist, his most famous song was probably *Hallelujah*, recorded by more than 300 different artists. At the age of 60, he moved to California, where he lived as a Buddhist monk for five years. One of his muses was Marianne Jensen, the Norwegian woman who he lived with on the Greek island of Hydra and for whom he wrote the song *So Long, Marianne*. Her death in early 2016 inspired his final album, *You want it darker*.

9 **Died 27 December 2016 aged 60**

She was the daughter of actress Debbie Reynolds and singer Eddie Fisher and it was the role of Princess Leia in the first Star Wars film which made her famous. From 1977 to 1983, she dated musician Paul Simon, who she met on the set of Star Wars, and she was later very close friends with the singer James Blunt.

---

2 GRAMMAR relative clauses

a Cover the text. Complete the relative clauses with *who*, *whose*, *which*, or *where*. Who are the extracts about?

1 She wrote *To Kill a Mockingbird*, _____ is considered a classic of modern literature.
2 At the age of 60, he moved to California, _____ he lived as a Buddhist monk for five years. One of his muses was Marianne Jensen, the Norwegian woman _____ he lived with on the Greek island of Hydra.
3 It was the role of Princess Leia in the first Star Wars film _____ made her famous.
4 He also became a prominent civil rights figure, _____ campaigned for black equality.
5 She was a world-famous architect, _____ Aquatic Centre at the 2012 London Olympics was probably her best-known work in the UK.

b ⓖ **p.150 Grammar Bank 10A**

c In pairs, look at the photos in **1** again. Cover the texts.

A Say a sentence about each person beginning *He / She is the actor / writer*, etc. *who / that / whose…*
B Try to add some more information.

3 SPEAKING

a Look at the quiz questions. How many can you answer?

What do you call…?

1 a person who appears in crowd scenes in films
2 the place with black and white stripes where you cross the road
3 the part of the body you use to taste
4 the thing which covers the top of a house
5 a man who a woman is going to marry

b ⓒ **Communication** Relative clauses quiz **A p.110 B p.114** Write and ask quiz questions.

4 WRITING

Ⓦ **p.124 Writing** A biography Write a biography of an interesting or successful person.

5 LISTENING

a 🔊 **10.3** Look at four famous examples of British design which featured on stamps. Do you have, or have you seen, any of these things? In which decade do you think they were created? Listen and check.

b 🔊 **10.4** Now listen to an audio guide for an exhibition about British design. Make notes about the following things.

1 The red phone box
- the Post Office
- Liverpool Cathedral and Tate Modern
- red, silver, and blue
- the Royal Academy of Arts in Piccadilly
- libraries and art galleries

2 The Anglepoise lamp
- suspension systems for cars
- Carwardine's company going bankrupt
- the human arm
- the Anglepoise model 1227
- hospital theatres and military aeroplanes

3 The Penguin book covers
- Allen Lane and a railway platform in 1935
- his secretary
- Edward Young and London Zoo
- Agatha Christie and Ernest Hemingway
- orange, blue, and green covers

4 The miniskirt
- the Beatles and the first man on the moon
- 'Bazaar' in the King's Road
- Mary Quant's school uniform
- tap dancers and the Mini
- Coco Chanel

c Compare your answers with a partner. Then listen again and add more information.

d Cover the notes and look at the design icons. What facts can you remember about them?

e Which of the four do you think has the most attractive design? What would you consider to be examples of iconic design in your country?

Glossary
a spring

The red phone box, designed by Giles Gilbert Scott

The Anglepoise lamp, designed by George Carwardine

British Design Classics

The Penguin book covers, designed by Edward Young

The miniskirt, designed by Mary Quant

6 SPEAKING

a Write the names of people, things, or places in as many of the rectangles as you can.

a famous dead person (who) you admire

Captain R. Scott, polar explorer

a famous living person (that) you admire

Malala Yousafzai, activist for women's education

an iconic landmark (that) you really like

St Paul's cathedral, London

a company whose design you love

Apple logo

an everyday object (that) you own that you think has a beautiful design

Aalto vase

an object (which) you would like to own whose design you love

Eames lounge chair

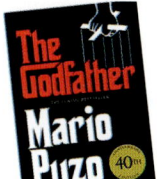

a DVD cover, film poster, or book cover (that) you think has a great design

The Godfather book cover

b In groups, talk about your people, things, and places. Explain why you admire them.

7 VOCABULARY & PRONUNCIATION
compound nouns; word stress

a Match a noun from column A to a noun from column B to make compound nouns.

A	B
paper	manufacturer
book	lamp
child	box
car	cover
desk	writer
song	back
phone	prodigy

b 🔊10.5 Listen and check. Which two are written as one word? Is the first or second noun usually stressed? Practise saying the compound nouns in **a** with the correct stress.

c In pairs, try to answer all the questions in **three minutes** with compound nouns from Files 1–10.

Compound nouns race

1 What do you call part of a road that only bicycles can use?

2 What do you call the busy time of day when many people are going to work or going home?

3 What might you have to pay if you park in a place where you shouldn't?

6 What should you put on when you get into a car?

5 What do you call a long line of cars that can't move?

4 What do you need to book if you want to play tennis with someone?

7 What do you call the person who is in charge of a school?

8 What do you call the music in a film?

9 What kind of books or films are about the future, often outer space?

12 What do you call a school which is paid for by the government?

11 If you are in a lift and you press G, where do you want to go?

10 What can you use to transfer files from one computer to another if the internet isn't working?

🔄 Go online to review the lesson

G question tags **V** crime **P** intonation in question tags

> You were a detective with Scotland Yard, weren't you?

> Yes, I was.

1 VOCABULARY & READING
crime

a Have you heard of Jack the Ripper? Do you know anything about him?

b Match the words in the list to definitions 1–9.

detectives /dɪˈtektɪvz/   evidence /ˈevɪdəns/
murder /ˈmɜːdə/   murderer /ˈmɜːdərə/
prove /pruːv/   solve /sɒlv/   suspects /ˈsʌspekts/
victims /ˈvɪktɪmz/   witnesses /ˈwɪtnəsɪz/

1 _____ *noun* police officers who investigate crimes
2 _____ *noun* people who see something which has happened and then tell others (e.g. the police) about it
3 _____ *noun* people who are hurt or killed by somebody in a crime
4 _____ *noun* a person who kills another person deliberately
5 _____ *noun* the crime of killing a person illegally and deliberately
6 _____ *noun* the facts, signs, etc. which tell you who committed a crime
7 _____ *noun* people who are thought to be guilty of a crime
8 _____ (a mystery) *verb* to find the correct answer to why something happened
9 _____ (sth) *verb* to use facts and evidence to show something is true

c 🔊 **10.6** Listen and check. Practise saying the words.

d Read the article about an unsolved crime and complete the gaps with words from **b**.

e Read the article again and find the answer to these questions.
1 Where and when did the murders take place?
2 How many murders were there?
3 How long did the murders go on for?
4 What kind of people have been suspects?

luck',
yours truly
Jack the Ripper
ind one giving the trade nam

THE GREATEST UNSOLVED CRIME

One of the greatest unsolved ¹*murder* mysteries of all time is that of Jack the Ripper.

In the autumn of 1888, a brutal ²_____ walked the dark, foggy streets of Whitechapel, in east London, terrorizing the inhabitants of the city. The ³_____ were all women and the police seemed powerless to stop the murders. There were no ⁴_____ to the crimes, so the police had no idea what the murderer looked like. Panic and fear among Londoners was increased by a letter sent to Scotland Yard by the murderer. In the letter, he made fun of the police's attempts to catch him and promised to kill again. It finished, 'Yours truly, Jack the Ripper'. This was the first of many letters sent to the police. The murders continued – five in total. But in November, they suddenly stopped, three months after they had first begun.

Jack the Ripper was never caught, and for more than a century, historians, writers, and ⁵_____ have examined the ⁶_____ and tried to discover and ⁷_____ his identity. Hundreds of articles and books have been written and many films made about the murders. But the question, 'Who was Jack the Ripper?' has remained unanswered. There have been plenty of ⁸_____, including a doctor, a businessman, a painter, a sailor, a singer, and even a member of the royal family, and all sorts of people over the years have tried to ⁹_____ this real-life murder mystery.

2 LISTENING

a ◀️ 10.7 Listen to Part 1 of an interview with a retired police inspector, who is an expert on Jack the Ripper. Who is Jan Bondeson's suspect? Write 1 in the box and complete his occupation.

| 1 Jan Bondeson | 2 Bruce Robinson | 3 Patricia Cornwell |

| ☐ Walter Sickert, a _____ | ☐ Hendrik de Jong, a _____ | ☐ Michael Maybrick, a _____ |

Glossary
the Freemasons a secret society whose members help each other and communicate using secret signs
Isle of Wight an island off the south coast of England
DNA the chemical in the cells of animals and plants that carries genetic information

b Listen again and make notes about Jan Bondeson's theory in the chart.

	1 Jan	2 Bruce	3 Patricia
what evidence there is			
what Inspector Morton thinks			

c ◀️ 10.8, 10.9 Repeat for Part 2 (Bruce Robinson's theory) and Part 3 (Patricia Cornwell's theory).

d Which of the three suspects do you think is the most / least credible? Do you know of any famous unsolved crimes in your country?

3 GRAMMAR question tags

a Look at four questions from the interview and complete the gaps.

1 'You were a detective with Scotland Yard, _____ _____?'
2 'It's incredible, _____ _____?'
3 'But he was never arrested, _____ _____?'
4 'But you don't think she's right, _____ _____?'

b ◀️ 10.10 Listen and check. Now make the direct questions for 1–4. What's the difference between the two types of question?

c Ⓖ p.151 **Grammar Bank 10B**

4 PRONUNCIATION & SPEAKING
intonation in question tags

a ◀️ 10.12 Listen and complete the conversation between a policeman and a suspect.

P Your surname's Jones, ¹_____?
S Yes, it is.
P And you're 27, ²_____?
S Yes, that's right.
P You weren't at home last night at 8.00, ³_____?
S No, I wasn't. I was at the theatre.
P But you don't have any witnesses, ⁴_____?
S Yes, I do. My wife was with me.
P Your wife wasn't with you, ⁵_____?
S How do you know?
P Because she was with me. At the police station. We arrested her yesterday.

b ◀️ 10.13 Listen and repeat the statements and question tags. Copy the rhythm and intonation.

c Ⓒ**Communication** Just checking A p.110 B p.114 Role-play a police interview.

d Which TV detective series or murder mystery films are popular in your country at the moment? Do you enjoy watching these kinds of programmes?

5 READING & LISTENING

a Do you enjoy reading crime novels? If yes, do you have a favourite author?

b 🔊 10.14 Read and listen to Part 1 of a short story. Then with a partner, explain what the highlighted phrases refer to.

1 June, however, was both, and her sunny personality brought her many admirers. *l.05*

2 During that time, May almost became beautiful, but the intensity of her passion frightened Mrs Thrace. *l.09*

3 It was all very unfortunate, Mrs Thrace said over and over again. *l.15*

4 'She's ruined my life.' *l.21*

5 This thought was the only thing that comforted her. *l.31*

c 🔊 10.15 Now read and listen to Part 2. Then answer the questions with a partner.

1 How did May react to her sister at a) her father's funeral, b) her brother-in-law's funeral?

2 Why did June invite May to live with her?

3 Why do you think June didn't want to talk about her life with Walter?

4 Why did May search the house for letters or presents from Walter?

5 Why do you think May started wearing her engagement ring again?

d Search the text. In Part 1, find...

1 two adjectives: from *change* (v), *wealth* (n)

2 two negative adjectives: from *fortunate* (adj), *known* (adj)

3 two adverbs: from *extreme* (adj), *passion* (n)

In Part 2, find...

4 two nouns: from *die* (v), *marry* (v)

5 two compound nouns with *ring* (n)

May and June By

Part 1

Mr and Mrs Thrace called their daughters May and June because of the months when they were born.

May was the oldest. She was changeable like the month, sometimes warm, sometimes cold, and neither pretty nor clever.
05 June, however, was both, and her sunny personality brought her many admirers. When May was twenty, she met a young lawyer called Walter. He was extremely good-looking and his father was wealthy. May fell passionately in love with him. He asked her to marry him and of course she accepted. During that time,
10 May almost became beautiful, but the intensity of her passion frightened Mrs Thrace.

June was away from home studying to be a teacher when May and Walter got engaged, so Walter had never met her. But a month before the wedding, June came home for the summer
15 holidays. It was all very unfortunate, Mrs Thrace said, over and over again. If Walter had left May for some unknown girl, they would have been furious. But what could they say or do when he had fallen in love with their younger daughter?

May became violent and tried to attack June with a knife.
20 'We're all terribly sorry for you, darling,' said Mrs Thrace. 'I shall never marry now,' said May. 'She's ruined my life. She stole my husband.' 'He wasn't your husband, May,' her mother replied.

When June and Walter came to visit, May always went out,
25 but she knew about them because she always read June's letters to her mother. She knew that they had a big house, that they collected furniture and pictures, and that they didn't have any children. She knew where they went for their holidays and who their friends were. But she could never discover if Walter loved
30 June or not. She thought that perhaps he was sorry that he had married June and not her. This thought was the only thing that comforted her.

Ruth Rendell

Part 2

May never married and she continued to live at home for over 30 years, until her parents died. Mrs Thrace
35 died in March and her husband, six months later. At her father's funeral, May saw Walter and June again. Walter was still good-looking and May wanted to die when she saw him. 'Please come and speak to your sister,' he said to her. But May refused.

40 It was only at another funeral that they were reconciled. May learnt of Walter's death from the newspaper and the pain was as great as when her mother had told her that Walter wanted to marry June. Inside the church, her sister came up to May and asked
45 her to forget about the past. 'Now you know what it's like to lose him,' May said.

Two days later May got a letter from June. June asked her to come and live with her, now that they were both alone. 'Now that you've retired and haven't got
50 very much money, I'd like to share my beautiful house with you,' she wrote. 'Perhaps this way I can give you something in return for what I took away from you.'

May decided to accept. She thought it was right. During their first evening together, she asked June to
55 talk about her marriage, about her life with Walter. But June didn't want to talk. May looked in the house for letters or presents from Walter, jewellery, or pictures. She couldn't find anything. Even June's wedding ring wasn't as beautiful as the engagement ring Walter had
60 given May all those years ago. 'He never really loved her,' she thought. 'All these years, he loved me.' She decided to start wearing her engagement ring again – on her little finger, which was the only one it now fitted.

e Do you think May and June are going to live happily together? How do you think the story is going to end?

f 🔊 10.16 Listen to Part 3. Were you right?

g Listen again. Answer the questions.
1 Why did May forgive June?
2 What did May think had happened when she heard the noise and looked out of the window?
3 What was the living room like when she went in?
4 What had June done?
5 What effect did the letter have on May?
6 What did she do?
7 What excuse did May give for touching the gun?

h Do you feel sorry for May or June?

6 ▶ VIDEO LISTENING

a Watch the documentary *Queens of Crime*. Who do you think had a more interesting life? Who do you think had a happier life?

b Complete the chart with notes on what you remember about the two writers' lives and books.

	Ruth Rendell	Agatha Christie
her life • born • parents • marriages • other things		
her books • first novel • detectives • pseudonyms • films • approach to crime writing		

c Compare your notes with a partner. Then watch the documentary again. Are there any facts that you both missed?

d Have you read any books by Ruth Rendell or Agatha Christie? Did you like them? Are there any other crime novelists whose books you enjoy?

🔴 **Go online** to watch the video and review the lesson

GRAMMAR

Circle a, b, or c.

1 If you ____ on time, we wouldn't have missed the start of the film.
   a arrived   b 'd arrived
   c would have arrived

2 What ____ if that man hadn't helped you?
   a you would do
   b you would have done
   c would you have done

3 If she ____ me that she was arriving this morning, I would have gone to the airport to pick her up.
   a told   b would tell   c had told

4 I would have finished the exam if I ____ about another ten minutes.
   a would have had   b had had
   c would have

5 I'm afraid there's ____ time left.
   a no   b none   c any

6 There are ____ good programmes on tonight. I don't know what to watch.
   a lots of   b a lot   c plenty

7 Is there ____ in the car for me, too?
   a room enough   b enough room
   c too much room

8 Most people have ____ close friends.
   a very little   b very few   c not much

9 Is he the man ____ you met at the party?
   a –   b whose   c which

10 Is that the woman ____ husband is a famous writer?
   a who   b that   c whose

11 *The Starry Night*, ____ was painted in 1889, is by Vincent van Gogh.
   a which   b what   c that

12 I'm very fond of Susan, ____ I used to share a flat with at university.
   a who   b –   c that

13 They're very rich, ____?
   a are they   b aren't they   c isn't it

14 Your brother's been to New Zealand, ____?
   a wasn't he   b isn't he   c hasn't he

15 You won't be late, ____?
   a will you   b won't you   c are you

VOCABULARY

a Complete the sentences with a word formed from the **bold** word.

1 I left home late, but _____ I got to work on time. **luck**
2 He's _____ with his work. It's always full of mistakes. **care**
3 This sofa is really _____. It's much too hard. **comfort**
4 I love this jacket, but _____ it's too expensive. **fortunate**
5 Don't be so _____! The bus will be here soon. **patience**

b Complete with a verb.

1 It was too hot in the room, so I _____ the heating down.
2 I need to _____ my alarm for 5.30, as I have an early flight.
3 It's a good idea to _____ your computer during a storm.
4 Could you _____ up the volume? I can't hear very well.
5 If you're not watching the TV, please _____ it off.

c Complete the words from the definitions.

1 you use this to change the TV channel   r_____ c_____
2 you use this on a computer to write   k_____
3 you use this to convert a European plug to a British one   a_____
4 it's the place on the wall where you plug things in   s_____
5 you use this to move the cursor on a computer   m_____

d Complete the compound nouns.

1 b_____ cover   4 s_____ writer
2 ch_____ prodigy   5 phone b_____
3 desk l_____

e Complete the words.

1 The d_____ was convinced that the man's alibi was false.
2 I'm sure he's guilty, but I can't pr_____ it.
3 Jack the Ripper's v_____ were all women.
4 They are sure they will be able to s_____ the mystery.
5 Walter Sickert is a s_____ in the Jack the Ripper case.

PRONUNCIATION

a Practise the words and sounds.

Vowel sounds   Consonant sounds

up   horse   clock   tourist   flower   witch   yacht   vase

b **P p.166-7 Sound Bank** Say more words for each sound.

c What sound in **a** do the pink letters have in these words?

1 caught   2 cough   3 enough   4 solve   5 tough

d Underline the stressed syllable.

1 comfor|ta|ble   3 ca|ble   5 e|vi|dence
2 a|dap|tor   4 wit|ness

CAN YOU understand this text?

a Read the article once. Complete headings 1–4.

1 _____ IS THE LONDON DUNGEON?

The London Dungeon brings together amazing actors, special effects, stage performances, scenes, and rides in a truly unique and exciting experience that you see, hear, touch, smell, and feel. It's dark, atmospheric, hilarious, and sometimes a bit scary.

2 _____ DOES IT WORK?

We've been entertaining audiences at The London Dungeon for over 40 years and it's one of the capital's 'must-see' attractions. We take you on a 110-minute journey through 1,000 years of London's unpleasant past. You and your companions walk through the Dungeon, moving from show to show, guided by our professional actors.

The shows are based on real London history and legends, without the boring bits! You'll get up close and personal with scary characters including Jack the Ripper and the infamous barber of Fleet Street, Sweeney Todd.

It's a theatrical experience. That means authentic sets and theatrical storytelling. On your journey, you'll pass through foggy East London streets and houses and the horrific torture chamber. Believe us, it's better than a sightseeing trip or boring museum tour of London.

3 _____ 'S IT FOR?

The London Dungeon is scary fun for everyone except very young guests and very sensitive adults! Our recommended age is 12 years old and above, and guests who are under 16 years of age must be accompanied by an adult over 18 years of age.

4 _____ AHEAD!

The London Dungeon is particularly brilliant for people who can plan ahead and book online! Not only will you save money, you won't have to wait on the day. We get busy, so make things easy on yourself and book in advance!

Adapted from the website

b Read the article again. Mark the sentences **T** (true), **F** (false), or **DS** (doesn't say).

1 The London Dungeon is both funny and frightening.
2 The Dungeon isn't very popular.
3 You're not allowed to talk to the actors.
4 You can spend as long as you like at the Dungeon.
5 The characters and stories are all historically accurate.
6 The Dungeon is suitable for very young children.
7 Tickets for children under 16 cost half the adult price.
8 Booking online is cheaper than paying on the day.

▶ CAN YOU understand these people?

◄))10.17 Watch or listen and choose a, b, or c.

1 Sean   2 Adrian   3 Nick   4 Emma   5 Coleen

1 Sean helped a little girl who had ____.
  a left her toy panda on a train
  b dropped her toy panda in the station
  c lost her toy panda in the car park
2 Because of Google maps, Adrian no longer ____.
  a uses his car's satnav   b plans his route in advance
  c buys maps
3 Nick's favourite detective is ____.
  a a female detective in *The Killing*
  b a male detective in *The Bridge*
  c a female detective in *The Bridge*
4 Emma is going to buy a dress by Maggie Sottero ____.
  a because she's getting married
  b although they're very expensive
  c because she saw some in a magazine
5 Coleen considers she has been lucky ____.
  a because she has never had a car accident
  b on many occasions
  c because she recently survived a car accident

CAN YOU say this in English?

Tick (✓) the box if you can do these things.

Can you…?

1 ☐ complete these three sentences:
If you'd told me about the party earlier,…
I would have bought those shoes if…
I wouldn't have been so angry if…

2 ☐ describe something that you do too much and something that you don't do enough

3 ☐ describe a person that you admire, saying who they are, what you know about them, and why you admire them

4 ☐ check five things you think you know about somebody using question tags

Go online to watch the video, review Files 9 & 10, and check your progress

Communication

6B JUDGING BY APPEARANCES
Students A+B

1 **Dominic McVey** is a British entrepreneur. He was born in London. At the age of 13, he set up a business importing micro-scooters from the US, and he was a millionaire by the age of 15 (in this photo he's 25). His business interests now include fashion, music, media, and cosmetics.

2 **Deshun Wang** is a model, also known as 'the world's hottest grandpa'. He was born in 1936 in Shenyang, China. He's only been modelling since he was 79 years old – before that he was an actor. He has two children and a granddaughter.

3 **Luz Acosta** is a Mexican weightlifter. She was born in 1980. She competed in the Olympics in Beijing in 2008 and in London in 2012. She won a bronze medal from London in 2017, five years after the Games, when a competitor was disqualified for taking drugs.

4 **Ilhan Omar** is a politician. She was born in 1982 in Somalia. Her family emigrated to the United States in 1995. She studied political science and international studies at university, and in 2016 she was elected to the Minnesota House of Representatives. She is the first Somali-American politician in the United States.

7A UNIVERSITY OR NOT?
Student A

a Read about Jack.

> **Jack Turner, 23, studied Fine Art in London.**
>
> When I was at university, my friends and I were free to do what we wanted from the first day of the first year to the last day of the third year. We painted ten hours a day, we partied with our tutors, we shared ideas. I loved it.
>
> After graduating, I moved to Manchester with my girlfriend. She had a good job and I was flexible. I planned to get any job that paid the bills and spend my free time painting. Since then, I've applied for at least 100 jobs and most of them never got in touch. I realize now that I spent too much time at uni focusing on art and not enough getting real-world experience.
>
> Now I'm unemployed. I admit that I sometimes ask myself the question, 'Why did I study Fine Art?' But I'm still applying for jobs and I'm optimistic. As soon as I get one that gives me some financial security, I'll start making art again. I just want to be able to enjoy Manchester with my girlfriend and to paint. It's difficult at the moment, but I'm very happy I studied Fine Art. It was a once-in-a-lifetime experience and it will always be a big part of who I am.

b Ask **B** your questions about Emily-Fleur.

When did Emily-Fleur leave school?

When she was…

Questions about Emily-Fleur
1 When did Emily-Fleur leave school?
2 Why didn't she go to university?
3 Where did she get her idea for her business?
4 What was the first wedding she photographed?
5 How did she get more bookings?
6 When did she buy her equipment?
7 Why does she think it was good to start a business young?
8 Why doesn't she envy her friends at university?

c Now answer **B**'s questions about Jack.

7B GUESS THE SENTENCE Student A

a Look at sentences 1–6 and think of the missing verb phrase (⊞ = positive, ⊟ = negative). **Don't write anything yet!**

1 I'd cook dinner every day if I _____ earlier from work. ⊞
2 If we _____ this summer, maybe we can afford to get a new car. ⊟
3 I think you _____ more if you see it in 3D. ⊞
4 I'd see my grandparents more often if they _____. ⊞
5 I _____ the fish if I were you. It isn't usually very good here. ⊟
6 I _____ if the water was a bit warmer. ⊞

b Read sentence 1 to **B**. If it isn't right, try again until **B** tells you, 'That's right'. Then write it in. Continue with 2–6.

c Now listen to **B** say sentence 7. If it's the same as your sentence 7 below, say, 'That's right'. If not, say 'Try again', until **B** gets it right. Continue with 8–12.

7 I'll **never be able to** buy a house unless my parents help me.
8 If I met my ex in the street, **I wouldn't say hello** to him.
9 If it **wasn't so late**, I'd stay a bit longer.
10 The flight **will be more comfortable** if we go in business class.
11 I wouldn't mind the winter so much if it **didn't get dark** so early.
12 If I had more money, **I'd buy a house** with a beautiful garden.

8A MATCH YOUR PERSONALITY TO THE JOB
Students A+B

In which group(s) do you have most ticks (✓)? Read the appropriate paragraph to find out which jobs would suit you. Would you like to do any of them?

> **If you have most ticks in 1–4,** the best job for you would be in the 'caring professions'. If you are good at science, you could consider a career in medicine, for example, becoming a doctor or nurse. Alternatively, teaching or social work are areas which would suit your personality.
>
> **If you have most ticks in 5–8,** you should consider a job involving numbers, for example, becoming an accountant, or working in the stock market. The world of business would also probably appeal to you, especially sales or marketing.
>
> **If you have most ticks in 9–12,** you need a creative job. Depending on your specific talents, you might enjoy a job in the world of music, art, or literature. Areas that would suit you include publishing, journalism, graphic design, fashion, or the music industry.
>
> **If you have most ticks in 13–16,** you have an analytical mind. You would suit a job in computer science or engineering. You also have good spatial sense, which would make architecture and related jobs another possibility.

8A DRAGONS' DEN Student A

Read what happened. Think about the questions below. Then tell your group.

– Did any of the Dragons like the product?
– Did they decide to invest?
– Was the product successful in the end?

Tingatang

The Dragons quickly decided that they didn't like the idea. Comments included, 'I immediately don't like it.' and 'The best place for you to start is by giving up this ridiculous idea.' So they didn't invest anything. Gill and Sarah didn't give up and carried on selling their pendants and rings at singles clubs and on dating websites, but the idea never really took off and the jewellery is no longer available.

8B GOING THE EXTRA MILE
Students A+B

A ⇨ **Nordstrom**
Finally, they looked through **all the dirt in their vacuum cleaners and found the woman's diamond**!

B ⇨ **Morton's, The Steakhouse**
He was joking, but amazingly, when he got off the plane, in the Arrivals area there was **a Morton's waiter with a bag that contained a steak, potatoes, bread, napkins, and a knife and fork, and it was all free**.

C ⇨ **Ritz-Carlton Hotels**
In it was Joshie, a present of a Frisbee and a football, and a photograph of **Joshie by the hotel pool**.

D ⇨ **Trader Joe's**
Half an hour later, the food arrived at her father's house, with **a note saying that it was free**!

E ⇨ **Apple**
They refunded his money, but they also sent the iPad back to him with another Post-it note saying, **'Apple said yes'**.

8B I WANT TO SPEAK TO THE MANAGER
Student A

Look at the situations and spend a few minutes preparing what you are going to say. Then role-play the conversations.

1 **You're a customer.** You bought something in a clothes shop in the sales yesterday (decide what) and there's a problem (decide what).
Go back to the shop. **B** is the shop assistant. You'd like to change it for another identical one. If you can't, you'd like a refund.
You start.

Excuse me. I bought…

2 **You're the manager of a restaurant.** Your normal chef is off this week and you have a temporary chef who is not very good. One of the waiters has had a problem with a customer, who would like to speak to you. **B** is the customer. When customers complain, you usually offer them a free drink or a coffee. If it's absolutely necessary, you might give a 10% discount on their bill, but you would prefer not to.
B will start.

9A GUESS THE CONDITIONAL Student A

a Look at sentences 1–6 and think of the missing verb phrase (⊞ = positive, ⊟ = negative). **Don't write anything yet!**

1 We _____ the hotel if we hadn't had satnav. ⊟
2 If I _____ that it was your birthday, I would have bought you something. ⊞
3 If I _____ about the concert earlier, I would have been able to get a ticket. ⊞
4 The burglar wouldn't have got in if you _____ the window open. ⊟
5 If our best player hadn't been sent off, we _____ the match. ⊞
6 I wouldn't have recognized her if you _____ me who she was. ⊟

b Read sentence 1 to **B**. If it isn't right, try again until **B** tells you, 'That's right'. Then write it in. Continue with 2–6.

c Now listen to **B** say sentence 7. If it's the same as your sentence 7 below, say, 'That's right'. If not, say, 'Try again' until **B** gets it right. Continue with 8–12.

7 If we hadn't taken a taxi, we **would have missed** the train.
8 If I hadn't gone to the party that night, I **wouldn't have met** my wife.
9 If I'd known that programme was on last night, I **would have watched** it.
10 If I'd listened to my friends, I would never have married James.
11 I **would have gone out** with you last night if I hadn't had to work late.
12 I **wouldn't have been** so angry if you had told me the truth right from the start.

PE5 ASKING POLITELY FOR INFORMATION Student A

a You are a tourist in **B**'s town. You are going to stop **B** in the street. You want to ask questions 1–5 and you want to be very polite. Rewrite 2–5 as indirect questions.

1 Do shops open on Sundays?
Could you tell me *if shops open on Sundays*?
2 Is there a post office near here?
Do you know _____?
3 What time do banks close here?
Could you tell me _____?
4 Where's the railway station?
Do you know _____?
5 Does the number 21 bus go to the city centre?
Can you tell me _____?

b Ask **B** your indirect questions 1–5. Always begin *Excuse me.*

c Now **B** is a tourist in your town. **B** stops you in the street and asks you some questions. Answer politely with the necessary information.

10A THE YEAR OUR HEROES DIED Students A+B

1 David Bowie
2 Alan Rickman
3 Harper Lee
4 Johan Cruyff
5 Zaha Hadid
6 Prince
7 Muhammad Ali
8 Leonard Cohen
9 Carrie Fisher

10A RELATIVE CLAUSES QUIZ Student A

a Complete the questions with a relative clause to describe the **bold** words. Start the clause with *who, which, that, whose,* or *where,* or no relative pronoun when there is a new subject.

1 **a pedestrian** What do you call somebody…?
2 **a loan** What do you call some money…?
3 **fans** What do you call people…?
4 **a boarding school** What do you call a place…?
5 **a coach** What do you call the person…?
6 **traffic lights** What do you call the things…?
7 **golf course** What do you call the place…?
8 **selfish** What do you call somebody…?
9 **a router** What do you call the thing…?

b Ask **B** your question 1.

c Now answer **B**'s question 1.

d Continue with 2–9.

10B JUST CHECKING Student A

a You are a police inspector. **B** is a suspect in a crime. Ask **B** the questions below, but **don't write anything down**. Try to remember **B**'s answers.

- What's your name?
- Where do you live?
- How old are you?
- Where were you born?
- Are you married?
- What do you do?
- What car do you drive?
- How long have you lived in this town?
- What did you do last night?
- Where were you at 7.00 this morning?

b Now check the information with **B** using a question tag.

Your name's Ivan Horváth, isn't it?
You live in Bratislava, don't you?

c Change roles. Now you are the suspect and **B** is the police inspector. Answer **B**'s questions. You can invent the information if you want to.

d **B** will now check the information he / she has. Say, 'Yes, that's right', or 'No, that's wrong' and correct the wrong information.

a   Read about Emily-Fleur.

> **Emily-Fleur Sizmur, 17, runs her own photography business.**
>
> I left school at 16. I've never been very interested in school or academic achievement. I still don't know my GCSE results – a friend went to school to pick them up for me, but I've never opened the envelope!
>
> When I left school, I was ready to start a business. Three of my sisters were getting married and I saw a gap in the market for wedding photographers in our area. I'd always loved taking photos and I saw an opportunity to make money doing something I liked. One of my science teachers was getting married and I asked her if I could take some pictures. She agreed and I put up my photos on Facebook the following day. Within a week, I had bookings for two more weddings. When I'd done six weddings, I spent £3,000 on better equipment.
>
> I don't think my age was a disadvantage, in fact, I think starting out young has been a huge help. People are more prepared to give someone young a chance. If I was 30 and starting out in this business with no experience, I think it would be much more difficult. A lot of my friends are going to university soon, but I don't envy them. They'll have to get out into the real world one day and I'm already here.

Glossary
GCSEs national exams taken by English and Welsh schoolchildren at the age of 16

b   Answer **A**'s questions about Emily-Fleur.

c   Now ask **A** your questions about Jack.

What did Jack study at university?
He studied...

Questions about Jack
1 What did Jack study at university?
2 What did he do on a typical day?
3 What did he do after he graduated?
4 What did he plan to do in Manchester?
5 How many jobs has he applied for?
6 What's he doing at the moment?
7 Is he enjoying life?
8 Does he regret studying Fine Art?

7B GUESS THE SENTENCE Student B

a Look at sentences 7–12 and think of the missing verb phrase (⊞ = positive, ⊟ = negative). **Don't write anything yet!**

7 I'll _____ buy a house unless my parents help me. ⊟

8 If I met my ex in the street, I _____ to him. ⊟

9 If it _____, I'd stay a bit longer. ⊟

10 The flight _____ if we go in business class. ⊞

11 I wouldn't mind the winter so much if it _____ so early. ⊟

12 If I had more money, I _____ with a beautiful garden. ⊞

b Listen to **A** say sentence 1. If it's the same as your sentence 1 below, say, 'That's right'. If not, say 'Try again', until **A** gets it right. Continue with 2–6.

1 I'd cook dinner every day if I **got home** earlier from work.

2 If we **don't go on holiday** this summer, maybe we can afford to get a new car.

3 I think you**'ll enjoy the film** more if you see it in 3D.

4 I'd see my grandparents more often if they **lived nearer**.

5 I **wouldn't have** the fish if I were you. It isn't usually very good here.

6 I**'d go swimming** if the water was a bit warmer.

c Now read sentence 7 to **A**. If it isn't right, try again until **A** tells you, 'That's right'. Then write it in. Continue with 8–12.

8A DRAGON'S DEN Student B

Read what happened. Think about the questions below. Then tell your group.

– Did any of the Dragons like the product?
– Did they decide to invest?
– Was the product successful in the end?

Slappie watches

Two of the Dragons were prepared to give David the money he wanted, although only in exchange for 45% of the company. David decided to accept Dragon Nick Jenkins's offer. Minutes after the programme was broadcast, Slappie's website crashed because it was unable to cope with the 'insane' numbers of people trying to buy watches. Since then, the company has grown and Slappie watches are now available on many different websites, including Amazon.

8B I WANT TO SPEAK TO THE MANAGER Student B

Look at the situations and spend a few minutes preparing what you are going to say. Then role-play the conversations.

1 **You're a shop assistant in a clothes shop. A** is a customer and is going to come to you with a problem with something he / she bought in the sales yesterday. You can't change it for an identical one because there are no more in his / her size. Try to persuade **A** to change it for something else, because you don't usually give refunds during the sales. **A** will start.

2 **You're a customer in a restaurant.** You have just finished your meal and you didn't enjoy it at all (decide what was wrong with it). You complained to the waiter, but the waiter didn't solve the problem. You have asked the waiter to call the manager. **A** is the manager. Try to get at least a 50% discount on your meal. **You** start.

Good evening. Are you the manager?

9A GUESS THE CONDITIONAL Student B

a Look at sentences 7–12 and think of the missing verb phrase (⊞ = positive, ⊟ = negative). **Don't write anything yet!**

7 If we hadn't taken a taxi, we _____ the train. ⊞

8 If I hadn't gone to the party that night, I _____ my wife. ⊟

9 If I'd known that programme was on last night, I _____ it. ⊞

10 If I _____ to my friends, I would never have married James. ⊞

11 I _____ with you last night if I hadn't had to work late. ⊞

12 I _____ so angry if you had told me the truth right from the start. ⊟

b Listen to **A** say sentence 1. If it's the same as your sentence 1 below, say 'That's right'. If not, say 'Try again' until **A** gets it right. Continue with 2–6.

1 We **wouldn't have found** the hotel if we hadn't had satnav.

2 If I **had remembered** that it was your birthday, I would have bought you something.

3 If I**'d known** about the concert earlier, I would have been able to get a ticket.

4 The burglar wouldn't have got in if you **hadn't left** the window open.

5 If our best player hadn't been sent off, we **would have won** the match.

6 I wouldn't have recognized her if you **hadn't told me** who she was.

c Now read sentence 7 to **A**. If it isn't right, try again until **A** tells you 'That's right'. Then write it in. Continue with 8–12.

PE5 ASKING POLITELY FOR INFORMATION Student B

a You are a tourist in **A**'s town. You are going to stop **A** in the street. You want to ask questions 1–5 and you want to be very polite. Rewrite 2–5 as indirect questions.

1 Do shops close at lunchtime?
Could you tell me *if shops close at lunchtime*?
2 Is there a cash machine near here?
Do you know _____?
3 Where's the nearest chemist's?
Can you tell me _____?
4 What time do buses stop running at night?
Do you know _____?
5 Do banks open on Saturday mornings?
Could you tell me _____?

b **A** is a tourist in your town. **A** stops you in the street and asks you some questions. Answer politely with the necessary information.

c Now ask **A** your indirect questions 1–5. Always begin *Excuse me*.

10A RELATIVE CLAUSES QUIZ Student B

a Complete the questions with a relative clause to describe the **bold** words. Start the clause with *who*, *which*, *that*, *whose*, or *where*, or no relative pronoun when there is a new subject.

1 **shy** What do you call somebody…?
2 **a remote control** What do you call the thing…?
3 **a referee** What do you call the person…?
4 **a cycle lane** What do you call the place…?
5 **a thriller** What do you call a film…?
6 **a receipt** What do you call the piece of paper…?
7 **a taxi rank** What do you call the place…?
8 **a colleague** What do you call a person…?
9 **a scooter** What do you call a thing…?

b Answer **A**'s question 1.

c Now ask **A** your question 1.

d Continue with 2–9.

10B JUST CHECKING Student B

a You are a suspect in a crime. **A** is a police inspector. Answer **A**'s questions. You can invent the information if you want to.

b **A** will now check the information he / she has. Say, 'Yes, that's right', or 'No, that's wrong' and correct the wrong information.

c Change roles. Now you are a police inspector and **A** is a suspect. Ask **A** the questions below, but **don't write anything down**. Try to remember **A**'s answers.

- What's your name?
- Where do you live?
- How old are you?
- Where were you born?
- Are you married?
- What do you do?
- What car do you drive?
- How long have you lived in this town?
- What did you do last night?
- Where were you at 7.00 this morning?

d Now check the information with **A** using a question tag.

Your name's John Hatton, isn't it?
You live in New York, don't you?

8A DRAGON'S DEN Student C

Read what happened. Think about the questions below. Then tell your group.

– Did any of the Dragons like the product?
– Did they decide to invest?
– Was the product successful in the end?

Tangle Teezer

The Dragons listened patiently to Shaun's pitch, but when it came to investing in his business, they responded unanimously, 'I'm out!' One Dragon called it 'a waste of time' and Deborah Meaden said it was like a 'horse brush'. However, they were wrong. The brushes are now sold all over the world and have revolutionized the hairdressing industry. A few years after his Dragons' Den appearance, Shaun sold the company for over £100 million. And as he owned it entirely himself, he was the one who enjoyed the profits.

CLASSIC FILMS YOU MUST SEE
PLEASE POST YOUR SUGGESTIONS

The Force Awakens (2015)

1. *The Force Awakens* is the seventh film in the Star Wars saga, created by George Lucas. The film was ¹_____ by J.J. Abrams. It ²_____ John Boyega as Finn, Daisy Ridley as Rey, and Harrison Ford as Han Solo. It was ³_____ for five Oscars in 2016, but it didn't win any.

2. The film is ⁴_____ a long time ago in a galaxy far, far away. It was ⁵_____ in the UK, Ireland, and Abu Dhabi.

3. The story begins 30 years after the events of *Star Wars: Episode VI Return of the Jedi*. Finn, a stormtrooper, leaves the evil organization called the First Order. He follows a little robot, BB-8, who has information about how to find Luke Skywalker, a Jedi who can use a special energy called the Force. Finn and BB-8 are helped by a young woman called Rey, and together they escape and find Han Solo, a space pilot, and his alien friend, Chewbacca. They help Finn and Rey in their search for Skywalker and their mission to destroy the First Order's new superweapon.

4. I strongly ⁶_____ *The Force Awakens*. It has ⁷_____, drama, a great ⁸_____, and a good plot, but above all, amazing ⁹_____. I think I will always prefer the classic Star Wars films, because I watched them when I was young, but I loved this film, too.

a Read the description of a film and complete the gaps with a word from the list.

> action   directed   filmed   nominated
> recommend   set   soundtrack
> special effects   stars

b Read the description again and number the paragraphs in order 1–4.

Paragraph		the plot
Paragraph		the name of the film, the director, the stars, and any prizes it won
Paragraph		why you recommend the film
Paragraph		where and when it is set, where it was filmed

c Look at paragraph 3 again. What tense do we use to tell the story of a film or book?

d Have you seen *The Force Awakens*? If yes, do you agree with the review? If no, does the review make you want to see it?

> 🔍 **Describing a film**
> *It was directed / written by…*
> *It is based on a true story / the book…*
> *It stars…*
> *It is set in…*
> *It was filmed in…*
> *The film is about…*
> *In the end…*
> *I strongly recommend (the film) because…*

e **Write** a description of a film you would recommend to people. **Plan** what you are going to write in the four paragraphs, using the paragraph notes in **b**. Use the language from the **Describing a film** box and **Vocabulary Bank** Cinema p.159 to help you.

f **Check** your description for mistakes (grammar, vocabulary, punctuation, and spelling).

← p.59

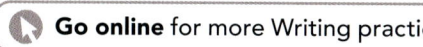

6 DESCRIBING A HOUSE OR FLAT

a The website HomeRent.com is for people who want to rent out their houses for holidays. Read two posts from the website. Which description makes you want to rent the house / flat? Why?

b Read about the flat in Florence again. <u>Underline</u> any adjectives which help to 'sell' the flat? What do they mean?

c Now read about the villa in Turkey again. Improve the description by replacing the word *nice* with one of the underlined adjectives. Often there is more than one possibility.

> 🔍 **Describing location**
> It is *perfectly situated in…*
> *walking distance from…*
> *a (15-minute) walk from…*
> *a short drive from…*
>
> *The neighbourhood is (safe, friendly, etc.)…*
>
> *It's a (beautiful) area…*

d **Write** a description of your house or flat for the website. **Plan** what you're going to write using the paragraph notes below. Use the language in the **Describing location** box and **Vocabulary Bank Houses p.162** to help you.

Paragraph 1	A brief introduction. What kind of house / flat is it? Where is it exactly?
Paragraph 2	Describe the house / flat. What rooms does it have? Does it have any special features?
Paragraph 3	Describe the neighbourhood. How far is it from places of interest? What public transport is there?
Paragraph 4	Who is the house / flat suitable for? Are there any restrictions?

e **Check** your description for mistakes (grammar, vocabulary, punctuation, and spelling).

⬅ p.73

HomeRent.com

Beautiful one-bedroom flat in Florence

#12900152

This flat is perfectly situated with a stunning view of the Palazzo Vecchio and Piazza della Signoria. It is on the second floor of a lovely old building.

This attractive flat has a spacious double bedroom, a sunny living room, a fully-equipped kitchen with a dining area, and a large bathroom with shower. There is a flat-screen TV in the living room and there is also wi-fi and air conditioning.

The neighbourhood, San Giovanni district, is in the centre of the city. The area is mainly pedestrian and the Uffizi Gallery, Piazza della Repubblica, and Piazza del Duomo are just a short walk away.

The flat is ideal for a couple who would like to go sightseeing in this beautiful city. It is a no-smoking house and no pets are allowed.

Beach villa in Kusadası, Turkey

#36499011

Kusadası is a *nice* [*beautiful*] holiday resort on the west coast of Turkey, about 80 km south of Izmir.

The house has three double bedrooms, a living room, a *nice* kitchen, and two bathrooms. All the rooms have air conditioning and the bedrooms have their own balconies. There is a *nice* terrace with table and chairs, so you can eat outside. There are *nice* views of the beach and the mountains. There is a *nice* garden and a communal swimming pool, which we share with the other nearby houses.

The house is walking distance from several *nice* beaches, where you can do lots of water sports. It's also a short drive from the mountains, where you can go hiking.

This house is *nice* for a family with children or for three couples. The house is not suitable for pets.

7 A COVERING EMAIL

We are looking for dedicated, enthusiastic, and energetic people to work at the forthcoming World Athletics Championships.

There are vacancies in the following areas:

• Administration

• Hospitality and catering

• Translation and language services

• Medical support

All applicants must be appropriately qualified and a B1 level of English is a minimum requirement.

Send your CV and a covering email (in English) to:

recruitment@wac.com

a   Look at the job advertisement. Which job could you apply for?

b   Ricardo Suarez wants to apply for a job and is submitting his CV. Read the covering email to go with it. Circle the best phrase in 1–6.

From: Ricardo Suarez <suarezr@chatchat.com>
To: recruitment@wac.com
Subject: Job application

Dear Sir / Madam,

¹ *I am writing / I'm writing* to apply for a job in Medical support at the forthcoming World Athletics Championships.

I am a qualified physiotherapist and ² *I've been working / I have been working* at a rehabilitation centre in Bristol since January 2016.
³ *My English is great / I speak English very well (level C1).*

⁴ I *enclose / attach* my CV.

⁵ *Hope to hear from you soon! / I look forward to hearing from you.*

⁶ *Yours sincerely, / Yours faithfully,*

Ricardo Suarez

c   **Write** a covering email (to send with your CV) to apply for a job at the next World Athletics Championships. **Plan** what you're going to write. Use the language in the **A formal email** box to help you.

> 🔍 **A formal email**
> You don't know the person's name:
>   • start *Dear Sir / Madam,*
>   • finish *Yours faithfully,*
>
> You know the person's name:
>   • start *Dear + Mr / Ms / Mrs (Garcia),*
>   • finish *Yours sincerely,*
>
> Style:
> • Don't use contractions.
> • Use formal language.

d   **Check** your email for mistakes (grammar, vocabulary, punctuation, and spelling).

 p.77

8 AN EMAIL OF COMPLAINT

From: Chris Mason <chrismason.1952@fastmail.com>
To: sandra.adams@johnleavis.com
Subject: Complaint

Sandra Adams
Head of Department
John Leavis Customer Service
PO Box 908
Swindon

May 19th 2018*

¹_____ Ms Adams,

A Last month, on 25 April, I ordered a coffee machine from your website (order ²_____, #CE437184). Before placing the order, I read the conditions carefully and the item was ³_____. Your website says that items in stock are ⁴_____ in 48 hours.

B Two weeks passed and nothing arrived. ⁵_____, I noticed that payment had been taken from my credit card. I phoned your customer service line and the person that I spoke to, Becky, was rude and ⁶_____. She said that the item was not in stock and that she didn't know when it would arrive. She could not explain why the money had been taken from my card.

C I have bought many things from you over the years, both from your London shop and your website, and I have always had good ⁷_____. I can only imagine that this is a departure from your usual high standards and I am sure you will be able to resolve the situation in a satisfactory way.

I look ⁸_____ to hearing from you.

⁹_____ sincerely,

Chris Mason

> *** Note** A formal email and a formal letter are exactly the same. We always include the address and the date in a formal letter.

a Read the email of complaint. Then answer the questions.

1 Who is Chris Mason complaining to?
2 What item is he complaining about? Why?
3 Who did he contact first?
4 What problem did he have when he phoned to complain?

b Match paragraphs A, B, and C in the email to what they say.

Paragraph	something positive about the company (if possible), and that you expect them to do something
Paragraph	an introduction that gives the context of the problem
Paragraph	a detailed explanation of the problem

c Read the email again and complete the gaps with a word from the list.

Dear   delivered   forward   However   in stock
reference   service   unhelpful   Yours

d **Write** an email of complaint about something you bought online. **Plan** what you're going to write. Write three main paragraphs. Use the paragraph notes in **b** and the language in the **A formal email** box on p.121 to help you.

e **Check** your email for mistakes (grammar, vocabulary, punctuation, and spelling).

→ p.83

9 AN ARTICLE – ADVANTAGES AND DISADVANTAGES

Wikipedia, for and against

Wikipedia is ¹a online encyclopaedia. It has become the main information source for ²milions of people every day. It is a wonderful resource, but it has both advantages and disadvantages.

The first advantage of Wikipedia is that it has information about more or less everything and the information is easy to find. Secondly, Wikipedia ³usualy gives a good basic introduction to a topic. Thirdly, it gives links and references to other sources, so it's easy to find out more if you want to.

⁴In the other hand, there ⁵is also disadvantages. For example, the information on Wikipedia is sometimes inaccurate, which is a problem if ⁶its your only information source. Also, you don't know who has ⁷writen the articles. It may be an expert, but it may be an amateur, and sometimes there is a personal or political bias.

⁸To conclusion, if ⁹your looking for information, Wikipedia is an excellent place to start. But it shouldn't be your only source – it's important ¹⁰get your information from other places too.

a   Read the article about the advantages and disadvantages of Wikipedia. Then cover it and answer the questions from memory.

   1 What are the three advantages of Wikipedia?
   2 What are the two disadvantages?
   3 In general, is the writer for or against Wikipedia?

b   Read the article again. There are ten mistakes (grammar, vocabulary, punctuation, and spelling). Can you correct them?

c   You are going to write a similar article about smartphones. Make a list of the advantages and disadvantages.

Advantages	Disadvantages

d   Now decide which are the three biggest advantages and number them 1–3 (1 = the biggest). Do the same with the disadvantages.

> 🔍 **Writing about advantages and disadvantages**
>
> Listing advantages:
> *First / Firstly,...   Secondly,...*
> *Thirdly,...*
>
> Listing disadvantages:
> *On the other hand, there are also (some) disadvantages...*
>
> *For instance / For example...*
>
> *Also,...*
>
> Conclusion:
> *In conclusion / To sum up, I think...*

e   **Write** an article called 'Smartphones – essential for modern life?' Start the article with this introduction.

> Most people today have a smartphone. But are they really essential for modern life? I think there are both advantages and disadvantages.

Write three more paragraphs. **Plan** what you're going to write using the paragraph notes below. Use the language in the **Writing about advantages and disadvantages** box to help you.

Paragraph 2	two or three advantages
Paragraph 3	two or three disadvantages
Paragraph 4	conclusion – say if you think smartphones are essential for modern life or not

f   **Check** your article for mistakes (grammar, vocabulary, punctuation, and spelling).

↩ p.93

UMBERTO ECO

(1932–2016)

Umberto Eco was a novelist, critic, and academic. When he was young, he loved reading everything from comics to classic novels. His father wanted him to be a lawyer, but he decided to study philosophy and literature at the University of Turin.

After he graduated, he worked for Radiotelevisione Italiana. During this time he wrote his first book.

In September 1962, he married Renate Ramge. They had a son and a daughter. They lived in an apartment in Milan. During the 1980s and 1990s Eco was a visiting professor at Harvard and Columbia Universities in the USA.

Eco is best known for his novel *The Name of the Rose*. The book is a murder mystery, set in a 14th-century Italian monastery.

Eco died in Milan in 2016.

a Read the short biography of Umberto Eco. Do you know anything else about him?

b Rewrite sentences 1–7 from the biography with the extra information below. Use non-defining relative clauses.

1 Umberto Eco was a novelist, critic, and academic. He was born in Italy in 1932.
   Umberto Eco, who was born in Italy in 1932, was a novelist, critic, and academic.

2 After he graduated, he worked for Radiotelevisione Italiana.
   At Radiotelevisione Italiana he became friends with artists, painters, musicians, and writers.
   _____
   _____

3 In September 1962, he married Renate Ramge.
   Renate Ramge was a German art teacher.
   _____
   _____

4 They lived in an apartment in Milan.
   Eco had a library of 30,000 books in the apartment.
   _____
   _____

5 Eco is best known for his novel *The Name of the Rose*.
   It was published in 1980 and made into a film six years later.
   _____
   _____

6 The book is a murder mystery set in a 14th-century Italian monastery.
   It sold 15 million copies and made him an international literary star.
   _____
   _____

7 Eco died in Milan in 2016.
   He had been diagnosed with cancer.
   _____
   _____

c **Write** a short biography of an interesting or successful person you know about. **Plan** what you're going to write and try to use some relative clauses.

d **Check** your biography for mistakes (grammar, vocabulary, punctuation, and spelling).

⟵ p.97

Listening

Part 1

Interviewer So tell me, how did you get involved in the film, Dagmara?

Dagmara Well, as you probably know, *Schindler's List* was shot in Krakow, in Poland, which is where I live. I was a university student at the time, studying English. And the film company set up their production office here three months before they started shooting the film and I got a job there as a production assistant, preparing and translating documents and the script.

Interviewer But how did you get the job as Steven Spielberg's interpreter?

Dagmara Well, it was a complete coincidence. Just before the shooting started, there was a big party in one of the hotels in Krakow for all the actors and the film crew, and I was invited too. When I arrived at the party the Polish producer of the film came up to me and said, 'The woman who was going to interpret for Steven Spielberg can't come, so we need you to interpret his opening speech.'

Interviewer How did you feel about that?

Dagmara I couldn't believe it! I was just a student – I had no experience of interpreting – and now I was going to speak in front of hundreds of people. I was so nervous that I drank a couple of glasses of champagne to give myself courage. I must have done a pretty good job though, because soon afterwards Spielberg came up to me to say thank you and then he said, 'I'd like you to be my interpreter for the whole film.' I was so stunned I had to pinch myself to believe that this was happening to me.

Part 2

Interviewer So what exactly did you have to do?

Dagmara I had to go to the film set every day and translate Spielberg's instructions to the Polish actors, and also to the extras. I had to make them understand what he wanted them to do. It was really exciting, and I often felt as if I was a director myself.

Interviewer So, was it a difficult job?

Dagmara Sometimes it was really hard. The worst thing was when we had to shoot a scene again and again because Spielberg thought it wasn't exactly right. Some scenes were repeated as many as 16 times – and then sometimes I would think that maybe it was my fault – that I hadn't translated properly what he wanted, so I'd get really nervous. I remember one scene with lots of actors in it which we just couldn't get right and Spielberg started shouting at me because he was stressed. Eventually we got it right and then he apologized, and I cried a little, because I was also very stressed – and after that it was all right again.

Interviewer So, was Spielberg difficult to work with?

Dagmara Not at all. I mean he was very demanding, I had to do my best every day, but he was really nice to me. I felt he treated me like a daughter. For instance, he was always making sure that I wasn't cold – it was freezing on the set most of the time – and he would make sure that I had a warm coat and gloves and things.

Interviewer Did you ever get to be an extra?

Dagmara Yes, twice! I was going to be in two party scenes, and I got to wear beautiful long dresses and high heels. Unfortunately, one scene didn't make it to the final cut of the film, and before we started shooting the other one I tripped walking down some stairs and twisted my ankle really badly. I was in so much pain that I couldn't take part in the filming. And that was the end of my 'acting career'. I still have the photos of me looking like a girl from the 40s, though!

Interviewer Have you ever worked with Spielberg again?

Dagmara Yes. A year later he invited me to interpret for him again, this time during the premiere of *Schindler's List* in Poland, which was broadcast live on national television! Before that, he had also asked me to come to work as a production assistant on his next movie in Hollywood. I was very tempted and thought really hard about it, but I hadn't finished my studies yet, and all my family and friends were in Poland – so in the end I decided not to go.

Interviewer Do you regret it?

Dagmara Not at all. I had my moment, and it was unforgettable, but that was it!

Danish Sheikh tells me that people with charisma do two basic things. They project their own personality but at the same time they also make other people feel important. Sheikh's lessons are designed to help me to do both of these things, and in the next 48 hours I learn a lot.

Projecting your own personality is difficult to learn. Nobody likes people who talk about how fantastic they are, but nobody remembers people who don't say anything about themselves. Sheikh says the solution is to talk about yourself enough, but not too much.

People with charisma also feel confident. Sheikh gives me advice to help me feel more confident for example, when I walk into a meeting or a party. He tells me to remember a time in the past when I was successful. This positive memory will stop me from feeling afraid or anxious.

Body language is also important. We practise it together, including how to stand like a gorilla, with your feet apart and your arms wide – this shows that you're an important person. Sheikh also tells me how to enter a room. You have to have your chin up and your shoulders back. He tells me to make eye contact with the people I'm talking to, but not for too long – maximum four seconds – it's important not to stare. We also study hand gestures – you shouldn't use them too much.

Finally, conversation. I learn that it's important not to speak too fast or too slowly. You need to vary your speed to keep your listener's attention. But the most important thing of all is listening carefully. If you show interest in people, it makes them feel special. But if you're not really listening, the person you're talking to notices very quickly, so you need to make sure you really concentrate on what they're saying.

At the end of the two days, I have a practical test…

At the end of the two days, I have a practical test. I go to a pub with Sheikh, and I have to talk to strangers. I start talking to people and it goes OK. I don't think English people really like it when a stranger starts speaking to them, but we laugh and I have some interesting conversations. Occasionally, Sheikh gives me advice. He reminds me to make eye contact with everyone I'm talking to, and tells me not to cross my arms, that kind of thing.

As we leave the pub, we shake hands. He says that the course has been good for me, and he gives me a thumbs up. So have I changed? Am I more charismatic? Not exactly – I'm never going to stand like a gorilla again, for example. But perhaps charisma is simpler than that anyway; it's about understanding who you are better, and showing the best version of yourself.

Week 1

On the first day of week 1 students change their normal school uniforms for Chinese-style tracksuits. They start the day much earlier than usual, at 7.00 in the morning, with 30 minutes of physical exercise. In Britain, PE is usually fun, and students only have two hours a week, but in the Chinese system, students do PE every day. Then lessons begin, and students get another shock – all 50 of them are together in one class. In Britain, the maximum is usually 30. In China it's common to have 50 kids in one room. They stop for lunch early, at 11.30. Classes finish at 5.00 but they're not allowed to go home. They have dinner at school, and after dinner they still have a lot of homework and self-study. When they finish, at 7.00, they have to clean the classroom. The school day is 12 hours long. British students find this exhausting!

Weeks 2 and 3

There are big differences between Chinese and British teaching styles. The Chinese teachers teach very fast. Everything is done in books and on paper, and there is a lot of copying from the board. In Britain, for example, in science, the approach is to let students do experiments and discover things by themselves, with less help from the teacher. Discipline is also very different in British and Chinese schools. In China, the teachers have complete authority, but in Britain, the same teachers are having problems. They're surprised that the students don't take school seriously. When her students don't pay attention, Miss Yang, the science teacher, makes them stand and look at the wall, but it doesn't seem to work very well. As Rosie, one of the students, says, 'It probably works in China, because everybody does what their teacher says. But here we don't care. We think it's funny.' By week three there is a serious problem with discipline. Some students like the Chinese system, but a lot of others are behaving badly in class, and some students stop coming to class completely. The Chinese teachers are losing control, and realize they need to change the way they are teaching or their students will fail the tests in week four. They start to teach the children about Chinese culture and food, and they add Chinese face-massage to their daily lessons. They also try to teach patience and concentration using traditional Chinese games. During a meeting with the parents, the Chinese teachers try to get them to help and to encourage their children to work hard. The parents are impressed, and the Chinese teachers are filled with new energy and confidence.

Week 4

During the last week of the experiment the children in the Chinese class are behaving better. At the end of the week all the students from the classes with Chinese teachers and the classes with British ones take tests in maths, science, and Mandarin. These tests will decide which style of teaching has worked better. So what do the results show?

In the maths test, the children taught by British teachers get an average of 54%, and the class taught by Chinese teachers gets…68%. In science, British-taught students get 50% and Chinese-taught students get…58%. And in Mandarin, British-taught students get 37%, and Chinese-taught students get…46%. The Chinese teachers are delighted and their students are really grateful and happy.

So the Chinese teachers get better results, but does that mean their teaching methods are better? Neil Strowger, the head teacher at the school, says, 'It clearly gets good results, but the discipline is too strict for some students.' The Chinese teachers agree that their method doesn't help to develop personality or creativity. Perhaps the last word should go to Miss Li, the Mandarin teacher. As she says, 'It's very hard to say which system is better… but I think we both learnt from each other.'

 7.21

Welcome to the Handel Hendrix house.

Handel's House

In 1712, the German composer Georg Frideric Handel decided to settle permanently in England, where he was employed as musician to the English court. After living in Surrey for some years, he moved to London and during the summer of 1723, he rented a house at 25 Brook Street. He was the first occupant of the house, but as a foreigner, he was not allowed to buy it. However, after becoming a British citizen five years later, he decided to continue renting the house. In 1742, his annual rent for Brook Street was £50.

The plan of the house in Brook Street was usual for a modest London townhouse of the period. There was a basement containing the kitchens and on the ground floor there was a room at the front for receiving visitors. On the first floor there were bigger rooms where Handel entertained and worked. In the largest room, he kept his instruments (a harpsichord and a little house organ) and he occasionally rehearsed there. The room next to it is where he composed many of his most famous works, including the *Messiah*.

The second floor contained the bedroom at the front, with a dressing room at the back where he kept his clothes. In the attic at the top of the house, the servants had their rooms.

During the last decade of his life, Handel's eyesight got worse and by 1754 he was completely blind. He died at his Brook Street house on 14th April 1759. He was buried in Westminster Abbey and more than 3,000 people attended his funeral.

Hendrix's Flat

Although Jimi Hendrix's career only lasted four years, he is widely regarded as one of the most influential electric guitarists in the history of rock music.

The flat on the upper floors of 23 Brook Street was found by Jimi's girlfriend Kathy Etchingham, when she saw an advert in one of the London evening newspapers in June 1968, while he was in New York. He moved in briefly in July before returning to the United States for an extensive tour. He spent some time decorating the flat to his own taste. He bought curtains and cushions from the nearby John Lewis department store, as well as ornaments from Portobello Road market and elsewhere. He told Kathy that this was 'my first real home of my own'. In January the following year, he gave a series of press and media interviews and photo shoots in the flat. He also appeared on the BBC and gave two concerts in February at the Royal Albert Hall.

In March 1969, he went back to New York again and although Kathy stayed at Brook Street for a while longer, Jimi did not live there again. He died in London in 1970, at the age of 27, but in a hotel, not in the Brook Street flat.

Over the years, his flat was used as an office until it was taken over in 2000 by the Handel House Trust. It opened to the public on Wednesday 10th February 2016.

The whole house is now a museum and a concert venue where both men's music can be heard in live performances.

 8.9

Part 1

Interviewer Whose idea was it to go on the programme?

Joe It was my idea. I applied without telling my business partner Jake. Of course, I never really expected to get on it. But then they phoned me from the BBC and said 'you're on the programme', so that's when I told him.

I Did you spend a long time preparing your pitch?

J Yes. We worked really hard, and we practised a lot so that we knew the pitch word for word. The evening before the show we actually went for a run – up in Manchester, where it's filmed – and we went running together just repeating the pitch over and over again.

I How did you feel when you arrived at the Den?

J Erm, well, we were told to get to the set at about 11.00 the night before, because you had to prepare everything in advance, like any furniture you need, things like that. It was freezing cold, and we were exhausted – we didn't get back to our hotel until the middle of the night – and a car came to pick us up a few hours later, at half five in the morning.

I What time did you actually do your pitch?

J Erm, 11.30. So we were lucky because we were the first in that particular programme.

I Why lucky?

J Because we didn't have to wait too long. The other contestants spent ages just waiting around. Some of them – the ones who are on last – had to wait 12 hours!

I Did you meet the Dragons before you went in to do the pitch?

J No. You're not allowed to. Like, if you go to the toilet before you go on, someone has to escort you in case you meet a Dragon. So the first time you see them is when you go into the Den.

 8.10

Part 2

I What were the Dragons like?

J Well, they're obviously told by the producers to be really unfriendly and aggressive. So I remember thinking, when the doors opened and we walked in, what I wanted to do was just to smile at one of them. That was my way of making myself relaxed. And I looked at Deborah Meaden, because she was in the middle, and I smiled at her, but she just, you know, stared at me, stony-faced, to make me feel nervous. And it worked.

I Did you think you did a good presentation?

J Yeah, we did. But Jake, who usually never gets anything wrong, he forgot his first words, and he just never does that. So we both thought, when he got the introduction wrong, that it was going to go badly, but it didn't.

I So what happened after you'd done your pitch?

J Yeah, well, four of the Dragons said 'I'm out', they said they weren't interested. So we were feeling pretty depressed, pretty negative.

I And then?

J The last Dragon was Peter. And he's quite scary – he's incredibly tall – over two metres. And at first he really criticized us. But then he told us he had a big chain of camera shops called Jessops and they were starting online printing and photo framing as part of their business. And then he said 'I've got 15 guys in Hong Kong trying to do what you guys are doing, but you guys are doing it better. I'm going to offer you both a job.'

I Were you very surprised?

J Totally, because it had never happened on *Dragons' Den* before. In ten years they'd never offered someone a job.

I So he offered you jobs just like that?

J Well, his offer was that he wanted to have our business, and for us to work with him at Jessops.

I With a good salary?

J Very.

I So what did you do?

 8.11

Part 3

J It was very stressful because we knew we had to make a decision immediately. So Jake said 'Yes, let's take the jobs', but I said, 'You don't want to work for Jessops.' And he stayed silent and I said, 'I don't want to work for Jessops.' I mean neither of us were in a position where we could have dropped everything and gone and worked for Jessops full-time. It was completely…it was ridiculous.

I So you said no?

J That's right.

I Have you ever regretted saying no?

J No, not for a second. It was still early days for us then, so we were still kind of having fun and enjoying running our own business. And things worked out well for us. Frame Again was successful, and eventually we sold the business this year.

I But not to one of the Dragons?

J No, but that would have been perfect!

 8.12

Jake Good morning. I'm Joe and this is Jake. Oh no, sorry, I'm Jake and this is Joe, and we're here to tell you about our new product, Frame Again.

Joe Frame Again is an online service for printing and framing your photos. At the moment it's easy to take a photo, but it's difficult to print and frame it attractively. With Frame Again it couldn't be simpler. First you upload your photo to the Frame Again website, straight from your phone, tablet, or computer. Then you choose the colours of your frame. Then we print, frame, and deliver your photo to you the very next day. It's quick and it's easy. The product's great, and the service is great.

Jake Frame Again is for today's smartphone photographers and Instagram users. That's why we designed a modern frame which is square – perfect for framing Instagram photos. We think it will be very popular, because the frames look great in any home or office.

Joe One photo, printed, framed, and delivered to your door, will cost £12.99.

Jake Our slogan is 'Printed, framed, and delivered in 24 hours.'

 8.19

Hello and welcome to *How's Business*? Today we're going to look at how social media can affect businesses. And I'd like to start with the story of Dave Carroll, an American singer-songwriter, who had a very bad experience with United Airlines. Dave and his band were flying with United Airlines from Halifax, in Nova Scotia, to Omaha, in Nebraska, with a stopover in Chicago. As they were waiting to get off the plane in Chicago, they heard another passenger say, 'My God! They're throwing guitars out there!'

As Dave and the other band members looked out of the plane window, they were horrified to see that the baggage handlers, who were taking the luggage off the plane, were throwing the band's guitars to each other. They couldn't believe what they were seeing. They immediately complained to United Airlines employees in Chicago, but nobody listened to them.

When they arrived in Omaha, Dave discovered that the neck of his very expensive Taylor guitar had been broken. It cost him $1,200 to get it repaired. For nine months he tried to claim compensation from United Airlines. He phoned and emailed their offices in Halifax, Chicago, and New York without success. In the end he even suggested that instead of money, they could give him $1,200 of flight tickets. But after all his complaints and suggestions, United simply said 'No'.

So, what else could a singer-songwriter do? Dave wrote a song about his experience, and produced a music video to go with it. The song was called *United Breaks Guitars*. He posted it on YouTube and it was a huge hit. The song reached number 1 on the iTunes music store within a week, and the video has had over 16 million views.

After 150,000 views, United Airlines contacted Dave and offered him a payment if he agreed to take the video off YouTube. He refused, and suggested they gave the money to charity. Of course, the impact of Dave's song went far beyond YouTube. Soon newspapers, websites, TV and radio stations all over North America were doing stories about the song. Dave was interviewed on many radio and TV shows where, of course, he retold the story of how *United Breaks Guitars*. He did over 200 interviews in the first three months!

Dave Carroll's favourite guitar was broken, but in the end United Airlines were the bigger losers. After the video had gone viral, the BBC reported that United Airlines' share price had dropped by 10% within four weeks of the release of the video, which means that the company lost an incredible $180 million. It would have been much cheaper to repair Dave's guitar!

 9.2

The ticket inspector touched my arm. 'Listen,' he said, 'when we get to Peterborough station, run as fast as you can to Platform 1. The Leeds train will be there.'

I looked at him, without really understanding what he had said. 'What do you mean?' I said. 'Is the train late or something?' 'No, it's not late,' the ticket inspector said. 'I've just radioed Peterborough station. The train is going to wait for you. As soon as you get on, it'll leave. The passengers will complain, but let's not worry about that. You'll get home, and that's the main thing.' And he walked away.

I suddenly realised what an amazing thing he had done. I got up and went after him. I wanted to give him everything I had, all the money in my wallet – but I knew he would be offended. I grabbed his arm. 'I, er, just wanted to…' but I couldn't continue. 'It's OK,' he said. 'No problem.'

'I wish I had a way to say thank you,' I said. 'I really appreciate what you've done.'

'No problem,' he said again. 'Listen, if you want to thank me, the next time you see someone in trouble, help them. That will pay me back. And tell them to do the same to someone else. It'll make the world a better place.'

When the train stopped, I rushed to Platform 1 and sure enough the Leeds train was there waiting, and a few hours later I was with my mum in hospital. Even now, years later, whenever I think of her, I remember the Good Ticket Inspector on that late-night train to Peterborough. It changed me from a young man who was nearly a criminal into a decent human being. I've been trying to pay him back ever since then.

🔊 9.3

Story 1
When I was seven, my family were on holiday in the USA and one day we drove to the Grand Canyon. The car window was open, and at one point, my favourite blanket flew out the window and was gone. I was devastated. It was my security blanket and I couldn't sleep without it. Soon after, we stopped for petrol at a service station. I was sitting in the car feeling miserable eating a sandwich when a biker gang, you know, a group of guys on motorbikes in leather jackets, drove into the petrol station. A huge frightening man with a grey-and-black beard got off his bike and came to the car. He knocked on the window and then pulled my blanket

from his jacket pocket and handed it to my mum. He then went back to his motorbike. I was so happy I ran up to him and gave him my sandwich.

Story 2
This happened about 20 years ago, but the memory is still really vivid. I was recently married, my wife was pregnant, and we had very little money because I only had a part-time job. It was a few days before payday and I went to a food store to get only what we absolutely needed. In all, I bought about $10 worth of stuff. At the checkout, I swiped my debit card. The cashier said, 'Sorry. It says 'Declined'. Try again.' I asked her to take one item out of the basket, and then I swiped again. There was now a line of customers behind me. The cashier, said, 'Sorry. Declined again.' I went on taking things out until the only thing I had left was a loaf of bread, and then the card was accepted. I took my bread and left – I was feeling absolutely humiliated. A few seconds later I heard the voice of a little girl behind me, a girl who was standing with her mother right behind me in the line. She gave me a grocery bag full of all the things I'd put back. Her mother had bought them for me. I still cry when I remember that moment and think how such a small act can mean so much for a person in need.

Story 3
I'm a painter and a couple of years ago I was travelling by plane to see friends and I'd taken my painting things with me. I forgot about the rules about not being able to take liquids in carry-on luggage, so when I got to security at the airport, the man took away all my paints. I was really angry with myself for being so stupid. But when I came back a week later, the security man was there at the baggage reclaim area with my paints. Not only had he kept them for me, but he'd also looked up the date and time of my return flight so that he could be there to meet me.

🔊 9.13

Technology addiction is real, and it's creating mental health problems all over the world. According to a recent survey, one in three UK adults is so addicted to their phone that they regularly check it in the middle of the night. So it's no surprise that the idea of a 'digital detox' is growing in popularity. But what is it actually like to go on one?

Time to Log Off is an organization which runs three-day digital detoxes in an old country house in Dorset in the south-west of England. People who go on them are not allowed to use digital devices at all for three days.

Journalist Anna Magee felt she was addicted to her smartphone, so when she read about the detoxes, she decided to go on one.

'When I arrived, the first thing I discovered was that there was no mobile phone coverage so I couldn't cheat even if I wanted to! Suddenly I felt cut off and panicky. What if something happened to my husband? What if something terrible happened in the world?

There were eight other people on the detox with me. At 6 p.m. we met in the living room and handed in our devices, our phones or tablets or whatever. People looked scared. I was worried there were going to be lots of lectures on psychology, things like that, but no. Instead, there was yoga, and walks through the countryside where we picked fruit and had lots of conversations with real-life humans. The first night I slept really well for the first time in months.

But it wasn't always easy. The second evening without my phone, I felt really disconnected and lonely. At yoga that night, I burst into tears, and I felt awful not being able to call a friend. But by the third and final day I had changed. When we went on our walk, I really noticed the beauty of the countryside. And I was able to sit still on the sofa, reading a book for nearly half an hour without losing concentration. I started colouring in pictures

in books. I was even eating more slowly, in a more relaxed way.

At lunchtime the next day we got our devices back, and said goodbye. When I finally managed to get coverage, I hungrily checked my phone for messages, likes, comments, news. But nothing had really happened. I managed the whole two-hour train journey back without checking my phone again, just noticing the countryside instead.

It's now three weeks since I went on the detox and though I can't quite believe it, I have managed to control my use of technology. I have one full day unplugged each week, on Saturdays, and I feel incredibly rested on Sundays as a result. I don't do email after 8 p.m., and that really helps me to sleep. I know they're tiny steps, but I feel that I've changed. When I'm chatting to friends I feel that I'm much more present, I'm really focusing on them and not getting distracted by my phone. And I find that when I have a break, instead of wanting to scroll through Twitter or check WhatsApp, what I really want is real-life conversation.'

🔊 10.4

1 The red phone box
In 1924, the Post Office organized a competition to design a new phone box. The winner was the architect Giles Gilbert Scott, who also designed Liverpool Cathedral and the building that is now Tate Modern. The first phone box was built in London in 1926. It was painted red to make it easy to see at a distance, although Scott had originally suggested silver with a blue interior. With the arrival of mobile phones in the 21st century, people didn't need phone boxes any more, and most of them have now been removed. However, today they are considered design icons of historic importance, and several are now tourist attractions, including one of the original ones next to the Royal Academy of Arts in Piccadilly. Others have found new lives in local communities, as mini-libraries or art galleries, and a very few still survive as working phones.

2 The Anglepoise lamp
George Carwardine was an engineer who specialised in suspension systems for cars. He worked for car manufacturers for several years, but when the company he was working for went bankrupt, he decided to set up a small company on his own. He had a little workshop in his garden, and there he designed a lamp which could be moved in different directions, inspired by the human arm. He licensed his design to a company which made the springs for his lamps, and in 1935 they brought out the three-spring Anglepoise desk lamp. It was an instant success, and the exact same model, the Anglepoise 1227, is still made today. Carwardine later developed many variations on the original design, including lamps for hospital operating theatres and for military aeroplanes. But it is the classic ever-popular Anglepoise 1227 which is today considered an iconic British design.

3 The Penguin book covers
Penguin books was started in 1935, although the classic cover was not designed until eleven years later. In 1935 publisher Allen Lane was at a bookstall on a railway platform looking for something to read, but he could only find magazines. He decided that people needed to be able to buy books that were good quality fiction, but cheap, and not just in traditional bookshops but also on railway stations and in chain stores.

Lane wanted a dignified but amusing symbol for the new books and his secretary suggested a penguin, so graphic designer Edward Young was sent to London Zoo to make drawings of penguins. The first Penguin paperbacks appeared in the summer of 1935. They included the works of Agatha Christie and the American writer Ernest Hemingway. The classic book cover was designed by Young in 1946. The books were colour coded – orange for fiction, blue for biography, and green for crime. The way people thought about books had changed forever – the paperback revolution had begun.

The cover designs of Penguin books have changed a lot over the years, but the original 1946 cover, which is considered a design icon, was recently brought back, and is also used on mugs, notebooks, and other items.

4 The miniskirt

The 1960s was famous for many things from The Beatles to the first man on the moon, but the miniskirt remains one of the decade's most long-lasting icons. Mary Quant was a British fashion designer who had a boutique called Bazaar in the King's Road, the most fashionable shopping street of the time. As a girl, she had always tried to make her school uniform skirts shorter, 'to be more exciting-looking'. In 1966, she saw a group of tap dancers at a nearby school in very short skirts, with socks and dance shoes. This inspired her to create the miniskirt, which she named after her favourite car, the Mini. However, the miniskirt was not popular with everyone. Coco Chanel described it as 'just awful'. But Quant's customers loved it. Before the 1960s, young women had been expected to dress like their mothers, but this was about young people looking young. Although 1960s fashion soon changed to the long hippy clothes of the 1970s, the miniskirt

🔊 10.7

Part 1

Interviewer Good morning and thank you for coming, Mr Morton – or should it be Inspector Morton – you were a detective with Scotland Yard, weren't you?

Inspector Morton Yes, that's right. For 25 years. I retired last year.

Interviewer People today are still fascinated by the identity of Jack the Ripper, over 130 years after the crimes were committed. It's incredible, isn't it?

Inspector Morton Well, it's not really that surprising. People are always interested in unsolved murders – and Jack the Ripper has become a sort of cult horror figure.

Interviewer So what can you tell us about some of the new theories about his identity?

Inspector Morton Well, a recent new theory was put forward by a crime historian called Jan Bondeson. He thinks that Jack the Ripper was a Dutch sailor called Hendrik de Jong.

Interviewer What evidence does he have?

Inspector Morton Well, de Jong was definitely a murderer. He killed four women in Holland and Belgium, including two of his ex-wives. He also travelled to London a lot, and he was there when the Jack the Ripper murders took place. He also matches the descriptions we have of Jack the Ripper.

Interviewer How credible is his theory?

Inspector Morton Well, even Dr Bondeson says that it's impossible to know for certain if de Jong was Jack the Ripper. I would say it's possible, but there isn't really enough conclusive evidence.

🔊 10.8

Part 2

Interviewer The next recent theory I'm interested in comes from the film director Bruce Robinson, who wrote a book in 2016 called *They All Love Jack*. What can you tell us about it?

Inspector Morton Bruce Robinson is convinced that Jack the Ripper was in fact Michael Maybrick, the brother of one of the original suspects, James Maybrick. He thinks that the style of the murders indicates that there was a connection with the Freemasons - which both brothers were.

Interviewer What did Michael do?

Inspector Morton He was a popular singer and composer of songs at the time, and Robinson thinks that the Ripper's letters are similar in style to some of his songs, and the fact that they were posted from so many different parts of the UK makes sense because Michael was on tour at the time. Robinson thinks he was a psychopath, and was responsible for at least 16 more murders that took place in England later. He even thinks that Michael went on to murder his brother James.

Interviewer But he was never arrested, was he?

Inspector Morton No, he wasn't. However, Bruce thinks that by 1893 the police had begun to suspect him, but because many of the police themselves were Freemasons they allowed him to escape to the Isle of Wight, where he lived for the rest of his life.

Interviewer And what do you do think?

Inspector Morton I think the book is well researched, but I don't really believe his conspiracy theory, that the police knew it was Michael and let him get away. I think the reason the Ripper was never caught was because the police were incompetent, not corrupt.

🔊 10.9

Part 3

Interviewer Finally, let's talk about Patricia Cornwell's research. In her 2002 book *Jack the Ripper – Case Closed* she said that she had identified the murderer and that she was convinced that Jack the Ripper was in fact Walter Sickert, the painter. What evidence did she put forward to support this claim?

Inspector Morton Well, she mainly used DNA analysis. She actually spent over £2,000,000 buying 32 paintings by Sickert. She cut up one of them to get the DNA from it – people in the art world were furious.

Interviewer I can imagine.

Inspector Morton And then she compared the DNA from the painting with DNA taken from the letters that Jack the Ripper sent to the police. Patricia Cornwell said that she was 99% certain that Walter Sickert was Jack the Ripper.

Interviewer And now she's written a new book with more evidence.

Inspector Morton Yes, it's called *Ripper: the Secret Life of Walter Sickert*. She says she's found new evidence, including letters which were written by Jack the Ripper and by Walter Sickert on the same very unusual type of paper. She also points out that some of his paintings are very violent and frightening.

Interviewer But you don't think she's right, do you?

Inspector Morton Well, I think she might be right. She has a lot of evidence, although I don't think it's completely reliable. And a lot of people think she's wrong!

Interviewer So, who do you think the murderer was?

Inspector Morton I can't tell you because I don't know.

Interviewer Do you think we'll ever solve the mystery?

Inspector Morton Yes, I think one day the mystery will be solved. Some new evidence will appear that proves 100% who Jack the Ripper was, and we'll be able to say that the case is finally closed. But at the moment it's still a mystery, and people like a good mystery.

6A

Passive (all tenses)

1 A lot of films **are shot** on location.
When **is** our car **being repaired**?
Andy's bike **has been stolen**.
The director died when the film **was being made**.
You**'ll be picked up** at the airport by one of our staff.
This bill **must be paid** tomorrow.
I love **being given** a massage.
2 The new concert hall **will be opened by** the Queen.
Gladiator **was directed by** Ridley Scott.

🔊 6.1

1 We often use the passive (*be* + past participle) when it isn't said, known, or important who does an action.
Andy's bike has been stolen. (= somebody has stolen Andy's bike, but we don't know who). In passive sentences, the object of the verb becomes the new subject.

2 If we want to say who did the action, we use *by*.

- We can often say things in two ways, in the active or in the passive. Compare:
Gladiator was directed by Ridley Scott. (= we want to focus more on the film)
Ridley Scott directed Gladiator. (= we want to focus more on the director)

- We form negatives and questions in the same way as in active sentences.
*Some films **aren't shot** on location.*
*Is your car **being** repaired today?*

- We often use the passive to talk about processes, for example, scientific processes, and in formal language, such as news reports.
*Then the water **is heated** to 100 degrees…*
*Many buildings in the city **have been damaged** by the earthquake.*

a Circle the correct form, active or passive.

The college *built /* (*was built*) in the 16th century.

1 The costumes for the show *are making / are being made* by hand.
2 The story *inspired / was inspired* him to make a film.
3 This castle *hasn't inhabited / hasn't been inhabited* for nearly a century.
4 His latest film *set / is set* in France in the 1960s.
5 The film *will shoot / will be shot* in the autumn.
6 The actors *aren't recording / aren't being recorded* the dialogue until next week.
7 The house *wasn't using / wasn't being used* by the owners during the winter.
8 The make-up artist *has transformed / has been transformed* the actor into a monster.
9 They *hadn't owned / hadn't been owned* the company for very long before they went bankrupt.
10 The photo *took / was taken* by my husband on the balcony of our hotel.

b Complete with the passive so that the meaning is the same. Only use *by* if necessary.

People don't use this room very often. This room *isn't used very often*.

1 They subtitle a lot of foreign films.
A lot of foreign films _____.
2 García Márquez wrote *Love in the Time of Cholera* in 1985.
Love in the Time of Cholera _____ in 1985.
3 Someone is repairing my laptop at the moment.
My laptop _____ at the moment.
4 They haven't released the DVD of the film yet.
The DVD of the film _____.
5 They won't finish the film until the spring.
The film _____ until the spring.
6 You have to collect the tickets from the box office.
The tickets _____ from the box office.
7 They hadn't told the actor about the changes in the script.
The actor _____ about the changes in the script.
8 Damien Chazelle directed *La La Land*.
La La Land _____.
9 They've already recorded the soundtrack.
The soundtrack _____.
10 They were interviewing the director about the film.
The director _____ about the film.

🔴 p.57

modals of deduction: *might, can't, must*

might (when you think something is possibly true)

> Tony's phone is switched off. He **might** be on the plane now, or just boarding.
> Laura **might not** like that skirt. It's not really her style.
> 🔊 6.11

can't (when you are sure something is impossible / not true)

> Nigel **can't** earn much money in his job. He's still living with his parents.
> That woman **can't** be Jack's wife. Jack's wife has dark hair.
> 🔊 6.12

must (when you are sure something is true)

> The neighbours **must** be out. There aren't any lights on in the house.
> Your sister **must** have a lot of money if she drives a Porsche.
> 🔊 6.13

The neighbours must be out.
There aren't any lights on in the house.

- We often use *might, can't,* or *must* to say how sure or certain we are about something (based on the information we have).
- In this context, the opposite of *must* is *can't*. Compare:
  The neighbours must be out. There aren't any lights on in the house.
  The neighbours can't be out. All the lights are on in the house. **NOT** *~~The neighbours mustn't be out.~~*
- We can use *may* instead of *might* and we can use *could* in positive sentences.
  Jack could (or may) be at the party – I'm not sure.
- We don't use *can* instead of *might / may.* **NOT** *~~He can be on the plane now.~~*
- We often use *be + gerund* after *might / must / can't.*
  They must be having a party – the music's very loud.

The neighbours can't be out.
All the lights are on in the house.

a Match the sentences.

	He might be American.	D
1	He can't be a university student.	
2	He must be cold.	
3	He might be going to the gym.	
4	He could be lost.	
5	He must be married.	
6	He must be a tourist.	
7	He can't be enjoying the party.	
8	He may not have a job.	
9	He can't be a businessman.	

A He's carrying a sports bag.
B He's carrying a camera and a guide book.
C He's looking at a map.
D ~~He's wearing a baseball cap.~~
E He's looking at job adverts in the newspaper.
F He isn't talking to anybody.
G He isn't wearing a suit.
H He's wearing a wedding ring.
I He's wearing school uniform.
J It's freezing and he isn't wearing a jumper.

b Complete with *must, might (not),* or *can't.*

A What does Pete's new girlfriend do?
B I'm not sure, but she *might* be a doctor. I think she works at the hospital.

1 **A** Do you know anyone who drives a Ferrari?
  B Yes, my nephew. I don't know his salary, but he _____ earn a fortune!
2 **A** Why don't you buy this dress for your mum?
  B I'm not sure. She _____ like it. It's a bit short for her.
3 **A** My sister works as an interpreter for the EU.
  B She _____ speak a lot of languages to work there.
4 **A** Did you know that Andy's parents have split up?
  B Poor Andy. He _____ be very happy about that.
5 **A** Are your neighbours away? All the curtains are closed.
  B I'm not sure. I suppose they _____ be on holiday.
6 **A** Where's your colleague today?
  B She _____ be ill. She called to say that she was going to the doctor's.
7 **A** I'm looking forward to seeing Jane! I haven't seen her for years.
  B You _____ recognize her – she's lost a lot of weight.
8 **A** My daughter has failed all her exams again.
  B She _____ be working very hard.
9 **A** Why is Tina so happy?
  B I'm not sure, but she _____ have a new partner.
10 **A** Where does your boss live?
   B I don't know, but he _____ live near the office because he commutes every day by train.

p.61

first conditional and future time clauses + *when*, *until*, etc.

first conditional sentences: *if* + present simple, *will* / *won't* + infinitive

1 If you **work** hard, you**'ll pass** your exams.    7.13
  The teacher **won't be** very pleased if we**'re** late for class.
2 **Come** and see us next week if you **have** time.
3 Alison **won't get** into university unless she **gets** good grades.
  I **won't go** unless you **go** too.

The teacher won't be very pleased if we're late for class.

- We use first conditional sentences to talk about a possible / probable future situation and its consequence.
  1 We use the present tense (**NOT** the future) after *if* in first conditional sentences. **NOT** ~~If you'll work hard, you'll pass all your exams.~~
  2 We can also use an imperative instead of the *will* clause.
  3 We can use *unless* + present simple ⊞ instead of *if...not* in conditional sentences. Compare: *Alison won't get into university **if** she **doesn't get** good grades.*

future time clauses

We**'ll have** dinner when your father **gets** home.   7.14
As soon as you **get** your exam results, **call** me.
I **won't go** to bed until you **come** home.
I**'ll have** a quick lunch before I **leave**.
After I **finish** university, I**'ll** probably **take** a year off and travel.

- We use the present tense (**NOT** the future) after *when*, *as soon as*, *until*, *before*, and *after* to talk about the future.

---

a Complete with the present simple or future with *will* and the verbs in brackets.

  If I fail my exams, I*'ll take* them again next year. (take)
1 That girl _____ into trouble if she doesn't wear her uniform. (get)
2 If you give in your homework late, the teacher _____ it. (not mark)
3 Don't write anything unless you _____ sure of the answer. (be)
4 Gary will be expelled if his behaviour _____. (not improve)
5 They'll be late for school unless they _____. (hurry)
6 Ask me if you _____ what to do. (not know)
7 Johnny will be punished if he _____ at the teacher again. (shout)
8 My sister _____ university this year if she passes all her exams. (finish)
9 I _____ tonight unless I finish my homework quickly. (not go out)
10 Call me if you _____ some help with your project. (need)

b (Circle) the correct word or expression.

  I won't go to university (*if*) / *unless* I don't get good results.
1 Don't turn over the exam paper *after* / *until* the teacher tells you to.
2 Please check the water's not too hot *before* / *after* the kids get in the bath.
3 Your parents will be really happy *when* / *unless* they hear your good news.
4 I'll look for a job in September *before* / *after* I come back from holiday.
5 The schools will close *unless* / *until* it stops snowing soon.
6 The job is very urgent, so please do it *after* / *as soon as* you can.
7 We'll stay in the library *as soon as* / *until* it closes. Then we'll go home.
8 Harry will probably learn to drive *when* / *until* he's 18.
9 You won't be able to speak to the head teacher *unless* / *if* you make an appointment.
10 Give Mummy a kiss *before* / *after* she goes to work.

← p.68

---

second conditional, choosing between conditionals

second conditional sentences: *if* + past simple, *would* / *wouldn't* + infinitive

1 If I **had** a job, I**'d get** my own flat. 🔊 7.15
If David **spoke** good English, he **could get** a job in that new hotel.
I **would get on** better with my parents if I **didn't live** with them.
I **wouldn't do** that job **unless** they **paid me** a really good salary.

2 If your sister **were** here, she**'d know** what to do.
If it **was** warmer, we **could have** a swim.

3 If I **were** you, I**'d buy** a new computer.

- We use the second conditional to talk about a hypothetical / imaginary present or future situation and its consequence. *If I had a job…* (= I don't have a job, I'm imagining it)

1 We use the past simple after *if* and *would* / *wouldn't* + infinitive in the other clause.

- We can also use *could* instead of *would* in the other clause.

2 After *if*, we can use *was* or *were* with *I*, *he*, and *she*.

3 We often use second conditionals beginning *If I were you, I'd…* to give advice. We don't normally use *If I was you…*

> 🔍 **Choosing between the first or second conditional**
> Using a first or second conditional usually depends on how probable you think it is that something will happen.
> *If I have time, I'll help you.* (= this is a real situation, it's possible that I'll have time – first conditional)
> *If I had time, I'd help you.* (= this is a hypothetical / imaginary situation, I don't have time – second conditional)
>
> ***would* / *wouldn't* + infinitive**
> We also often use *would* / *wouldn't* + infinitive (without an *if* clause) when we talk about imaginary situations.
> *My ideal holiday **would be** a week in the Bahamas.*
> *I**'d** never **buy** a car as big as yours.*

If I were you, I'd buy a new computer.

a Write second conditional sentences and questions.

I *wouldn't live* with my parents if I *didn't have to*.
(not live, not have to)
Would you *have* a dog if you *didn't live* in a flat?
(have, not live)

1 Nick _____ commute every day if he _____ from home. (not have to, work)
2 If they _____ such a noisy dog, they _____ better with their neighbours. (not have, get on)
3 I _____ that bike if I _____ you – it's too expensive. (not buy, be)
4 _____ we _____ our house if somebody _____ us enough money? (sell, offer)
5 If my mother-in-law _____ with us, we _____ divorced. (live, get)
6 _____ you _____ a flat with me if I _____ half the rent? (share, pay)
7 If my sister _____ her room more often, it _____ such a mess. (tidy, not be)
8 You _____ me like this if you really _____ me. (not treat, love)
9 If we _____ the kitchen white, _____ it _____ bigger? (paint, look)
10 I _____ a house with a garden if I _____ gardening so much. (not buy, not enjoy)

b First or second conditional? Complete with the correct form of the verb in brackets.

I*'ll stay* with my sister if I have to go to London for my job interview. (stay)
I'd buy my own flat if I *had* enough money. (have)

1 My kids _____ earlier if they didn't go to bed so late. (get up)
2 Where _____ you _____ if you go to university? (live)
3 If you _____ your exams, what will you do? (not pass)
4 I'd buy a bigger house if I _____ sure we could afford it. (be)
5 We couldn't have a dog if we _____ a garden. (not have)
6 How will you get to work if you _____ your car? (sell)
7 If we sit in the shade, we _____ sunburnt. (not get)
8 If you could change one thing in your life, what _____ it _____? (be)
9 He won't be able to pay next month's rent if he _____ a job soon. (not find)
10 If she made less noise, her neighbours _____ so often. (not complain)

⟵ p.71

choosing between gerunds and infinitives

gerund (verb + -ing)

> 1 I'm not very **good at working** in a team. 🔊 8.6
>   Katie's **given up smoking**.
> 2 **Looking for** a job can be depressing.
>   **Shopping** is my favourite thing to do at weekends.
> 3 I **hate not being** on time for things.
>   I **don't mind getting up** early.

- We use the gerund (verb + -ing)
  1 after prepositions and phrasal verbs.
  2 as the subject of a sentence.
  3 after some verbs, e.g. *hate, don't mind*.
- Common verbs which take the gerund include: *admit, avoid, deny, dislike, enjoy, feel like, finish, hate, keep, like, love, mind, miss, practise, prefer, recommend, spend time, stop, suggest*, and some phrasal verbs, e.g. *give up, go on*, etc.
- The negative gerund = *not* + verb + *-ing*.

> 🔍 *like, love, and hate*
> In American English, *like, love,* and *hate* are followed by the infinitive with *to*. This is becoming more common in British English too, e.g. *I like to listen to music in the car.*

the infinitive with *to*

> 1 My flat is very **easy to find**. 🔊 8.7
> 2 Liam is saving money **to buy** a new car.
> 3 My sister has never **learned to drive**.
>   **Try not to make** a noise.

- We use the infinitive + *to*:
  1 after adjectives.
  2 to express a reason or purpose.
  3 after some verbs, e.g. *want, need, learn*.

- Common verbs which take the infinitive include: (*can't*) *afford, agree, decide, expect, forget, help, hope, learn, need, offer, plan, pretend, promise, refuse, remember, seem, try, want, would like*. More verbs take the infinitive than the gerund.
- The negative infinitive = *not to* + verb.
- These common verbs can take either the infinitive or gerund with no difference in meaning: *start, begin, continue*.
  It started to rain. It started raining.

> 🔍 **Verb + person + infinitive with *to***
> We also use the infinitive with *to* after some verbs + person, e.g. *ask, tell, want, would like*.
> Can you ask the manager **to come**?
> She told him not **to worry**.
> I want you **to do** this now.
> We'd really like you **to come**.

the infinitive without *to*

> 1 I **can't drive**. 🔊 8.8
>   We **must hurry**.
> 2 She always **makes** me **laugh**.
>   My parents didn't **let** me **go** out last night.

- We use the infinitive without *to*:
  1 after most modal and auxiliary verbs.
  2 after *make* and *let*.

> 🔍 **Verbs that can take a gerund or an infinitive, but the meaning is different**
> **Try to be** on time. (= make an effort to be on time)
> **Try doing** yoga. (= do it to see if you like it)
> **Remember to phone** him. (= don't forget to do it)
> I **remember meeting** him years ago. (= I have a memory of it)

---

a Circle the correct form.

I'm in charge of *recruiting* / *to recruit* new staff.

1 It's important for me *spending* / *to spend* time with my family.
2 *Applying* / *Apply* to go to university abroad can be complicated.
3 I want *to do* / *doing* my shopping this morning.
4 My boss wants *open* / *to open* a new office.
5 Be careful *not asking* / *not to ask* her about her boyfriend – they've split up.
6 We went on *working* / *to work* until we finished.
7 Dave is very good at *solving* / *to solve* problems.
8 The best thing about weekends is *not going* / *not to go* to work.
9 Layla gave up *modelling* / *to model* when she had a baby.
10 I went on a training course *to learning* / *to learn* about the new software.

b Complete with a verb from the list in the correct form.

~~not buy~~   commute   do   leave   lock   ~~not make~~   retire   ~~set up~~   wear   not worry

~~not buy   commute   do   leave   lock   not make   retire~~
~~set up~~   wear   not worry

I'd like *to set up* my own company.

1 My parents are planning _____ before they are 65.
2 Rob spends three hours _____ to work and back every day.
3 Mark and his wife agreed _____ about the problems he had at work.
4 Did you remember _____ the door?
5 In the end I decided _____ the shoes because they were very expensive.
6 The manager lets us _____ work early on Fridays.
7 All employees must _____ a jacket and tie at work.
8 Please try _____ any more mistakes in the report.
9 I don't mind _____ overtime during the week.

🔶 p.77

> 🔵 **Go online** to review the grammar for each lesson

reported speech: sentences and questions

reported sentences

direct statements	reported statements	8.13
'I like shopping.'	She said (that) she liked shopping.	
'I'm leaving tomorrow.'	He told her (that) he was leaving the next day.	
'I'll always love you.'	He said (that) he would always love me.	
'I passed the exam!'	She told me (that) she had passed the exam.	
'I've forgotten my keys.'	He said (that) he had forgotten his keys.	
'I can't come.'	She said (that) she couldn't come.	
'I may be late.'	He said (that) he might be late.	
'I must go.'	She said (that) she had to go.	

- We use reported speech to report (i.e. to tell another person) what someone said.
- When the reporting verb (*said*, *told*, etc.) is in the past tense, the tenses in the sentence which is being reported usually change like this:

  present → past
  will → *would*
  past simple / present perfect → past perfect

> **When tenses don't change**
>
> When you report what someone said very soon after they said it, the tenses often stay the same as in the original sentence.
> **Adam** '*I can't come tonight.*'
> *I've just spoken to Adam and he said that he can't come tonight.*
> **Jack** '*I really enjoyed my trip.*'
> *Jack told me that he really enjoyed his trip.*

- Some modal verbs change, e.g. *can* → *could*, *may* → *might*, *must* → *had to*. Other modal verbs stay the same, e.g. *could*, *might*, *should*, etc.
  '*I might come back next week.*' *He said he might come back next week.*
- We usually have to change the pronouns.
  '*I like jazz.*' *Jane said that she liked jazz.*
- Using *that* after *said* and *told* is optional.

- If you report what someone said on a different day or in a different place, some other time and place words can change, e.g. *tomorrow* → *the next day*, *here* → *there*, *this* → *that*, etc.
  '*I'll meet you here tomorrow.*' *He said he'd meet me there the next day.*

> **say and tell**
>
> Be careful – after *said*, <u>don't</u> use a person or an object pronoun.
> *Sarah said that she was tired.* **NOT** ~~Sarah said me that she was tired.~~
> After *told*, you <u>must</u> use a person or object pronoun.
> *Sarah told me that she was tired.* **NOT** ~~Sarah told that she....~~

reported questions

direct questions	reported questions	8.14
'Are you married?'	She asked him if he was married.	
'Did Lucy phone?'	He asked me whether Lucy had phoned.	
'What's your name?'	I asked him what his name was.	
'Where do you live?'	She asked me where I lived.	

- When we report a question, the tenses change as in reported statements.
- When a question doesn't begin with a question word, we add *if* (or *whether*).
  '*Do you want a drink?*' *He asked me if / whether I wanted a drink.*
- We also have to change the word order to subject + verb and not use *do / did*.

---

a Complete using reported speech.

'I'm in love with you.'
My boyfriend told me *he was in love with me*.

1 'I'm selling all my books.'
My friend Tim said _____.

2 'I've booked the flights.'
Emma told me _____.

3 'Your new dress doesn't suit you.'
My mother told me _____.

4 'I may not be able to go to the party.'
Matt said _____.

5 'I won't wear these shoes again.'
Jenny said _____.

6 'I didn't buy you a present.'
My brother told me _____.

7 'I can't find anywhere to park.'
Luke told me _____.

b Complete using reported speech.

'Why did you break up?'
My friend asked me *why we had broken up*.

1 'When are you leaving?'
My parents asked me _____.

2 'Have you ever been married?'
She asked him _____.

3 'Will you be home early?'
Anna asked Robert _____.

4 'Where do you usually buy your clothes?'
My sister asked me _____.

5 'Did you wear a suit to the job interview?'
We asked him _____.

6 'Do you ever go to the theatre?'
I asked Lisa _____.

7 'Can you help me?'
Sally asked the policeman _____.

 p.80

third conditional

If I'**d known** you had a problem, I **would have helped** you. 🔊9.4
If Paul **hadn't gone** to Brazil, he **wouldn't have met** his wife.
Would you **have gone** to the party if you'**d known** Lisa was there?
You **wouldn't have lost** your job if you **hadn't been** late every day.

- We normally use third conditional sentences to talk about hypothetical / imaginary situations in the past, i.e. how things could have been different in the past. Compare:
  Yesterday I got up late and missed my train. (= the real situation)
  If I hadn't got up late yesterday, I wouldn't have missed my train. (= the hypothetical or imaginary past situation)
- To make a third conditional, we use *if* + past perfect and *would have* + past participle. **NOT** ~~If I would have known you had a problem...~~
- The contraction of both *had* and *would* is *'d*.
  If I'd known you had a problem, I'd have helped you.
- We can use *might* or *could* instead of *would* to make the result less certain.
  If she'd studied harder, she might have passed the exam.

a Match the sentence halves.

Billy wouldn't have injured his head	D	A if you'd gone to university?
1 If I hadn't seen the speed camera,		B you wouldn't have caught a cold.
2 Jon might have got the job		C if she'd told you the truth?
3 She would have hurt herself badly		D if he'd worn his helmet.
4 If Katy and Luke hadn't caught the same train,		E they wouldn't have met.
5 What would you have studied		F if he'd been on time for his interview.
6 How would you have got to the airport		G if they'd come with us.
7 If you'd worn a warmer coat,		H if she'd fallen down the stairs.
8 Your parents would have enjoyed the trip		I I wouldn't have slowed down.
9 Would you have been annoyed		J if the trains had been on strike?

b Complete the third conditional sentences with the correct form of the verbs in brackets.

If Tom *hadn't gone* to university, he *wouldn't have got* a job with that company. (not go, not get)

1 If you _____ me to the station, I _____ my train. (not take, miss)
2 We _____ the match if the referee _____ us a penalty. (not win, not give)
3 You _____ the weekend if you _____ with us. (enjoy, come)
4 If I _____ the theatre tickets online, they _____ more expensive. (not buy, be)
5 Mike _____ his wife's birthday if she _____ him. (forget, not remind)
6 If the police _____ five minutes later, they _____ the thief. (arrive, not catch)
7 If you _____ me the money, I _____ to go away for the weekend. (not lend, not be able)
8 That girl _____ in the river if you _____ her arm! (fall, not catch)
9 We _____ the hotel if we _____ the signpost. (not find, not seen)
10 If I _____ about the job, I _____ for it. (know, apply)

🔙 p.87

quantifiers

large quantities

1	My daughter has **a lot of** apps on her phone. 🔊 9.15 Nina has **lots of** clothes. I've been there **loads of** times.
2	James eats **a lot**.
3	There aren't **many** cafés near here. Do you have **many** close friends? Do you watch **much** TV? I don't eat **much** chocolate.
4	Don't run. We have **plenty of** time.

1 We use *a lot of* or *lots of* in ⊞ sentences. We can also use *loads of*, but it's more informal.
2 We use *a lot* when there is no noun, e.g. *He talks a lot.* **NOT** *He talks a lot of.*
3 *much / many* are normally used in ⊟ sentences and ?, but *a lot of* can also be used.
4 We use *plenty of* in ⊞ sentences. (= more than enough)

small quantities

1	**A** Do you want some more ice cream? 🔊 9.16 **B** Just **a little**. The town only has **a few** cinemas.
2	I'm so busy that I have **very little time** for myself. Sarah isn't popular and she has **very few friends**.
3	I have **less free time** than I used to have. There are **fewer flights** in the winter than in the summer.

1 We use *little* + uncountable nouns, *few* + plural countable nouns.
• *a little* and *a few* = some, but not a lot.
2 *very little* and *very few* = not much / many.
3 The comparative of *little* is *less* and the comparative of *few* is *fewer*.

more or less than you need or want

1	I don't like this city. It's **too big** and 🔊 9.17 it's **too noisy**. You're speaking **too quietly** – I can't hear you.
2	There's **too much** traffic and **too much** noise. There are **too many** tourists and **too many** cars.
3	There aren't **enough parks** and there aren't **enough trees**. The buses aren't **frequent enough**. The buses don't **run frequently enough**.

1 We use *too* + adjective or adverb.
2 We use *too much* + uncountable nouns and *too many* + plural countable nouns.
3 We use *(not) enough* before a noun, e.g. *(not) enough eggs / milk*, and after an adjective, e.g. *It isn't big enough*, or an adverb, e.g. *You aren't walking fast enough*.

zero quantity

1	There **isn't any** milk in the fridge. 🔊 9.18 We **don't have any** eggs.
2	There's **no** milk in the fridge. We **have no** eggs.
3	**A** How many eggs do we have? **B** **None**. I've used them all.

1 We use *any* + uncountable or plural noun for zero quantity with a ⊟ verb.
2 We use *no* + uncountable or plural noun with a ⊞ verb.
3 We use *none* (without a noun) in short answers.

---

a Circle the correct word or phrase. Tick (✓) if both are possible.

My husband has *too much* / ~~too many~~ gadgets.
1 I just have to reply to *a few* / *a little* emails.
2 Do you spend *much* / *many* time on social media?
3 My bedroom is a nice size. There's *enough room* / *plenty of room* for a desk.
4 I know *very few* / *very little* people who speak two foreign languages.
5 My brother has downloaded *a lot of* / *lots of* apps onto his new phone.
6 I have some cash on me, but not *a lot* / *a lot of*.
7 Their new TV is *too* / *too much* big. It hardly fits in the living room.
8 *There aren't any* / *There are no* potatoes. I forgot to buy some.
9 My niece isn't *old enough* / *enough old* to play with a games console.
10 I don't have *a lot of* / *many* close friends.

b Are the highlighted phrases right (✓) or wrong (✗)? Correct the wrong ones.

My nephew got lots of video games for his birthday. ✓
I don't post much photos online. *many photos*
1 'How many presents did you get?' 'A lot of!'
2 I buy fewer ebooks than I used to because I prefer physical books.
3 There isn't no time to walk there. We'll have to get a taxi.
4 Please turn that music down. It's too much loud!
5 There aren't many good programmes on TV tonight.
6 My broadband isn't enough fast for me to download films easily.
7 I get too much emails at work. It takes me ages to read them all!
8 **A** How much fruit do we have? **B** Any. Can you buy some?
9 There are only a little people that I can talk to about my problems.
10 Karen has plenty of money, so she always has the latest phone.

↩ p.92

relative clauses: defining and non-defining

defining relative clauses (giving essential information)

> 1 Harper Lee is the woman **who** (**that**) wrote 10.1
> *To Kill a Mockingbird*.
> I'm looking for a book **which** (**that**) teaches you how to relax.
> That's the house **where** I was born.
> 2 Is Frank the man **whose** brother plays for Manchester United?
> It's a tree **whose** leaves change colour in autumn.
> 3 I've just had a text from the girl (**who** / **that**) I met on the flight to Paris.
> This is the phone (**which** / **that**) I bought yesterday.

- We use a defining relative clause (= a relative pronoun + verb phrase) to give essential information about a person, place, or thing.
1 We use the relative pronoun *who* for people, *which* for things / animals, and *where* for places.
- We can use *that* instead of *who* or *which*.
2 We use *whose* to mean 'of who' or 'of which'.
3 In some relative clauses, the verb after *who*, *which*, or *that* has a different subject, e.g. *She's the girl who I met on the train* (the subject of *met* is *I*). In these clauses, *who*, *which*, or *that* can be omitted.
She's the girl I met on the train.
- *where* and *whose* can never be omitted. **NOT** ~~Is that the woman dog barks?~~
- We can't omit *who* / *which* / *that* / *where* if it's the same subject in both clauses. **NOT** ~~Julia's the woman works in the office with me.~~

non-defining relative clauses (giving extra non-essential information)

> This painting, **which** was painted in 1860, is worth 10.2
> millions of pounds.
> Last week I visited my aunt Jane, **who**'s nearly 90 years old.
> Burford, **where** my grandfather was born, is a beautiful little town.
> My neighbour, **whose** son goes to my son's school, has just remarried.

- We use a non-defining relative clause to give extra (often non-essential information) in a sentence. If this clause is omitted, the sentence still makes sense.
This painting~~, which was painted in 1860,~~ is worth millions of pounds.
- Non-defining relative clauses must go between commas (or a comma and a full stop).
- In these clauses, we <u>can't</u> leave out the relative pronoun (*who*, *which*, etc.).
- In these clauses, we <u>can't</u> use *that* instead of *who* / *which*.
NOT ~~This painting, that was painted in 1860, is worth millions of pounds.~~

a Complete with *who*, *which*, *where*, or *whose*.

Minneapolis is the city *where* Prince was born.
1 Rob and Corinna, _____ have twins, often need a babysitter.
2 Downing Street, _____ the British Prime Minister lives, is in central London.
3 The sandwich _____ you made me for lunch was delicious.
4 The woman _____ lived here before us was a writer.
5 David Bowie, _____ songs inspired us for nearly 50 years, died in 2016.
6 My computer is a lot faster than the one _____ I used to have.
7 The *Mona Lisa*, _____ has been damaged several times, is now displayed behind glass.
8 Look! That's the woman _____ dog bit me last week.
9 On our last holiday we visited Stratford-upon-Avon, _____ Shakespeare was born.
10 We all went to the match except Angela, _____ doesn't like football.
11 That man _____ you saw at the party was my boyfriend!
12 That's the park _____ I learned to ride a bike.

b Look at the sentences in **a**. Tick (✓) the ones where you could use *that* instead of *who* / *which*. Circle the relative pronouns which could be left out.

c Add commas (,) where necessary.

Caroline, who lives next door to me, is beautiful.
1 This is the place where John crashed his car.
2 The castle that we visited yesterday was amazing.
3 Beijing which is one of the world's biggest cities has a population of over 25 million.
4 Adele's *25* which was released in 2015 is one of the best-selling albums of the last ten years.
5 These are the shoes which I'm wearing to the wedding tomorrow.
6 Sally and Joe who got married last year are expecting their first baby.

⬅ p.97

10B

question tags

question tags

positive verb, negative tag	negative verb, positive tag 🔊 10.11
It's cold today, **isn't it**?	**She isn't** here today, **is she**?
You're Polish, **aren't you**?	**You aren't** angry, **are you**?
They live in London, **don't they**?	**They don't** eat meat, **do they**?
The match finishes at 8.00, **doesn't it**?	**Lucy doesn't** drive, **does she**?
Your sister worked in the USA, **didn't she**?	**You didn't** like the film, **did you**?
We've met before, **haven't we**?	**Mike hasn't** been to Rome before, **has he**?
You'll be OK, **won't you**?	**You won't** tell anyone, **will you**?
You'd lend me some money, **wouldn't you**?	**Sue wouldn't** resign, **would she**?

It's cold today, isn't it?

- Question tags (*is he?*, *aren't they?*, *do you?*, *did we?*, etc.) are often used to check something you already think is true.
  Your name's Maria, isn't it?
- To form a question tag, we use:
  – the correct auxiliary verb, e.g. *be / do / have / will / would*, etc. in the correct form, e.g. *do / don't*, etc. for the present, *did / didn't* for the past, *will / won't*, etc. for the future.
  – a pronoun, e.g. *he, it, they*, etc.
  – a negative auxiliary verb if the sentence is positive and a positive auxiliary verb if the sentence is negative or with *never*, e.g. *You never do the washing-up, do you?*

a Match the question halves.

You know that man,	*G*	A didn't you?
1 You're going out with him,		B will you?
2 You haven't told your family about him,		C did you?
3 You met him last month,		D won't you?
4 You were at the same party,		E have you?
5 You didn't know he was a criminal,		F weren't you?
6 You aren't happy in the relationship,		G ~~don't you?~~
7 You never want to see him again,		H are you?
8 You'll tell us the truth,		I aren't you?
9 You won't tell any lies,		J don't you?
10 You understand what I'm saying,		K do you?

b Complete with a question tag (*are you?*, *isn't it?*, etc.).

Your name's Jack, *isn't it*?

1 Your brother works at the police station, _____?
2 They don't have any proof, _____?
3 That man isn't the murderer, _____?
4 You were a witness to the crime, _____?
5 The police have arrested someone, _____?
6 The woman wasn't dead, _____?
7 That girl took your handbag, _____?
8 He won't go to prison, _____?
9 You haven't seen the suspect, _____?
10 They couldn't find enough evidence, _____?

← p.101

Cinema

1 KINDS OF FILM

a Match the kinds of films and photos.

an <u>ac</u>tion film /ˈækʃn fɪlm/
an ani<u>ma</u>tion /ænɪˈmeɪʃn/
a <u>com</u>edy /ˈkɒmədi/
1 a <u>dra</u>ma /ˈdrɑːmə/
a hi<u>sto</u>rical film /hɪˈstɒrɪkl fɪlm/
a <u>hor</u>ror film /ˈhɒrə fɪlm/
a <u>mu</u>sical /ˈmjuːzɪkl/
a <u>rom</u>-com /ˈrɒm kɒm/ (romantic comedy)
a <u>sci</u>ence <u>fic</u>tion film /ˌsaɪəns ˈfɪkʃn fɪlm/
a <u>thri</u>ller /ˈθrɪlə/
a <u>war</u> film /ˈwɔː fɪlm/
a <u>wes</u>tern /ˈwestən/

b  6.4 Listen and check.

ACTIVATION Talk to a partner.

Think of a famous film for each kind of film in **a**.

What kind of films do you / don't you like? Why?

2 PEOPLE AND THINGS

a Match the nouns and definitions.

<u>au</u>dience /ˈɔːdiəns/   <s>cast</s> /kɑːst/   <u>cri</u>tic /ˈkrɪtɪk/   <u>ex</u>tra /ˈekstrə/
plot /plɒt/   re<u>view</u> /rɪˈvjuː/   scene /siːn/   script /skrɪpt/
<u>se</u>quel /ˈsiːkwəl/   set /set/   <u>sound</u>track /ˈsaʊndtræk/
<u>spe</u>cial e<u>ffe</u>cts /ˈspeʃl ɪˈfekts/   star /stɑː/   <u>sub</u>titles /ˈsʌbtaɪtlz/
<u>trai</u>ler /ˈtreɪlə/

1	*cast*	all the people who act in a film
2	_____	(also *verb*) the most important actor in a film
3	_____	the music of a film
4	_____	the story of a film
5	_____	a part of a film which happens in one place
6	_____	the people who watch a film in a cinema
7	_____	a film which continues the story of an earlier film
8	_____	images often created by a computer
9	_____	a series of short scenes from a film, shown in advance to advertise it
10	_____	the words of a film
11	_____	a person who is employed to play a very small part in a film, usually as a member of a crowd
12	_____	the translation of the dialogue of a film on screen
13	_____	an article which gives an opinion about a new film
14	_____	the place where a film is being shot; the scenery used for a film or play
15	_____	a person who writes films reviews for the press

b  6.5 Listen and check.

3 VERBS AND VERB PHRASES

a Match sentences 1–6 to sentences A–F.

1 ☐ The film **is based on** the story of opera singer Florence Foster Jenkins.
2 ☐ It **is set in** New York during the 1940s.
3 ☐ It **is directed by** Stephen Frears.
4 ☐ Hugh Grant **plays the part of** Florence's husband and manager.
5 ☐ It **was shot (or filmed) on location** in Liverpool.
6 ☐ It **is dubbed** into other languages.

A It is situated in that place at that time.
B He is the director.
C This is his role in the film.
D The words are spoken in a different language by foreign actors.
E The film is an adaptation of a true story.
F It was filmed outside the studio.

b  6.6 Listen and check.

ACTIVATION Cover 1–6 and look at A–F. Remember 1–6. Then think of another film you know well and say sentences 1–6 about the film.

⟲ p.58

 Go online to review the vocabulary for each lesson

The body

1 PARTS OF THE BODY

a Match the words and photos.

- [ ] arms /ɑːmz/
- [ ] back /bæk/
- [ ] chin /tʃɪn/
- [ ] ears /ɪəz/
- [ ] eyes /aɪz/
- [ ] face /feɪs/
- [ ] feet /fiːt/ (*sing* foot /fʊt/)
- [ ] <u>fi</u>ngers /ˈfɪŋgəz/
- [ ] hands /hændz/
- [ ] head /hed/
- [ ] knees /niːz/
- [ ] legs /legz/
- [ ] lips /lɪps/
- [1] mouth /maʊθ/
- [ ] neck /nek/
- [ ] nose /nəʊz/
- [ ] <u>shoul</u>ders /ˈʃəʊldəz/
- [ ] <u>sto</u>mach /ˈstʌmək/
- [ ] teeth /tiːθ/ (*sing* tooth /tuːθ/)
- [ ] thumb /θʌm/
- [ ] toes /təʊz/
- [ ] tongue /tʌŋ/

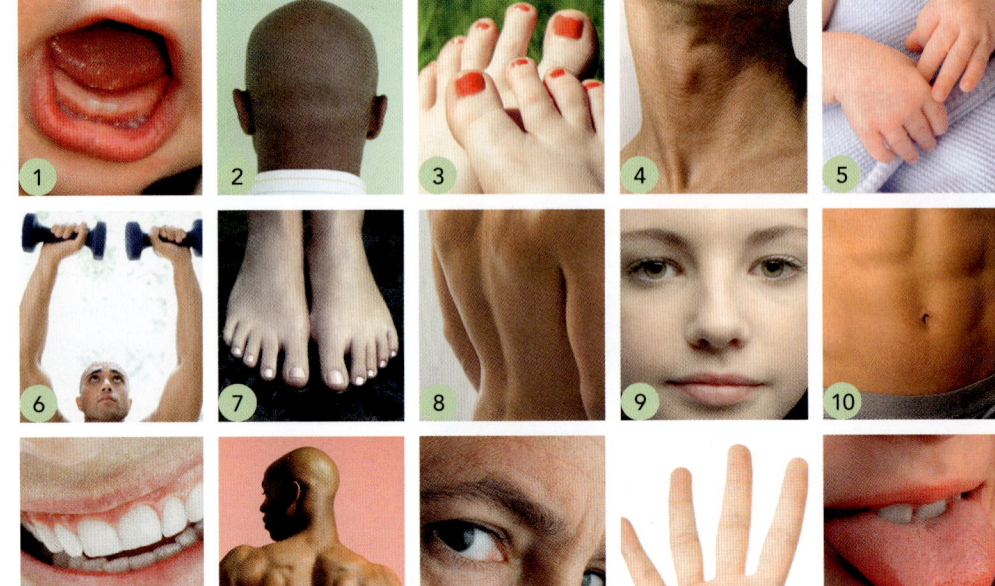

b ◉ 6.14 Listen and check.

ACTIVATION In pairs, point to a part of the body for your partner to say the word.

> 🔍 **Possessive pronouns with parts of the body**
> In English, we use possessive pronouns (*my*, *your*, etc.) with parts of the body.
> *Give me your hand.* **NOT** ~~Give me the hand.~~

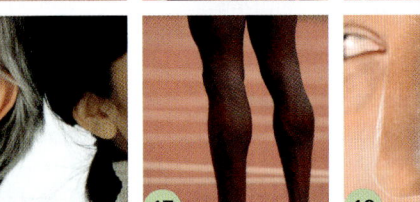
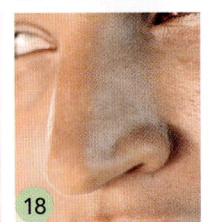
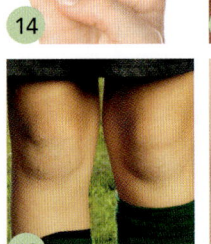

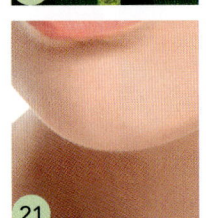
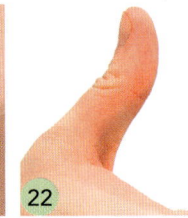

2 VERBS RELATED TO THE BODY

a Complete the sentences with a verb from the list in the correct tense.

<del>bite</del> /baɪt/   clap /klæp/   kick /kɪk/   nod /nɒd/
point /pɔɪnt/   smell /smel/   smile /smaɪl/   stare /steə/
taste /teɪst/   touch /tʌtʃ/   <u>whistle</u> /ˈwɪsl/
---

1 Don't be frightened of the dog. He won't <u>bite</u>.
2 Jason _____ the ball too hard and it went over the wall into the next garden.
3 Mmm! Something _____ delicious! Are you making a cake?
4 The stranger _____ at me for a long time, but he didn't say anything.
5 Can you _____ the sauce? I'm not sure if it needs more salt.
6 My dog always comes back when I _____.
7 Don't _____ the oven door! It's really hot.
8 The audience _____ when I finished singing.
9 The teacher suddenly _____ at me and said, 'What's the answer?' I hadn't even heard the question!
10 He's a very serious person – he never _____.
11 Everybody _____ in agreement when I explained my idea.

b ◉ 6.15 Listen and check. Which parts of the body do you use to do the things in **a**?

↩ p.62

Education

1 THE SCHOOL SYSTEM IN THE UK AND THE US

a Complete the text about the UK with words from the list.

boarding /'bɔːdɪŋ/   degree /dɪ'griː/   head /hed/   nursery /'nɜːsəri/   primary /'praɪməri/   private /'praɪvɪt/   pupils /'pjuːplz/   secondary /'sekəndri/   state /steɪt/   students /'stjuːdnts/   terms /tɜːmz/

In the UK

Children start [1] *primary* school when they're five. Before that, many children go to [2]_____ school, e.g. between the ages of two and four, but this is not compulsory. From 11–18, children go to [3]_____ school. The majority of schools in the UK (about 90%) are [4]_____ schools, which means that they are paid for by the government and education is free. The other 10% are [5]_____ schools, where parents have to pay. A few of these are [6]_____ schools, where children study, eat, and sleep. Children at primary school are often called [7]_____ and children at secondary school are usually called [8]_____, as are people who are studying at university. The person who is in charge of a school is called the [9]_____ teacher. The school year is divided into three [10]_____.

If you want to go to university, you have to take exams called A levels in your last year at school. If your results are good enough, you get a place. A person who has finished university and has a [11]_____ is called a graduate.

b ◑7.2 Listen and check.

c Complete the text about the US with words from the list.

college /'kɒlɪdʒ/   elementary /elɪ'mentəri/   grades /ɡreɪdz/   high /haɪ/   kindergarten /'kɪndəɡɑːtn/   semesters /sɪ'mestəz/   twelfth grade /'twelfθ ɡreɪd/

In the US

The school system is divided into three levels, [1] *elementary* school, middle school (sometimes called junior high school), and [2]_____ school. Schoolchildren are divided by age groups into [3]_____. The youngest children start in [4]_____ (followed by first grade) and continue until [5]_____, which is the final year of high school. The school year is divided into two [6]_____. Higher education in the US is often called [7]_____.

d ◑7.3 Listen and check.

ACTIVATION Cover the texts. With a partner, remember the different types of school (starting from the lowest level) in both countries.

2 DISCIPLINE AND EXAMS

a Complete the texts with a verb from the list in the right form.

~~not be allowed to~~ /nɒt biː ə'laʊd tə/   be expelled /bi ɪk'speld/   be punished /bi 'pʌnɪʃt/   cheat /tʃiːt/   let /let/   make /meɪk/   misbehave /mɪsbɪ'heɪv/

A Discipline is very strict in our school. We [1] *aren't allowed to* take our phones to school and they don't [2]_____ us bring unhealthy food for lunch, like crisps or fizzy drinks. Most children behave well, but if you [3]_____, for example, talk too much in class, you'll [4]_____ and the teacher will probably [5]_____ you stay behind after class. If you do something more serious, like [6]_____ in an exam, you might even [7]_____.

fail /feɪl/   pass /pɑːs/   result /rɪ'zʌlt/   revise /rɪ'vaɪz/   take /teɪk/ (or do)

B Marc has to [1]_____ an important English exam next week. He hopes he'll [2]_____, but he hasn't had much time to [3]_____, so he's worried that he might [4]_____. He won't get the [5]_____ until July.

b ◑7.4 Listen and check.

ACTIVATION Cover the texts and look at the verbs. Explain what they mean.

> 🔍 **make, let, and allow**
> My French teacher **made me do** extra homework. Our IT teacher **lets us play** games every Friday. The head **doesn't allow us to take** our phones to school.
>
> We use *make* and *let* with an object pronoun and the infinitive without *to*. We use *allow* with an object pronoun and the infinitive + *to*.
>
> *let* and *allow* have a similar meaning. We often use *allow* in the passive, e.g. *We're allowed to play games every Friday*, but we can't use *let* in the passive **NOT** ~~We're let play games…~~

← p.66

Houses

1 WHERE PEOPLE LIVE

a Complete the **Preposition** column with *in* or *on*.

	Preposition
1 I live ▢ **the country**, surrounded by fields.	*in*
2 I live ▢ **the outskirts** of Oxford, about three miles from the centre.	_____
3 I live ▢ **a village** (**a town** / **a city**).	_____
4 I live in Cromer, a small town ▢ **the east coast**.	_____
5 I live ▢ **the second floor** of a large block of flats.	_____
6 I live ▢ Croydon, **a suburb** of London about 15 miles from the city centre.	_____

b 🔊 **7.17** Listen and check.

c Cover the **Preposition** column. Say the sentences with the correct preposition.

ACTIVATION Talk to a partner. Describe where you live.

---

2 PARTS OF A HOUSE

a Match the words and pictures.

▢ attic /ˈætɪk/
▢ balcony /ˈbælkəni/
▢ basement /ˈbeɪsmənt/
▢ chimney /ˈtʃɪmni/
▢ entrance /ˈentrəns/
▢ gate /geɪt/
▢ ground floor /ɡraʊnd ˈflɔː/ (*AmE* first floor)
▢ path /pɑːθ/
1 roof /ruːf/
▢ steps /steps/
▢ terrace /ˈterəs/ (patio /ˈpætiəʊ/)
▢ top floor /tɒp ˈflɔː/
▢ wall /wɔːl/

b 🔊 **7.18** Listen and check.

3 DESCRIBING A HOUSE OR FLAT

a Match the descriptions and photos.

▢ I live in a cottage in the country. It's old and made of stone and the rooms have very low ceilings. There's an open fire in the living room and it's very cosy in the winter.

▢ I live in a modern flat in the city centre. It's spacious and very light, with wooden floors and big windows.

b 🔊 **7.19** Listen and check. Focus on how the highlighted phrases are pronounced.

ACTIVATION Cover the descriptions and look at the photos. Describe the rooms.

> 🔍 **chimney or fireplace?**
> In English, *chimney* only refers to the structure on the roof of the house.
> *Fireplace* is the place where you burn wood or coal. For some nationalities, *chimney* is a 'false friend'.
>
> **roof or ceiling?**
> *Roof* is the top part of a house. *Ceiling* is the top part of a room.

← p.72

Work

1 VERB PHRASES

a Complete the sentences with a verb or verb phrase from the list.

applied for /əˈplaɪd fɔː/   do /duː/   ~~do overtime~~ /duː ˈəʊvətaɪm/   got promoted /gɒt prəˈməʊtɪd/   resign /rɪˈzaɪn/   retire /rɪˈtaɪə/
run /rʌn/   set up /set ʌp/   was made redundant /wəz meɪd rɪˈdʌndənt/   was sacked /wəz sækt/   work shifts /wɜːk ʃɪfts/

1 Dan has to _do overtime_.	He has to work extra hours.
2 Matt _____ last week.	He was given a more important job.
3 Most nurses have to _____.	Sometimes they work during the day and sometimes at night.
4 A man in our department _____ yesterday. (or be fired)	The boss told him to leave.
5 Colin _____.	He lost his job because the company didn't need him any more.
6 The director of the company is going to _____. (AmE quit)	He has decided to leave his job.
7 Lilian is going to _____ next month.	She's 65 and she's going to stop working.
8 Angela has _____ a business selling clothes online.	She had the idea and has started doing it.
9 Everyone in the office has to _____ a training course.	They need to learn how to use the new software.
10 Mandy _____ a job online.	She replied to an advert and sent in her CV.
11 My parents _____ a language school in Brighton.	They employ six teachers, who teach English to foreign students.

b ◆8.2 Listen and check. Cover the first sentence and look at the second. Can you remember the verb?

ACTIVATION Do you know anybody who has applied for a job / got promoted / been made redundant / resigned / been sacked (fired) / retired recently?

2 SAYING WHAT YOU DO

a Match the adjectives and definitions.

freelance /ˈfriːlɑːns/   part-time /pɑːt taɪm/
self-employed /ˌself ɪmˈplɔɪd/   temporary /ˈtemprəri/
unemployed /ˌʌnɪmˈplɔɪd/

talking about people

1 I'm _____.	without a job
2 He's _____.	working for himself
3 He's a _____ designer.	working for different companies

talking about a job or work

4 It's a _____ job.	(opp permanent) only a short contract, e.g. for six months
5 It's a _____ job.	(opp full-time) only a few hours a day

b Complete the sentences with at, for, in, or of.

1 I **work** _for_ (in) a multinational company.
2 I'm _____ **charge** _____ the Marketing Department.
3 I'm **responsible** _____ customer loans.
4 I'm _____ school (university).
5 I'm _____ my third year at university.

c ◆8.3 Listen and check **a** and **b**.

3 WORD-BUILDING

a Make nouns from the verbs by adding -ment, -ion, or -ation. Make any other necessary changes.

	Noun			Noun
1 promote	promotion		4 employ	
2 apply			5 qualify	
3 retire			6 resign	

b Make nouns for the people who do the jobs by adding -er, -or, -ian, or -ist. Make any other necessary changes.

	Noun			Noun
1 science			4 pharmacy	
2 law			5 farm	
3 music			6 translate	

c ◆8.4 Listen and check **a** and **b**. Underline the stressed syllable in the new words.

ACTIVATION Cover the **Noun** columns and look at 1–6 in **a** and **b**. Remember the nouns. Then think of two more jobs ending in -er, -or, -ian, or -ist. ← p.76

Word-building

1 MAKING NOUNS FROM VERBS

a Make nouns from the verbs in the list and write them in the correct column.

achieve /əˈtʃiːv/   agree /əˈɡriː/   argue /ˈɑːɡjuː/
attach /əˈtætʃ/   choose /tʃuːz/   compensate /
ˈkɒmpənseɪt/   complain /kəmˈpleɪn/   consider /kənˈsɪdə/
deliver /dɪˈlɪvə/   demonstrate /ˈdemənstreɪt/
explain /ɪkˈspleɪn/   fail /feɪl/   improve /ɪmˈpruːv/
lose /luːz/   manage /ˈmænɪdʒ/   pay /peɪ/
respond /rɪˈspɒnd/   sell /sel/   serve /sɜːv/
succeed /səkˈsiːd/   tempt /tempt/   treat /triːt/
value /ˈvæljuː/

+ ation	+ ment	new word
	achievement	

b ◆8.20 Listen and check. Underline the stressed syllable in the nouns.

ACTIVATION Test a partner. Then change roles.

A (book open) Say the verb. **B** (book closed) Say the noun.

c Complete the questions with a noun from **a** in the singular or plural.

1 Have you ever been on a _demonstration_? What were you protesting about?
2 Have you ever opened an email _____ that contained a virus?
3 Do you often have _____ with your family? What about?
4 Do you prefer reading grammar _____ in your own language, or do you think it's better to read them in English?
5 Have you ever made a _____ to a company and got _____?
6 Do you think that there's too much _____ when you're shopping, e.g. for a new phone?
7 In a restaurant, what's more important for you, the food or the _____?

d ◆8.21 Listen and check.

ACTIVATION With a partner, ask and answer the questions in **c**.

← p.83

2 MAKING ADJECTIVES AND ADVERBS

> 🔍 **Adjective prefixes and suffixes**
> We often make adjectives from nouns by adding a suffix. Some common suffixes are: -y, e.g. sun – sunny; -ate, e.g. passion – passionate; -able / -ible, e.g. fashion – fashionable; -ful, e.g. use – useful. Nouns which end in -ence often make the adjective with -ent, e.g. violence – violent.
>
> To make a negative adjective, we usually add a prefix, e.g. un-, im-, etc. (See **Vocabulary Bank** Personality, **p.153**.) However, some adjectives that end in -ful make the negative by changing the suffix -ful to -less, e.g. useful – useless, hopeful – hopeless.

a Look at the adjectives and adverbs from the noun *luck* in the chart below. Complete the chart.

	adjectives		adverbs	
noun	+	−	+	−
luck	lucky	unlucky	luckily	unluckily
fortune	fortunate	unfortunate		
comfort				
patience				
care				

b ◆9.7 Listen and check.

c Complete the sentences with the correct form of the **bold** noun.

1 The beach was beautiful, but _unfortunately_ it rained almost every day.   **fortune**
2 My new shoes are very _____. I wore them all day yesterday and they didn't hurt at all.   **comfort**
3 He did the exam quickly and _____ and so he made lots of mistakes.   **care**
4 We were really _____. We missed the flight by just five minutes.   **luck**
5 Jack is a very _____ driver! He can't stand being behind someone who is driving slowly.   **patience**
6 It was a bad accident, but _____ nobody was seriously hurt.   **luck**
7 It was raining, but fans waited _____ in the queue to buy tickets for tomorrow's concert.   **patience**
8 The roads will be very icy tonight, so drive _____.   **care**
9 The temperature dropped to minus 10 degrees, but _____, we were all wearing warm coats.   **fortune**
10 The bed in the hotel was incredibly _____. I hardly slept at all.   **comfort**

d ◆9.8 Listen and check.

← p.89

Irregular verbs

Infinitive	Past simple	Past participle
be /bi/	was /wɒz/ were /wɜː/	been /biːn/
beat /biːt/	beat	beaten /ˈbiːtn/
become /bɪˈkʌm/	became /bɪˈkeɪm/	become
begin /bɪˈgɪn/	began /bɪˈgæn/	begun /bɪˈgʌn/
bite /baɪt/	bit /bɪt/	bitten /ˈbɪtn/
break /breɪk/	broke /brəʊk/	broken /ˈbrəʊkən/
bring /brɪŋ/	brought /brɔːt/	brought
build /bɪld/	built /bɪlt/	built
buy /baɪ/	bought /bɔːt/	bought
can /kæn/	could /kʊd/	–
catch /kætʃ/	caught /kɔːt/	caught
choose /tʃuːz/	chose /tʃəʊz/	chosen /ˈtʃəʊzn/
come /kʌm/	came /keɪm/	come
cost /kɒst/	cost	cost
cut /kʌt/	cut	cut
do /duː/	did /dɪd/	done /dʌn/
draw /drɔː/	drew /druː/	drawn /drɔːn/
dream /driːm/	dreamt /dremt/ (also dreamed)	dreamt (also dreamed)
drink /drɪŋk/	drank /dræŋk/	drunk /drʌŋk/
drive /draɪv/	drove /drəʊv/	driven /ˈdrɪvn/
eat /iːt/	ate /eɪt/	eaten /ˈiːtn/
fall /fɔːl/	fell /fel/	fallen /ˈfɔːlən/
feel /fiːl/	felt /felt/	felt
find /faɪnd/	found /faʊnd/	found
fly /flaɪ/	flew /fluː/	flown /fləʊn/
forget /fəˈget/	forgot /fəˈgɒt/	forgotten /fəˈgɒtn/
get /get/	got /gɒt/	got
give /gɪv/	gave /geɪv/	given /ˈgɪvn/
go /gəʊ/	went /went/	gone /gɒn/
grow /grəʊ/	grew /gruː/	grown /grəʊn/
hang /hæŋ/	hung /hʌŋ/	hung
have /hæv/	had /hæd/	had
hear /hɪə/	heard /hɜːd/	heard
hit /hɪt/	hit	hit
hurt /hɜːt/	hurt	hurt
keep /kiːp/	kept /kept/	kept
know /nəʊ/	knew /njuː/	known /nəʊn/
learn /lɜːn/	learnt /lɜːnt/	learnt
leave /liːv/	left /left/	left

Infinitive	Past simple	Past participle
lend /lend/	lent /lent/	lent
let /let/	let	let
lie /laɪ/	lay /leɪ/	lain /leɪn/
lose /luːz/	lost /lɒst/	lost
make /meɪk/	made /meɪd/	made
mean /miːn/	meant /ment/	meant
meet /miːt/	met /met/	met
pay /peɪ/	paid /peɪd/	paid
put /pʊt/	put	put
read /riːd/	read /red/	read /red/
ride /raɪd/	rode /rəʊd/	ridden /ˈrɪdn/
ring /rɪŋ/	rang /ræŋ/	rung /rʌŋ/
run /rʌn/	ran /ræn/	run
say /seɪ/	said /sed/	said
see /siː/	saw /sɔː/	seen /siːn/
sell /sel/	sold /səʊld/	sold
send /send/	sent /sent/	sent
set /set/	set	set
shine /ʃaɪn/	shone /ʃɒn/	shone
shut /ʃʌt/	shut	shut
sing /sɪŋ/	sang /sæŋ/	sung /sʌŋ/
sit /sɪt/	sat /sæt/	sat
sleep /sliːp/	slept /slept/	slept
smell /smel/	smelt /smelt/ (also smelled)	smelt (also smelled)
speak /spiːk/	spoke /spəʊk/	spoken /ˈspəʊkən/
spend /spend/	spent /spent/	spent
stand /stænd/	stood /stʊd/	stood
steal /stiːl/	stole /stəʊl/	stolen /ˈstəʊlən/
swim /swɪm/	swam /swæm/	swum /swʌm/
take /teɪk/	took /tʊk/	taken /ˈteɪkən/
teach /tiːtʃ/	taught /tɔːt/	taught
tell /tel/	told /təʊld/	told
think /θɪŋk/	thought /θɔːt/	thought
throw /θrəʊ/	threw /θruː/	thrown /θrəʊn/
understand /ʌndəˈstænd/	understood /ʌndəˈstʊd/	understood
wake /weɪk/	woke /wəʊk/	woken /ˈwəʊkən/
wear /weə/	wore /wɔː/	worn /wɔːn/
win /wɪn/	won /wʌn/	won
write /raɪt/	wrote /rəʊt/	written /ˈrɪtn/

Consonant sounds

		usual spelling	! but also
🐟	fish	i bill dish fit pitch since ticket	pretty decided women busy village physics
🐑	tree	ee beef speed ea peach team e refund sequel	people magazine key niece receipt
🐱	cat	a mango tram tax bank carry crash	
🚗	car	ar garden charge starter a cast pass drama	aunt laugh heart
⏰	clock	o cost lorry bossy plot off on	watch want sausage because
🐴	horse	(o)or score floor al bald wall aw draw prawns	warm course thought caught audience board
🐑	bull	u full put oo cook look foot good	could should would woman
👢	boot	oo food moody cartoon u* rude argue ew few flew	suitcase juice move shoe soup through queue
💻	computer	Many different spellings. /ə/ is always unstressed. other nervous about complain information camera	
🐦	bird	er term prefer ir dirty circuit ur turn nursery	learn work world worse journey
🥚	egg	e lemon lend text spend plenty cent	friendly healthy jealous already many said
⬆️	up	u public subject unlucky duck hurry rush	money tongue someone couple touch enough

		usual spelling	! but also
🚂	train	a* save gate ai fail brain ay may say	break steak great weight grey they
☎️	phone	o* broke stone frozen slope oa coach roast	owe elbow although shoulders aubergine
🚲	bike	i* bite retire y cycle shy igh lights flight	buy eyes height
🦉	owl	ou hour mouth proud ground ow town brown	
🧒	boy	oi boiled noisy coin spoilt oy enjoy unemployed	
👂	ear	eer beer engineer ere here we're ear beard appearance	really idea serious
🪑	chair	air airport upstairs fair hair are stare careful	their there wear pear area
🧑	tourist	Not a very common sound. euro furious plural sure	
/i/		A sound between /ɪ/ and /iː/. Consonant + y at the end of words is pronounced /i/. happy angry hungry	
/u/		Not a very common sound. education usually situation	

* especially before consonant + e

◻️ short vowels   ◻️ long vowels   ◻️ diphthongs

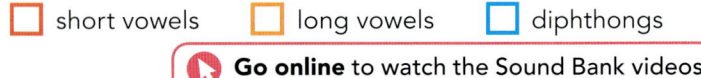 **Go online** to watch the Sound Bank videos

Vowel sounds

		usual spelling	! but also
parrot	**p** **pp**	**p**ro**p**ose **p**u**p**il trans**p**ort tri**p** a**pp**ly sho**pp**ing	
bag	**b** **bb**	**b**eans **b**ill pro**b**a**b**ly cra**b** du**bb**ed stu**bb**orn	
key	**c** **k** **ck**	**c**ourt s**c**ript **k**ind **k**i**ck** tra**ck** lu**ck**y	**ch**emist's s**ch**ool stoma**ch** a**cc**ount s**q**uid
girl	**g** **gg**	**g**olf **g**rilled for**g**et collea**g**ue a**gg**ressive lu**gg**age	
flower	**f** **ph** **ff**	**f**ood roo**f** **ph**armacy ne**ph**ew tra**ff**ic a**ff**ectionate	lau**gh** enou**gh**
vase	**v**	**v**an **v**egetables tra**v**el in**v**est pri**v**ate belie**v**e	o**f**
tie	**t** **tt**	**t**aste **t**idy s**t**adium s**t**rict a**tt**ractive co**tt**age	work**ed** pass**ed**
dog	**d** **dd**	**d**irector gra**d**uate come**d**y affor**d** a**dd**ress mi**dd**le	bor**ed** fail**ed**
snake	**s** **ss** **ce/ci**	**s**tep**s** like**s** bo**ss** a**ss**istant **ce**iling **ci**nema	**sc**ene **sc**ience **c**y**c**le
zebra	**z** **s, se**	la**z**y free**z**ing co**s**y love**s** toe**s** lo**se** no**se**	
shower	**sh** **ti (+ vowel)** **ci (+ vowel)**	**sh**ow puni**sh** ca**sh** self**ish** ambi**ti**ous explana**ti**on spa**ci**ous so**ci**able	**s**ugar **s**ure **ch**ef ma**ch**ine
television	Not a very common sound. confu**si**on deci**si**on revi**si**on u**s**ually cour**g**ette		

		usual spelling	! but also
thumb	**th**	**th**row **th**riller heal**th**y ma**th**s pa**th** tee**th**	
mother	**th**	**th**e **th**at wi**th** fur**th**er toge**th**er	
chess	**ch** **tch** **t (+ure)**	**ch**ange **ch**eat ma**tch** pi**tch** pic**t**ure fu**t**ure	
jazz	**j** **g** **dge**	**j**ealous **j**ust **g**enerous mana**g**er fri**dge** ju**dge**	
leg	**l** **ll**	**l**imit sa**l**ary re**l**iable unti**l** se**ll** rebe**ll**ious	
right	**r** **rr**	**r**esult refe**r**ee p**r**imary f**r**ied bo**rr**ow te**rr**ace	**wr**itten **wr**ong
witch	**w** **wh**	**w**ar **w**aste **w**estern motor**w**ay **wh**istle **wh**ich	**o**ne **o**nce
yacht	**y** **before u**	**y**et **y**ear **y**oghurt **y**ourself **u**niversity arg**u**e	
monkey	**m** **mm**	**m**ean ro**m**antic char**m**ing ar**m** su**mm**er swi**mm**ing	la**m**b
nose	**n** **nn**	**n**eck ho**n**est **n**one chim**n**ey ten**n**is win**n**er	**kn**ee **kn**ew
singer	**ng** **before g / k**	cook**ing** go**ing** bri**ng** spri**ng** tongue think	
house	**h**	**h**ands **h**elmet be**h**ave in**h**erit un**h**appy per**h**aps	**wh**o **wh**ose **wh**ole

OXFORD
UNIVERSITY PRESS

fourth edition

English File

Intermediate Multipack B

Workbook B Units 6–10

WITH KEY

Christina Latham-Koenig
Clive Oxenden
Jerry Lambert

with Jane Hudson

Paul Seligson and Clive Oxenden
are the original co-authors of
English File 1 and *English File 2*

Contents

How to use your Workbook and Online Practice

Student's Book

Use the Student's Book section in class with your teacher.

English File
fourth edition

ACTIVITIES · AUDIO · VIDEO · RESOURCES

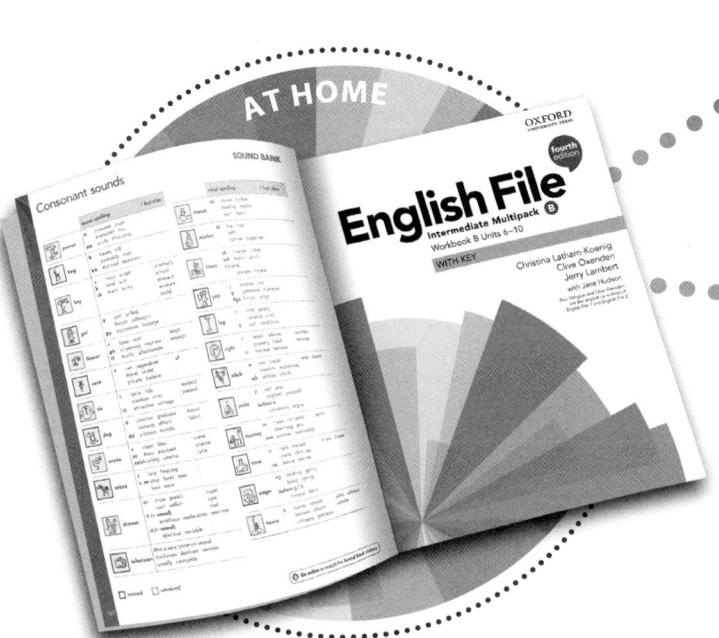

Go to **englishfileonline.com** and use the code on your Access Card to log into the Online Practice.

Workbook

Practise **Grammar**, **Vocabulary**, and **Pronunciation** for every lesson.

Online Practice

Look again at the Grammar, Vocabulary, and Pronunciation from the Student's Book section before you do the Workbook exercises.

Listen to the audio for the Pronunciation exercises.

Use the Sound Bank videos to practise English sounds.

Practise the **Practical English** for every episode.

Watch the Practical English videos before you do the exercises.

Use the interactive video for more Practical English practice.

Do the **Can you remember...?** exercises to check that you remember the Grammar, Vocabulary, and Pronunciation every two Files.

Look again at the Grammar, Vocabulary and Pronunciation if you have any problems.

Practise Reading, Listening, Speaking and Writing.

> All you need to make a movie is a girl and a gun.
> *Jean-Luc Godard, French director*

1 GRAMMAR passive (all tenses)

a Circle the correct form, active or passive.

1 The film *sets* / *is set* in Manchester in the 1980s.

2 A well-known comedy writer *wrote* / *was written* the script.

3 Special effects *will use* / *will be used* to create the monster.

4 Some of the extras *have invited* / *have been invited* to the film premiere.

5 Cinemas all over the country *are showing* / *are being shown* the musical.

6 The drama *is going to dub* / *is going to be dubbed* into other languages.

7 It was very windy while they *were filming* / *were being filmed* the final scenes.

8 Tickets for the show *can buy* / *can be bought* online.

b Complete the sentences with the correct passive form of the verbs in brackets.

1 The director's new film *is based* on a true story. (base)

2 I've just read that Jude Law _____ for an Oscar. I hope he wins! (nominate)

3 The final scene _____ in Africa right now. (film)

4 The actor looked very different because he _____ into an old man by the make-up artist. (transform)

5 The first *Star Wars* films _____ by George Lucas. (direct)

6 One of the workers fell off a ladder while the set _____. (build)

7 The sequel _____ next year. (release)

8 The scene had to _____ several times before the director was satisfied. (shoot)

c Read the article. Circle a, b, or c.

STEVEN SPIELBERG
Four decades of film history

Steven Spielberg [1]_____ films for over 40 years. The film that made him famous around the world was *Jaws*, which [2]_____ in 1975. *Jaws* [3]_____ the story of a holiday resort where swimmers [4]_____ by a huge great white shark. Spielberg had many problems with the mechanical sharks while the film [5]_____, but he managed to finish it in the end. *Jaws* was extremely successful, and it [6]_____ three Academy Awards. Since then, Spielberg [7]_____ many films which have since become classics, including *Close Encounters of the Third Kind*, *E.T.*, and *Jurassic Park*. He [8]_____ for an Oscar seven times and has won the award for Best Director twice: for *Schindler's List* and *Saving Private Ryan*. Today, Spielberg [9]_____ to be one of the most popular directors and producers in film history. Now in his seventies, he's still making films, and it seems unlikely that he [10]_____ any time soon.

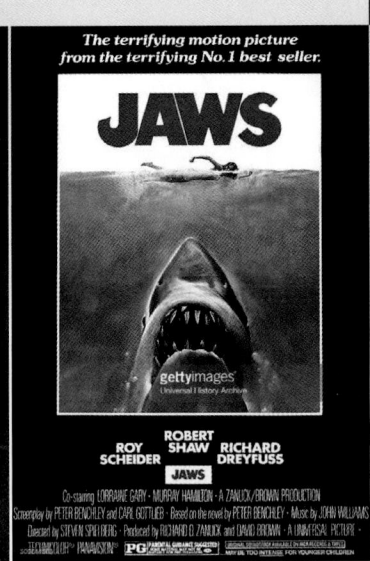

The terrifying motion picture from the terrifying No. 1 best seller.

JAWS

ROY SCHEIDER   ROBERT SHAW   RICHARD DREYFUSS

1 **a** has been making   **b** has been made   **c** is made

2 **a** is released   **b** released   **c** was released

3 **a** is told   **b** tells   **c** was told

4 **a** are being attacked   **b** are attacking   **c** attack

5 **a** was shot   **b** shoot   **c** was being shot

6 **a** was won   **b** won   **c** was being won

7 **a** has been directed   **b** has directed   **c** was directed

8 **a** nominated   **b** has nominated   **c** has been nominated

9 **a** considers   **b** is considered   **c** has been considered

10 **a** will retire   **b** will be retired   **c** is retired

2 PRONUNCIATION regular and irregular past participles

a Look at the past participles. Which sounds do the letters in **bold** have? Write the words from the list in the correct column in the chart.

s**ai**d sh**o**t t**a**ken t**o**ld us**ed** wait**ed** watch**ed** w**o**n w**or**n wr**i**tten

t tie	1 finish**ed** look**ed** releas**ed** *watched*
d dog	2 film**ed** play**ed** own**ed**
/ɪd/ /ɪd/	3 add**ed** direct**ed** repeat**ed**
fish	4 b**ui**lt g**i**ven h**i**t
cl**o**ck	5 c**o**st g**o**ne g**o**t
h**or**se	6 br**ough**t dr**aw**n t**augh**t
egg	7 f**e**lt l**e**ft m**ea**nt
up	8 d**o**ne dr**u**nk r**u**n
tr**ai**n	9 b**a**sed m**a**de p**ai**d
ph**o**ne	10 ch**o**sen fl**ow**n st**o**len

b ◐6.1 Listen and check. Then listen again and repeat the groups of words.

3 VOCABULARY cinema

a Match the words from the list to definitions 1–12.

action film animation ~~comedy~~ drama historical film horror film musical rom-com science fiction film thriller war film western

1 an amusing film that has a happy ending
   comedy

2 a film that has a lot of exciting events, e.g. fights and car chases
   _____

3 a film about imaginary events in the future
   _____

4 a film with a serious story
   _____

5 a film where the cast sing and dance
   _____

6 a film with an exciting story, often about a crime
   _____

7 a film based on real events in the past
   _____

8 a scary film
   _____

9 a film about soldiers fighting battles
   _____

10 a film about life in the past in the US
   _____

11 a film which is made with pictures that appear to move
   _____

12 a funny film about love
   _____

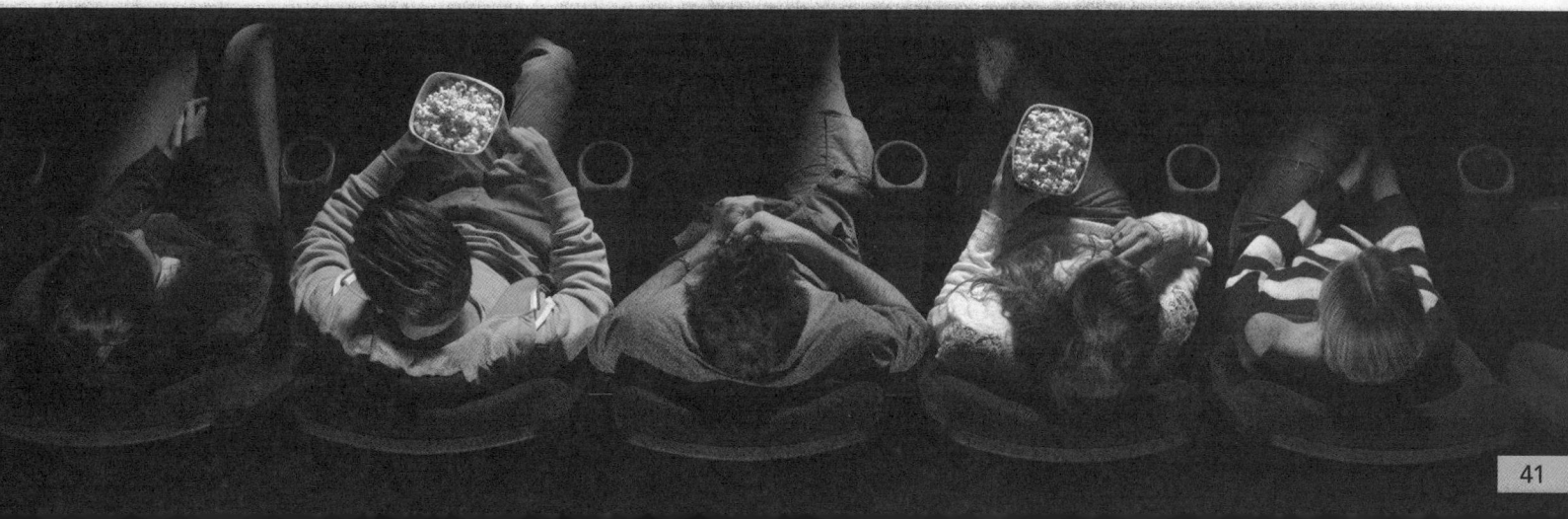

b Complete the sentences.

1 The st<u>ar</u>_____ of the film was a famous British actress.

2 I didn't understand the film because the pl_____ was very complicated.

3 The actor wanted to play the part as soon as he had read the sc_____.

4 Some of the a_____ were crying at the end of the film.

5 Most critics have given the film an excellent r_____.

6 They only had to shoot the sc_____ once.

7 It's a French film, but with English s_____.

8 You'll have to wait for the s_____ to find out what happens next.

9 My favourite s_____ is the music from *Guardians of the Galaxy*.

10 The best thing about the film was the sp_____ e_____. They were very realistic.

11 The director is looking for e_____ to act in the crowd scenes.

12 The c_____ was a mixture of British and American actors.

13 *The Times* film cr_____ didn't like the film at all.

14 The two actors first met on the s_____ of the film *La La Land*.

15 I've seen the tr_____, and it looks like a really interesting film.

c Complete the text with the phrases from the list.

is based on   ~~was directed by~~   was dubbed into
plays the part of   is set in   was shot

THE REVENANT

The Revenant is a 2015 American western. It [1] <u>was directed by</u> Mexican film director Alejandro G. Iñárritu. The film [2] _____ the north-western part of the US. It [3] _____ a novel about the experiences of Hugh Glass, a man who lived in the area in the early 1800s. *The Revenant* [4] _____ on location in Canada, the US, and Argentina. Leonardo DiCaprio [5] _____ Hugh Glass and won an Academy Award for his performance. *The Revenant* was made in English, but it [6] _____ other languages.

A FILM BY *ALEJANDRO G. IÑARRITU*

LEONARDO DiCAPRIO   TOM HARDY

BLOOD LOST. LIFE FOUND.
THE REVENANT
INSPIRED BY TRUE EVENTS
JANUARY 8

Go online for more practice

Take care of your body. It's the only place you have to live.
Jim Rohn, American businessman

G modals of deduction: *might, can't, must* **V** the body **P** diphthongs

1 GRAMMAR modals of deduction

a Circle the correct words.

1 That man *can't* / *must* be the new boss. Our new boss is a woman.

2 You *must* / *can't* be really tired. You've had a long trip.

3 I'm not sure what book to buy Oliver. He *might not* / *mustn't* like the same kind of things as me.

4 Paula *can't* / *could* be injured. She isn't running very well at all today. She's very slow.

5 Your neighbour *must* / *might not* have a good job. He has a very expensive car.

6 Luke and Molly *must* / *can't* have much money. They never go out.

b Complete the sentences with *must*, *might*, *might not*, or *can't*.

1 He lived in Argentina for five years, so he *must* speak good Spanish!

2 You _____ be very busy at work. You're always on Facebook!

3 I'm not sure, but the new assistant _____ be Italian. Her surname is Rossi.

4 Mark passed all his exams. His parents _____ be very proud.

5 **A** I think England will win tonight.
   B You _____ be serious! They have no chance!

6 Lucy wasn't feeling well this afternoon, so she _____ come to the party tonight. She said she'd let us know later today.

7 I thought our neighbour was away on holiday, but she _____ be – I've just seen her in her garden.

8 It's very cold and cloudy this evening. I think it _____ snow.

c Rewrite the highlighted sentences. Use *might (not)*, *can't*, or *must*.

1 They've been knocked out of the tournament. I'm sure they're disappointed.
   They *must be disappointed* _____ .

2 Emily's late. It's possible that she has a meeting.
   She _____ .

3 It's 8.30 and Tom's still in bed. I'm sure he isn't going to work today.
   He _____ .

4 Don't buy that jumper for Ruth. It's possible that she won't like it.
   She _____ .

5 We've only walked three kilometres. I'm sure you aren't tired already.
   You _____ .

6 Susie's been studying all night. I'm sure she has an exam tomorrow.
   She _____ .

7 We've been waiting ages for the lift. It's possible that it isn't working.
   It _____ .

8 My brother isn't answering his phone. It's possible that he's driving home from work.
   He _____ .

2 VOCABULARY the body

a Label the picture.

1 h<u>ead</u>

2 n_____

3 b_____

4 a_____

5 l_____

6 fe_____

7 f_____

8 n_____

9 ch_____

10 st_____

11 f_____

12 kn_____

b Look at the pictures. Complete the puzzle to find the hidden part of the body.

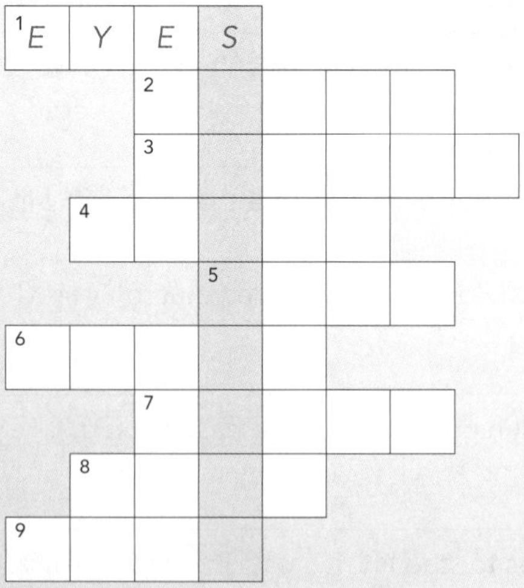

¹E	Y	E	S			
		2				
		3				
	4					
		5				
6						
	7					
8						
9						

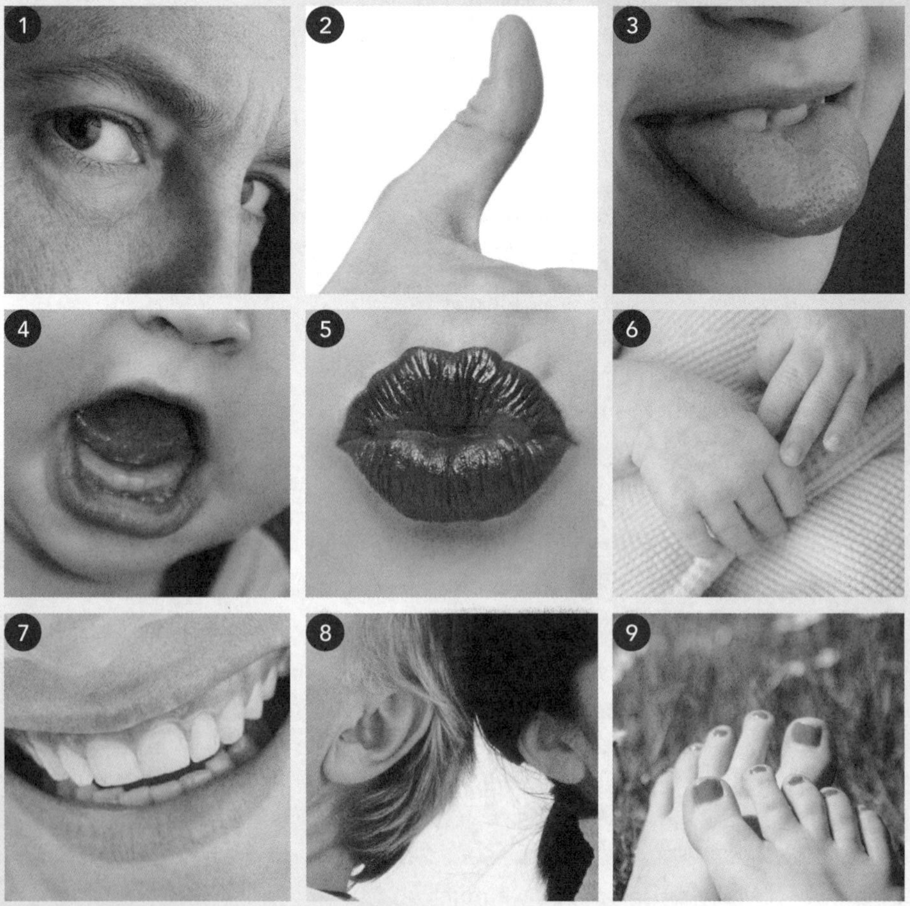

c Complete the sentences with a verb from the list.

bite clap kick nod point smell
smile ~~stare~~ taste throw touch whistle

1 It's rude to *stare* at people. It can make them feel uncomfortable.
2 You'll have to _____ the ball harder to score a goal.
3 Don't _____ that plant with your hand – it's poisonous.
4 If you're in another country and don't speak the language, you can _____ at the thing you want in a shop or café.
5 I can _____ something burning. Did you turn off the oven?
6 My grandparents always look unhappy in photos because they never _____ at the camera.
7 He was too embarrassed to speak, but he was able to _____ his head to show he had understood.
8 Did the audience _____ much at the end of the concert?
9 Lisa doesn't like dogs because she's afraid they'll _____ her.
10 I often _____ my favourite song when I'm in the shower.
11 Don't drop rubbish in the street. _____ it in the bin.
12 Can you _____ the soup? I think it might need more salt.

d Complete the sentences with a part of the body.

1 You kick with your *foot*.
2 You point with your _____.
3 You smile with your _____.
4 You taste with your _____.
5 You nod with your _____.
6 You stare with your _____.
7 You smell with your _____.
8 You touch with your _____.
9 You whistle with your _____.
10 You bite with your _____.
11 You clap with your _____.

3 PRONUNCIATION diphthongs

a (Circle) the word with a different sound.

aɪ bike	1 b**i**te	sm**i**le	h**eigh**t	(w**eigh**t)	
eɪ train	2 f**a**ce	gr**ea**t	**eye**s	t**a**ste	
əʊ phone	3 n**o**se	t**o**ngue	thr**ow**	t**oe**s	
aʊ owl	4 s**ou**nd	cr**ow**d	m**ou**th	sh**ou**lders	
eə chair	5 h**air**	h**ere**	st**are**	w**ear**	
ɪə ear	6 app**ear**ance	b**ear**d	f**air**	s**er**ious	

b 🔊 6.2 Listen and check. Then listen again and repeat the words.

7A Live and learn

One child, one teacher, one book, one pen can change the world.
Malala Yousafzai

G first conditional and future time clauses + *when*, *until*, etc. **V** education **P** the letter *u*

1 VOCABULARY education

a Complete the sentences. Order the letters to make school subjects.

1 *Physics*_____ (siphycs) is the scientific study of natural forces such as light, sound, heat, electricity, pressure, etc.

2 _____ (ogphyrage) is the study of the world's surface, physical qualities, climate, countries, products, population, etc.

3 _____ (lobigyo) is the scientific study of living things.

4 _____ (teturelira) is the study of poetry, drama, and fiction.

5 _____ (trymische) is the scientific study of substances and what happens to them in different conditions.

6 _____ (rytohis) is the study of past events.

7 _____ _____ (fortionmain nogytechlo) is the study of computers for collecting, storing and sending out information.

8 _____ (eticsmamath) is the study of numbers, quantities or shapes.

b Match the words from the list to definitions 1–11.

In the UK

boarding school   degree   head   nursery school
primary school   private school   ~~pupils~~
secondary school   state school   students   term

1 Children in school.
*pupils*_____

2 A school for children aged four to eleven.
_____

3 The teacher in charge of a school.
_____

4 A school controlled by the government.
_____

5 An official document that students gain by successfully completing a course at university.
_____

6 A school that parents pay for.
_____

7 A period of time that the school year is divided into.
_____

8 A school that children live at while they're studying.
_____

9 A school for children aged from about two to five.
_____

10 People who are studying at school or university.
_____

11 A school for children aged from eleven to eighteen.
_____

c Complete the sentences.

In the US

1 Very young children often go to k*indergarten*_.

2 Children start e_____ sch_____ when they're six.

3 Schoolchildren are divided by age group into gr_____.

4 The school year is divided into s_____.

5 After middle school, students go on to h_____ sch_____.

6 Students finish school in tw_____ gr_____.

7 When they leave school, some students go to c_____ to continue their education.

d Complete the texts with the past simple form of the verbs from the list.

~~be expelled~~   be punished   cheat   let   make
misbehave   (not) be allowed to

At my secondary school, discipline was very strict. Students who behaved badly [1]*were expelled*, so very few students [2]_____ in class. We [3]_____ talk during lessons, and the teacher [4]_____ us stand up every time another teacher came into the classroom. We had to wear a uniform, and we [5]_____ if we wore something different. We had to study a lot, and nobody [6]_____ in exams. In the final year, the teachers weren't as strict with us, and they [7]_____ us leave school during the lunch break.

fail   pass   revise   take

I was very nervous before my final exams at university. I [8]_____ for several weeks, and I didn't go out at all. I [9]_____ eight exams, and I was very relieved when I had finished. In the end, I [10]_____ all of them, but my friends weren't so lucky. They [11]_____ some of the exams, so they had to do them again.

2 PRONUNCIATION the letter *u*

a Circle the word with a different sound.

u: boot	1	fr**u**it (**lu**nch) sc**oo**ter tr**ue**	
↑ **u**p	2	c**ou**ple m**u**ssels p**u**ll t**o**ngue	
ʊ b**u**ll	3	c**u**t f**u**ll p**u**sh p**u**t	
/ju/ /ju/	4	m**u**sical st**u**pid s**u**btitles t**u**na	

b ◄))7.1 Listen and check. Then listen again and repeat the words.

3 GRAMMAR first conditional and future time clauses + *when*, *until*, etc.

a Match the sentence halves.

1 Will you buy a car   _e_
2 Mike's parents will be furious   ____
3 I'll have more time to help you   ____
4 You'll have to go to a new school   ____
5 He won't pass his exams   ____
6 Nina won't go back to work   ____
7 You'll need to buy the book   ____
8 I'll stay at home   ____

a unless he revises more.
b after I come back from my holiday.
c if he fails his exam again.
d before the classes start.
e ~~if you pass your driving test?~~
f when your family moves house.
g if I still don't feel well in the morning.
h until her daughter starts school.

b Complete the sentences with a word from the list. Use each word only once.

after   before   if   ~~unless~~   until   when

1 They won't be able to leave the school _unless_ the teacher gives them permission.
2 They'll have to wear a uniform _____ they go to secondary school.
3 I'll talk to my teachers _____ I choose my exam subjects.
4 Ella will be disappointed _____ she doesn't get good marks.
5 I'll have a long holiday _____ the course finishes.
6 The teacher won't start the class _____ all the pupils are quiet.

c Complete the sentences with the correct form of the verbs in brackets. Use the present simple or future (*will / won't*).

1 I _'ll do_ my homework as soon as I _get_ home. (do, get)
2 We _____ late unless we _____. (be, hurry)
3 I _____ a shower before I _____. (have, go out)
4 The school bus _____ for you if you _____ on time. (not wait, not be)
5 If the teacher _____, we _____ the exam. (not come, not have)
6 James _____ home until he _____ a job. (not leave, find)
7 Alice _____ buy a car unless her parents _____ her the money. (not be able to, lend)
8 As soon as my boyfriend _____ his results, he _____ me. (get, call)
9 She _____ primary school until she _____ five years old. (not start, be)
10 You _____ better if you _____ every day. (play, practise)

d Complete the sentences with your own ideas.

1 I'll charge my phone _when I get home tonight_____.
2 I'll go out tonight if _____.
3 I won't watch TV later unless _____.
4 I'll do my homework before _____.
5 I won't buy a (new) phone until _____.
6 I'll go to bed after _____.

Go online for more practice

The hotel of Mum and Dad

Home is a place you grow up wanting to leave and grow old wanting to get back to.
John Ed Pearce, US journalist

G second conditional, choosing between conditionals   **V** houses   **P** sentence stress, the letter *c*

1 GRAMMAR second conditional, choosing between conditionals

a Match the sentence halves.

1 If we had the time, _d_
2 I'd like my flat more, ____
3 You'd be able to find a job ____
4 If my sister didn't work so hard, ____
5 If we bought a bigger house in the country, ____
6 If they could live anywhere they wanted to, ____
7 We'd get on better ____
8 I wouldn't want to live in London, ____

a she could spend more time with her children.
b they'd move to France.
c if you spoke better English.
d ~~we'd do the housework ourselves.~~
e if we didn't have to share an office.
f unless I earned a lot of money.
g if it was on the top floor.
h we'd be able to have a dog.

b Complete the sentences with the correct form of the verbs in brackets. Use the second conditional.

1 If Tom _had_ more time, he_'d paint_ his room himself. (have, paint)
2 Lucy _____ happier if her flatmate _____ the kitchen more often. (be, clean)
3 I _____ to work if I _____ a parking space. (not drive, not have)
4 _____ you _____ working if you _____ a lot of money? (carry on, win)
5 I'm sure Sally _____ better if she _____ so much coffee. (sleep, not drink)
6 My parents _____ me the money if I _____ to buy a new car. (lend, need)
7 I _____ surprised if it _____ tonight. (not be, snow)
8 If our house _____ so small, you _____ all stay the night. (not be, can)
9 _____ you _____ if you _____ your alarm? (wake up, not set)
10 If we _____ another bathroom, there _____ a queue for the shower. (have, not be)

c Complete the sentences with the words in brackets. Use the first or second conditional.

1 If they offer me the job, _I'll take it_____. (I / take it)
2 If my car wasn't being repaired, _I'd give you a lift___. (I / give you a lift)
3 If I had Emily's number, _____. (I / call her)
4 You'll miss the train if _____. (you / not hurry up)
5 If I see John, _____. (I / tell him the news)
6 Rob wouldn't send you flowers if _____. (he / not love you)
7 If my mother didn't live on her own, _____. (she / be happier)
8 If it rains on Saturday, _____. (they / cancel the match)
9 You wouldn't spend so much money if _____. (you / not eat out every night).
10 Rita won't go to work tomorrow if _____. (she / not feel better)

2 PRONUNCIATION sentence stress, the letter *c*

a ◖))7.2 Listen and complete the sentences.

1 If I _did_____ more _exercise_____, I'd be a _lot fitter_____.
2 I'd _____ my own _____ if I had a _____.
3 Would you _____ a _____ if you _____?
4 If it were _____, I _____ the _____.
5 I _____ a _____ if I _____ in the _____.

b ◖))7.2 Listen again and repeat the sentences. Copy the rhythm.

c Say the pairs of words. Do the letters in **bold** have the same pronunciation or are they pronounced differently? Write **S** (same) or **D** (different).

1 **c**arpet   lo**c**ation   _S_
2 **c**abin   **c**eiling   _D_
3 **c**entre   **c**osy   ____
4 spa**c**ious   spe**c**ial   ____

5 **c**ity   **c**entre   ____
6 **c**astle   musi**c**ian   ____
7 de**c**ide   entran**ce**   ____
8 firepla**ce**   bal**c**ony   ____

d 🔊 7.3 Listen and check. Then listen again and repeat the words.

3 VOCABULARY houses

a Complete the sentences with *in* or *on*.

1 We're looking for a flat _in_ a suburb. We don't want to live in the city centre.
2 I'd love to live by the sea, maybe ____ the south coast.
3 All the bedrooms are ____ the first floor.
4 Sara bought a beautiful cottage ____ the country, where she can ride her horse.
5 Chris lives ____ the outskirts of the city, so he has to commute to the centre every day.
6 My grandparents live ____ a town north of Manchester called Blackburn.

b Complete the crossword.

DOWN ↓

1 one of the sides of a room or building joining the ceiling to the floor
2 the highest floor of a building
3
5 the space or room under the roof of a house
6
7
9 the part of the building that covers the top of it

ACROSS →

2 a flat, hard area, especially outside a house or restaurant, where you can sit, eat, and enjoy the sun
4
6 a room or rooms in a building, partly or completely below ground level
8 the floor of a building that is at street level
10
11

c   Complete the adverts. Circle a, b, or c.

JUST ADDED

FOR SALE

This ¹____ flat is on the top floor of a building with magnificent views of Regent Park. All the rooms are very ²____. It has three bedrooms, a bathroom, and a large ³____ kitchen. The living room has a ⁴____ floor, and there are carpets in all the bedrooms.

....

1	**a** modern	**b** recent	**c** young
2	**a** clear	**b** light	**c** lit
3	**a** big	**b** spacious	**c** tiny
4	**a** board	**b** rug	**c** wooden

VILLAGE LOCATION

FOR SALE

This 18th-century cottage is situated in a quiet village. It has a kitchen, bathroom, living room, and two small but ⁵____ bedrooms. All the rooms have low ⁶____, and the walls are made ⁷____ stone. There is an open ⁸____ in the living room, but the house also has central heating.

....

5	**a** cosy	**b** safe	**c** soft
6	**a** ceilings	**b** roofs	**c** walls
7	**a** by	**b** in	**c** of
8	**a** chimney	**b** fire	**c** heating

3 BEDROOMS

FOR SALE

This recently-built house is located on the ⁹____ of the city, with good public transport links. Downstairs there's a kitchen, a living room, and a dining room, while on the ¹⁰____ floor are three bedrooms and a stylish bathroom. Outside the house there are four ¹¹____ down to a small garden, where there's a ¹²____ which is perfect for outdoor entertaining.

....

9	**a** suburbs	**b** outskirts	**c** centre
10	**a** ground	**b** first	**c** second
11	**a** steps	**b** stairs	**c** paths
12	**a** terrace	**b** basement	**c** balcony

Go online for more practice   Go online to check your progress

Practical English Boys' night out

1 MAKING SUGGESTIONS

a Re-order the words to make phrases for making and responding to suggestions.

1 not / why
Why not _____?

2 very / fish / keen / not / I'm / on / raw
_____.

3 a / idea / great / that's
_____!

4 restaurant / don't / sushi / that / we / why / new / try
_____?

5 about / Chinese / having / what / a
_____?

6 shall / lunch / go / we / where / for
_____?

7 cab / could / to / time / get / we / a / save
_____.

8 Italian / to / going / how / an / restaurant / about
_____?

9 there / go / let's
_____.

b Complete the conversation with the phrases from **a**.

Jess I'm hungry. ¹*Where shall we go for lunch* _____?
Phil I think there's a burger bar near here. ² _____.

Jess Phil, you know I don't eat meat.
Phil Oops! Sorry, I forgot. Well, ³ _____?
    I fancy some pasta.
Jess Aren't you on a diet?
Phil Well, yes…
Jess No Italian for you, then. ⁴ _____?
Phil I'm not sure about Japanese food. ⁵ _____.
Jess Well, ⁶ _____?
    I know a place that does excellent fried rice.
Phil ⁷ _____? Is it very far?
Jess It's a couple of blocks away. ⁸ _____.
Phil ⁹ _____! Let's do that.

2 VERB FORMS

Complete the sentences with the correct form of a verb from the list.

eat out   go   meet   ~~order~~   play   watch

1 We could *order* _____ a pizza.
2 Shall we _____ a movie?
3 What about _____ at 9 p.m.?
4 Why don't we _____ cards?
5 How about _____ to the theatre?
6 Let's _____ tonight.

3 SOCIAL ENGLISH

Complete the conversation.

Ellie Joe?
Joe Hi, Ellie.
Ellie It's Mum's birthday, and you're late. Where are you, ¹a*nyway* _____?
Joe That's ²wh_____ I'm calling. I'm not going to ³m_____ it for dinner.
Ellie Why not?
Joe I'm at a friend's house. She's ⁴o_____ to Germany tomorrow to start her new job, and I wanted to say goodbye.
Ellie But why tonight? It's ⁵n_____ that I don't think you should say goodbye, but couldn't you do it tomorrow?
Joe Not really. I wanted to have a ⁶w_____ with her about something before she left.
Ellie Mum's going to be upset.
Joe Sorry, Ellie. It won't ⁷h_____ again. Tell Mum I'll see her tomorrow.

Go online to practise the Practical English phrases

1 GRAMMAR

Circle the correct words.

1 John and Mary are delighted because their son *gets / 's getting / will get* married next year.
2 He *plays / 's playing / 's been playing* tennis for ten years.
3 You *don't have to / ought to / mustn't* send text messages when you're driving. It's against the law.
4 I'd love to *can / be able to / could to* play the piano, but I can't.
5 If I *have / had / will have* time tonight, I'll send you those photos.
6 If I knew the answer, I *'ll tell / tell / 'd tell* you.

2 VOCABULARY

Circle the word that is different.

1 dishonest   irresponsible   sympathetic   unkind
2 borrow   charge   invest   salary
3 boarding   primary   state   head
4 arena   coach   sports hall   stadium
5 cast   extra   plot   star
6 lips   shoulder   teeth   tongue

3 PRONUNCIATION

Circle the word with a different sound.

k key	1 **c**arpet **c**ast **c**inema **c**ritic	
snake	2 **c**eiling **c**entre **c**osy terra**c**e	
shower	3 **c**ity musi**c**ian spa**c**ious spe**c**ial	
eɪ tr**ai**n	4 st**are** st**a**te t**a**ste tr**ai**ler	
aɪ b**i**ke	5 **eye**s f**ai**l h**igh** sm**i**le	

4 GRAMMAR & VOCABULARY

Read the article. Circle a, b, or c.

Alternative schooling

Mother-of-two, Sue Cowley, is an experienced teacher and author of many books on how to give children [1]____ education. These days, teachers [2]____ the first people to insist that children must be educated at school, not at home. However, Mrs Cowley doesn't agree. That's why she decided to take her children out of school for six months to go on a road trip. The route the family took [3]____ by the children themselves, Alvie and Edite, who were eleven and eight at the time.

In November 2014, they [4]____ in the family car and headed for the Netherlands, where they stayed in a mobile home on the [5]____ of Amsterdam. They visited Anne Frank's house and the Rijksmuseum. From there, they drove all around Europe before making their way to China. While their [6]____ were studying hard at school, Alvie and Edite [7]____ giant pandas at Beijing Zoo.

The children [8]____ get up early or study on their trip, but their mother [9]____ them write a page in their travel diary every day. Alvie and Edite learned a lot on their travels, including how to draw an accurate map of Europe and what to do if you become separated from your family on the underground.

[10]____ at school since they returned from their trip, but Mrs Cowley would like to take them on another adventure one day.

1 **a** better **b** best **c** the best
2 **a** are usually **b** usually are **c** used to be
3 **a** chose **b** was chose **c** was chosen
4 **a** set down **b** set off **c** set up
5 **a** coast **b** outskirts **c** suburbs
6 **a** classmates **b** colleagues **c** partners
7 **a** have visited **b** had visited **c** were visiting
8 **a** can't **b** didn't have to **c** mustn't
9 **a** allowed **b** let **c** made
10 **a** They're **b** They've been **c** They were

8A The right job for you

G choosing between gerunds and infinitives | **V** work | **P** word stress

1 VOCABULARY work

a Complete the text with words from the list.

applied ~~overtime~~ promoted ran redundant
resign retire sacked set up shifts training course

My father's first job was in a small local company. He had to do a lot of ¹*overtime*, which he really hated, but he knew he would be ²_____ if he didn't do it. One day, he decided to ³_____ from the job. He ⁴_____ for a new job with a multinational company. At first, he worked ⁵_____ in a factory. Then, he got ⁶_____ to supervisor. Later, he was made ⁷_____ because business was bad. After that, my dad did a ⁸_____ in Business Management, and he ⁹_____ his own business. He ¹⁰_____ the company for 20 years, and he didn't ¹¹_____ until he was 68 years old. This photo shows the party they organized for him on his last day.

b Complete the sentences with a preposition and a word from the list.

freelance full-time part-time permanent
~~self-employed~~ temporary unemployed

1 Maxine is a *self-employed* mechanic. She loves working *for* herself.
2 My niece is still _____ school, but she has a _____ job. She only works on Friday evenings and Saturdays.
3 Oliver is _____ his third year of medicine. He's hoping to get a _____ job as a waiter for the summer to earn some money.
4 Laura is _____ charge of IT at the public library. It's a _____ job – she works from 8 a.m. to 6 p.m. every day.
5 My cousin used to work _____ a large multinational company, but he's been _____ since he was made redundant last year.
6 My boyfriend has a _____ job in a bank, and he hopes to stay there until he retires. He's responsible _____ customer loans.
7 My sister is a _____ software developer. She works _____ lots of different companies.

c Complete the sentences with a noun form of the word in **bold**.

1 A _musician_ plays **music** for a living.
2 They're looking for a _____ to **translate** some documents into Polish.
3 The company **employs** 200 staff – 150 are in full-time _____.
4 Helen studied **pharmacy** because she wanted to be a _____.
5 When we **retire**, we'd like to spend our _____ with our grandchildren.
6 They're going to **promote** someone, but we don't know who's going to get the _____.
7 Colin's interested in **law**, so he'd like to be a _____.
8 My son is good at all the **sciences**, so I'm sure he'll be a _____ when he's older.
9 My colleague tried to **resign**, but our boss wouldn't accept his _____.
10 I **applied** for the job, but I sent in the _____ too late.
11 A _____ has to get up early to look after his **farm**.
12 He wasn't **qualified** for the job, because he didn't have any _____.

d Complete the sentences with the correct form of a word from the list. Use each word twice.

company   fire   market   run   work

1 I like spending time with John. I enjoy his _company_.
2 The police _____ their guns in the air.
3 I dropped my phone in the bath and now it doesn't _____.
4 I _____ five kilometres every evening.
5 Jane was _____ because she stole money from the company.
6 We always buy fruit and vegetables from our local _____.
7 My sister has applied for a job with an engineering _____.
8 There isn't a big _____ for this kind of product in Europe.
9 I _____ part-time in a café.
10 One day, I would like to _____ my own business.

2 PRONUNCIATION word stress

a Underline the stressed syllable.

1 ap|pli|ca|tion
2 ap|ply
3 em|ploy|ment
4 far|mer
5 free|lance
6 law|yer
7 mu|si|cian
8 per|ma|nent
9 phar|ma|cist
10 pro|mo|tion
11 qual|i|fi|ca|tion
12 qua|li|fy
13 re|dun|dant
14 re|sig|na|tion
15 re|tire
16 re|tire|ment
17 sci|en|tist
18 tem|pora|ry
19 trans|la|tion
20 un|em|ployed

b ◑ 8.1 Listen and check. Then listen again and repeat.

3 GRAMMAR choosing between gerunds and infinitives

a Circle a, b, or c.

1 It's difficult _____ a good job these days.
   a finding   **b** to find   **c** find
2 He isn't very good at _____ decisions.
   a making   **b** to make   **c** make
3 They promised _____ me at the end of the month.
   a paying   **b** to pay   **c** pay
4 I should _____. It's getting late.
   a going   **b** to go   **c** go
5 _____ an application form can take ages.
   a Filling in   **b** To fill in   **c** Fill in
6 My girlfriend told me _____ her later.
   a calling   **b** to call   **c** call
7 The film I saw last night made me _____.
   a crying   **b** to cry   **c** cry
8 Tim really enjoys _____ in a team.
   a working   **b** to work   **c** work
9 I went to the supermarket _____ some bread.
   a buying   **b** to buy   **c** buy
10 I gave up _____ basketball when I went to university.
   a playing   **b** to play   **c** play

b Correct any mistakes in the highlighted verbs. Tick (✔) the correct sentences.

1 I remember having my first job interview. I was really nervous!   ✔

2 Lift heavy weights can give you back problems.
   Lifting heavy weights _____

3 The interviewer asked me wait in reception. _____

4 I know you don't like my boyfriend, but please try to be nice to him. _____

5 Go on, tell me! I promise to not laugh. _____

6 The bus didn't come, so we started walking home. _____

7 Anna went on study until midnight. _____

8 It's impossible to read your writing! _____

9 If you're tired, I don't mind stay in tonight. _____

10 Everyone is afraid of being sacked. _____

c Complete the sentences with the correct form of the verbs in brackets.

1 I went to the bank _to get_____ some money. (get)

2 Try _____ to your boss. He might be able to help you. (talk)

3 I want you _____ me exactly what happened. (tell)

4 I didn't remember _____ the cooker, so the kitchen was full of smoke. (turn off)

5 Some couples can go on _____ to each other for days after an argument. (not speak)

6 I'm going out with Jamie because he makes me _____. (laugh)

7 _____ drive is one of the requirements of the job. (be able to)

8 The service had been so bad that the manager agreed _____ us for our meal. (not charge)

1 GRAMMAR reported speech

a Circle the correct words.

1 Matt said yesterday that he *will* / *would* come shopping with me.

2 We asked the sales assistant how much *it was* / *was it*.

3 My sister *said me* / *told me* that she had spent all her money in the sales.

4 I asked Lucy where *she bought* / *did she buy* her clothes.

5 You told me that you *may* / *might* go shopping on Saturday.

6 My brother asked me *if I can* / *if I could* lend him £50 until next weekend.

7 Kate said that she *had to* / *must* go to the supermarket.

8 I asked my sister whether *suited me the dress* / *the dress suited me*, and she said I looked great!

9 Helena asked me what *I wanted* / *did I want* from the shops.

10 Nick said that he couldn't pay me back, because he *'s forgotten* / *'d forgotten* his wallet.

b Complete the sentences with *said* or *told*.

1 Jackie *said* that she was thinking of buying a new car.

2 My boyfriend _____ me he wanted to see his friends more often.

3 You _____ you'd check the price online.

4 I _____ you I might be late.

5 Ryan _____ me that he couldn't find his credit card.

6 My sister _____ that she would buy me a new smartphone for my birthday.

c Report the conversations.

1 'Where do you buy your clothes?'
'I buy them online.'
I asked Kate *where she bought her clothes* _____.
She told *me (that) she bought them online* _____.

2 'Have you seen my wallet?'
'I don't know where it is.'
He asked me _____.
I said _____.

3 'Do your school shoes still fit you?'
'They fit me perfectly!'
I asked my daughter _____.
She told_____.

4 'How much did you pay for your jacket?'
'It was a bargain.'
I asked Oliver _____.
He said _____.

5 'Where are you going tomorrow?'
'I'm meeting some friends.'
Sophie asked me _____.
I told _____.

6 'Do you need anything from the shop?'
'I want some chocolate.'
I asked John _____.
He said _____.

7 'Did you enjoy your stay?'
'It's been very enjoyable.'
She asked us _____.
We told _____.

8 'When are you going shopping?'
'I may go on Saturday.'
Holly asked me _____.
I said _____.

2 VOCABULARY shopping, making nouns from verbs

a Complete the pairs of sentences with the correct word, a or b.

1 The sports section is on the top floor of the _b_ .
  You can find this _a_ in shopping centres all over the world.
  a chain store   **b** department store

2 He wasn't happy with his new trousers, so he asked for a ____.
  She paid with a twenty-pound note, so the shop assistant gave her some change with her ____.
  a receipt   **b** refund

3 Those trousers are too short – they don't ____ you.
  That dress is the right size, but it really doesn't ____ you.
  a fit   **b** suit

4 You can go to a ____ to buy your favourite author's latest novel.
  Instead of buying the book, she's going to borrow it from the ____.
  a bookshop   **b** library

5 The whole family comes with me when I do the monthly shop, and the children take turns pushing the ____.
  I only needed a few things, so I picked up a ____ at the entrance to the store.
  a basket   **b** trolley

6 This leather jacket was only £10. What a ____!
  There was a 50% ____ on sandals, so I bought two pairs.
  a bargain   **b** discount

7 I'd ____ a coat if I were you – it's cold outside.
  It would be a good idea to ____ that shirt before you buy it.
  a try on   **b** put on

8 You use a ____ when you want to pay at the end of the month.
  There's no extra charge if you pay by ____.
  a credit card   **b** debit card

b Complete the sentences with the noun form of the verbs in brackets.

1 The company made a _loss_ of two million pounds last year. (lose)

2 The ____ was very slow, so we didn't leave a tip. (serve)

3 Selina gets special ____ because she's the manager's niece. (treat)

4 We couldn't reach an ____ with our boss about salaries. (agree)

5 My exam marks this term are a big ____ on last term. (improve)

6 They've had an ____, and they aren't talking to each other. (argue)

7 They had to get a ____ of their house before they could sell it. (value)

8 His greatest ____ was winning an Olympic gold medal. (achieve)

9 It's a difficult ____ to make between my best friend's wedding or my sister's birthday party. (choose)

10 The restaurant had to close as a result of bad ____. (manage)

11 There's a ____ on Saturday against the closure of the hospital. (demonstrate)

12 The ____ of alcohol is often prohibited at sports matches. (sell)

13 After careful ____, we've decided to sell the company. (consider)

14 My attempt to run a marathon ended in ____ when I fell and broke my leg after the first kilometre. (fail)

15 I had to resist the ____ to have another cake – they were delicious! (tempt)

c Complete the text with the noun form of the verbs in brackets.

A month ago, I bought a video game online for my son's birthday. I got a confirmation email back, which said that ¹_delivery_____ (deliver) would take about ten days. Two weeks later, I began to worry. I knew the seller had received my ²_____ (pay), but the video game hadn't arrived. So I decided to make a ³_____ (complain). I sent an email to the seller with a copy of the order confirmation as an ⁴_____ (attach). I received a ⁵_____ (respond) immediately, which said that the seller would look into the incident. After that, I heard nothing for three days, so I sent another email demanding an ⁶_____ (explain). This time I had more ⁷_____ (succeed), and the seller said he would send another copy of the game. If I don't receive it before my son's birthday, I'm going to ask for ⁸_____ (compensate).

3 PRONUNCIATION the letters *ai*

a Circle the word where *ai* is pronounced differently.

1 barg**ai**n   mount**ai**n   tr**ai**ners
2 cert**ai**n   compl**ai**n   r**ai**n
3 p**ai**nting   s**ai**d   w**ai**t
4 **ai**rline   f**ai**r   r**ai**lway
5 capt**ai**n   pl**ai**n   em**ai**l
6 br**ai**n   h**ai**r   st**ai**rs

b ◀8.2 Listen and check. Then listen again and repeat the words.

9A Lucky encounters

G third conditional   **V** making adjectives and adverbs   **P** sentence rhythm, weak pronunciation of *have*

1 GRAMMAR third conditional

a Complete the sentences with *had* or *would have*.

1 If I'd known it was your birthday, I'*d have* _____ bought you a present.

2 It _____ been quicker if we'd gone by train. Our flight was very delayed.

3 Harry wouldn't have been late for work if the bus _____ been on time.

4 I'm sure that if David _____ seen you, he would have said hello.

5 I _____ gone to their party if they'd invited me, but they didn't.

6 If you'd got up earlier, you _____ had time to make your bed.

7 If Kim _____ paid attention in class, she would have known about the exam.

8 You wouldn't have fallen asleep at the cinema if you _____ had a rest this afternoon.

b Complete the sentences with the correct form of the verbs in brackets.

1 If you'd told me you weren't staying for dinner, I *wouldn't have made* so much food. (not make)

2 We _____ on time if we'd left half an hour earlier. (arrive)

3 If we _____ a table, we wouldn't have been able to have dinner there. (not book)

4 You'd have seen my message if you _____ your mobile phone. (check)

5 I'd have enjoyed the party more if the music _____ so loud. (not be)

6 If you'd concentrated on what you were doing, you _____ so many mistakes. (not make)

7 If I _____ it was going to be so cold today, I would have worn a warmer coat. (know)

8 We _____ Joe to dinner too if we'd known you didn't like him. (not invite)

9 If you _____ so rude about my mother, I wouldn't have got so angry. (not be)

10 My sister _____ promoted if she'd refused to do overtime. (not get)

c Complete the second sentence so it has a similar meaning to the first sentence.

1 I got to the restaurant late because I went to the wrong place first.
If I hadn't gone to the wrong place first, *I wouldn't have got to the restaurant late.*

2 I passed my final exams, so I went to university.
I wouldn't have gone to university if _____ _____.

3 Helen didn't have the right qualifications, so she didn't get the job.
If Helen had had the right qualifications, _____ _____.

4 We had lunch before we left, so we weren't hungry.
We would have been hungry if _____ _____.

5 We didn't play tennis this afternoon because it was windy.
If it hadn't been so windy this afternoon, _____ _____.

6 You got lost because you didn't follow my directions.
You wouldn't have got lost if _____ _____.

7 I didn't win that game because you cheated.
If you hadn't cheated, _____ _____.

8 Alex wasn't very careful with his glasses, so he broke them.
If Alex had been more careful with his glasses, _____ _____.

2 PRONUNCIATION sentence rhythm, weak pronunciation of *have*

a 🔊 9.1 Listen and complete the sentences.

1 If they hadn't played so badly, they
   would have won _____ the match.
2 If you'd told me about the meeting, I
   _____ .
3 She _____ the coat
   if it hadn't been so expensive.
4 If there had been room for us, we
   _____ the night.
5 We _____ to
   the cinema on time if we'd taken a taxi.
6 If I'd known you were moving house, I
   _____ you.

b Listen again and repeat the sentences. Copy the rhythm.

3 VOCABULARY making adjectives and adverbs

a Complete the chart with the two adjective forms of each noun from the list.

care   ~~comfort~~   fortune   luck   patience

	+	−
adjective ending in -*able*	¹ *comfortable*	² *uncomfortable*
adjective ending in -*ate*	3	4
adjective ending in -*ful / less*	5	6
adjective ending in -*ient*	7	8
adjective ending in -*y*	9	10

b Complete the sentences with the correct form of the words in brackets.

1 We were sitting *comfortably* on the sofa when there was a knock at the door. (comfort)
2 I was in a hurry, so I waited _____ for the lift to arrive. (patience)
3 She put down the glass _____, so it fell on the floor and broke. (care)
4 _____, I'd taken an umbrella because it began to rain before I'd got to my office. (fortune)
5 They were _____ to lose the basketball match because they'd played very well. (luck)

c Complete the charts.

noun	adjectives	
	+	−
success	¹ *successful*	² *unsuccessful*
possibility	3	4
self	5	6
use	7	8
suit	9	10

noun	adverbs	
	+	−
success	¹¹ *successfully*	¹² *unsuccessfully*
possibility	13	14
self	15	16
use	17	18
suit	19	20

d Complete the sentences with a word from the charts.

1 It's *possible* to see the English coast from France on a clear day.
2 She very _____ took both of the biscuits that were left on the plate.
3 You should throw that old umbrella away – it's completely _____ .
4 All of their children have been very _____ in their chosen careers.
5 They were very _____ dressed for the weather.

e Complete the text with the correct adjective or adverb of the nouns in brackets.

Unlucky teen's meeting with an alligator

An American teenager made a ¹*careless* (care) mistake yesterday when he jumped into a river without checking the area for alligators before going swimming.

Kaleb Langdale was at the Caloosahatchee River in Florida with friends when he decided to go for a swim. The ² _____ (patient) young man soon found himself in the ³ _____ (comfort) position of sharing the water with an alligator, which started to attack him. He was ⁴ _____ (luck) enough to escape the first attack and began to swim to the bank, where his friends were ⁵ _____ (desperation) waiting for him. ⁶ _____ (fortune), the three-metre animal attacked again, and this time it held on to Kaleb's arm. ⁷ _____ (luck), Kaleb managed to get away, but his arm was seriously injured in the process.

Kaleb is now recovering in hospital, and doctors say his condition is ⁸ _____ (comfort) despite his injuries. He recommends that anybody who goes swimming in the Caloosahatchee River should check the area ⁹ _____ (care) before going swimming.

Go online for more practice

G quantifiers **V** electronic devices **P** linking, *ough* and *augh*

1 VOCABULARY electronic devices

a Complete the words.

1 k <u>e</u> y b <u>o</u> <u>a</u> <u>r</u> d

2 p _ _ _ _ t _ _ _

3 s _ _ _ _ k _ _ _

4 a _ _ _ p _ _ _ r

5 r _ m _ _ _ _ _ c _ _ t _ _ _ l

6 s _ _ _ k _ _ _

7 ch _ _ _ g _ _ _

8 s _ _ _ t _ _ _

9 p _ _ _ g

10 U _ _ _ c _ b _ _ _

11 m _ m _ _ _ _ s _ _ _ _ k

12 r _ _ _ t _ _ _

b Complete the sentences with a word from **a**.

1 Let's turn the lights on. Where's the *switch*_____?

2 I've got the presentation on a _____ _____, so I don't need to take my laptop.

3 My battery's getting low. Can I borrow your _____?

4 Can I use your _____? I need to print out the boarding pass for my flight.

5 You'll need a _____ _____ if you want to connect your phone to your laptop.

6 Where's the '@' symbol on this _____?

7 Who's got the _____ _____ for the TV? I want to change channels.

8 You can't use European plugs in the UK if you haven't got an _____.

9 If you turn on the _____, you might be able to hear something!

10 Is the _____ working? I haven't got an internet connection.

11 Never take a _____ out of a _____ with wet hands – you might get an electric shock.

c Complete the crossword.

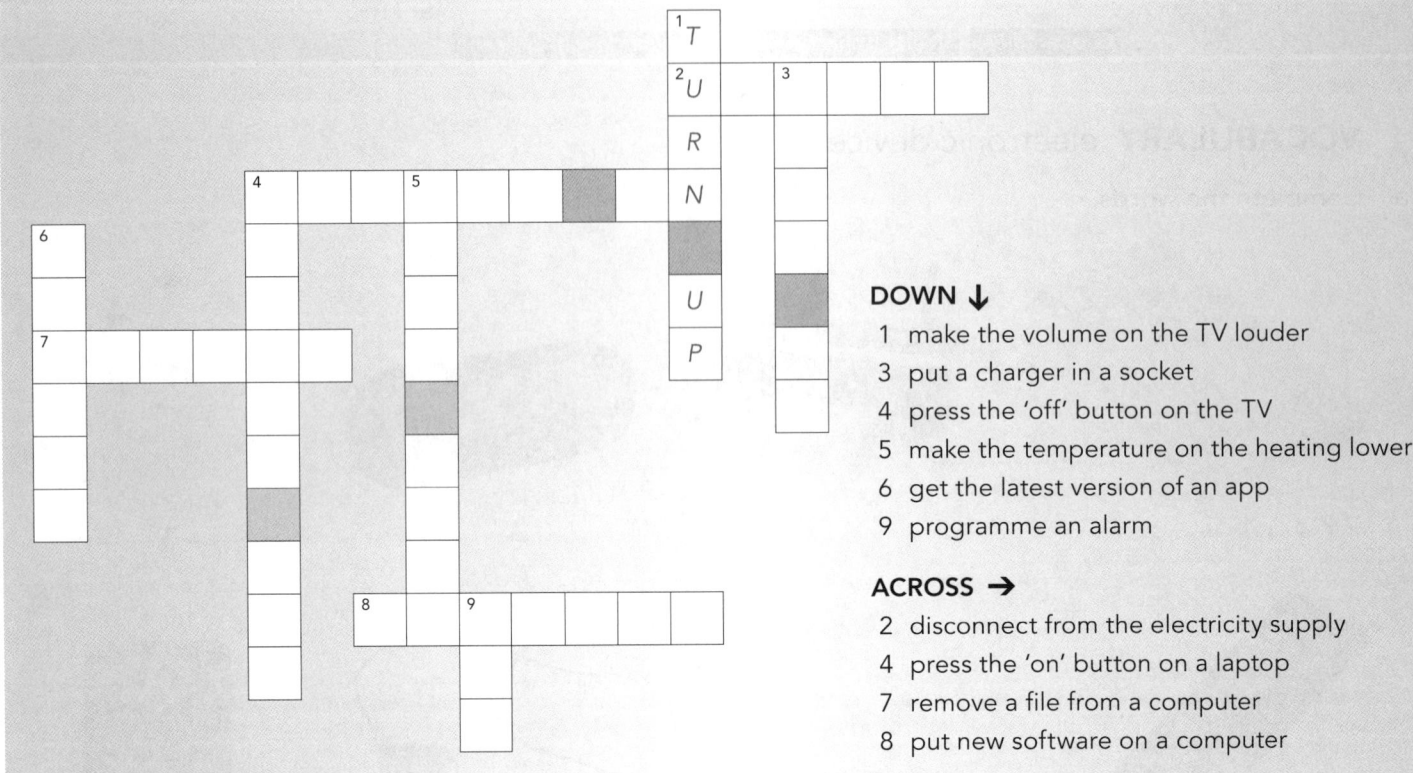

DOWN ↓
1 make the volume on the TV louder
3 put a charger in a socket
4 press the 'off' button on the TV
5 make the temperature on the heating lower
6 get the latest version of an app
9 programme an alarm

ACROSS →
2 disconnect from the electricity supply
4 press the 'on' button on a laptop
7 remove a file from a computer
8 put new software on a computer

2 GRAMMAR quantifiers

a Circle the correct answers. One, two, or three answers may be correct.

1 Do you eat ____ sweets?
  a many
  b a lot of
  c much

2 I sleep ____ when I'm on holiday.
  a a lot of
  b a lot
  c lots of

3 I don't drink ____ coffee.
  a many
  b a lot of
  c much

4 You can sit here. There's ____ room.
  a many
  b much
  c plenty of

5 My sister has ____ friends.
  a a lot of
  b lots of
  c loads of

6 Can I have ____ more cake please?
  It's delicious!
  a a few
  b a little
  c very little

7 My phone has ____ games because I never play them.
  a a few
  b very few
  c very little

8 There are ____ young people living in the village than there used to be.
  a fewer
  b less
  c little

9 I can't hear you. There's ____ noise.
  a enough
  b too many
  c too much

10 You aren't working ____.
  a hard enough
  b enough hard
  c too much hard

11 There isn't ____ milk in the fridge.
  a any
  b no
  c some

12 **A** How much bread is there?
   B ____. I've just finished it all.
  a Any
  b None
  c No any

b Complete each pair of sentences so that they have the same meaning. More than one answer may be possible.

1 There _aren't enough_ chairs.
 There are _too few_ chairs.

2 He can't afford it. He doesn't have _____ money.
 He can't afford it. It's _____ for him.

3 We only had _____ sleep last night.
 We didn't have _____ sleep last night.

4 There are _____ cars in the city centre.
 There aren't _____ parking spaces.

5 There's _____ petrol in the tank.
 There isn't _____ petrol in the tank.

6 She buys very _____ books these days.
 She doesn't buy _____ books these days.

c Complete the sentences with a quantifier and the words in brackets. Sometimes more than one answer is possible.

1 The party was a disaster. There weren't _many people_. (people)
2 I didn't have _____, so I only ordered a plate of chips. (money)
3 We'll have to drive. There aren't _____ on a Sunday. (buses)
4 It's raining, so there are _____ on the beach – just one or two. (people)
5 He can't drive yet. He isn't _____. (old)
6 Anna's worried because she's a freelance photographer, and she has _____ at the moment. (work)
7 You can't move in their living room. There's _____. (furniture)
8 We can't use the printer. There's _____. (paper)
9 It took us ages to get here. There was _____. (traffic)
10 I couldn't sleep on the plane. There were _____. (children)
11 I'll only be a moment. I have to make _____ before we leave. (phone calls)
12 This jacket doesn't fit me. It's _____. (small)

3 PRONUNCIATION linking, *ough* and *augh*

a ◉ 9.2 Listen and write the sentences.

1 I _switched it on_. 5 I _____.
2 I _____. 6 I _____.
3 I _____. 7 I _____.
4 I _____. 8 I _____.

b ◉ 9.2 Listen again and repeat the sentences. Try to link the words.

c Circle the word with a different sound.

1 horse	2 up	3 horse	4 horse
brought	although	bought	caught
⦸cough	enough	daughter	laughed
thought	tough	through	taught

d ◉ 9.3 Listen and check. Then listen again and repeat the words.

⦿ Go online for more practice ✓ Go online to check your progress

1 INDIRECT QUESTIONS

a (Circle) the correct words.

1 Can you tell me what time *(it is)/ is it*, please?
2 Do you know if this bus *does go / goes* to Windsor?
3 Could you tell me where *can I / I can* buy a ticket?
4 I wonder where *Lola is / is Lola* today.
5 Do you know whether this shirt *does come / comes* in a larger size?
6 I'd like to know where *are you / you're* going.
7 I wonder what time *the restaurant closes / does the restaurant close*.
8 Can you remember who *did you speak to / you spoke to*?

b Make questions 1–6 more indirect by using the beginnings given.

1 What time is the next bus for Boston?
   I'd like to know *what time the next bus for Boston is.*
2 What time does it arrive?
   Do you know _____?
3 Which stop does the bus go from?
   Could you tell me _____?
4 How much does a one way ticket cost?
   Could you tell me _____?
5 Do I need to change buses?
   I wonder _____.
6 How much discount do I get with a student card?
   Can you tell me _____?

c Complete the conversation with the indirect questions from **a**. There is one question you don't need to use.

Ticket clerk Can I help you?
Max Yes, please. [1] *I'd like to know what time the next bus for Boston is.*
Ticket clerk Well, the next bus leaves at 10 a.m.
Max Great. [2] _____
Ticket clerk Sure. It costs $35.95.
Max [3] _____
Ticket clerk With a student card you get a 20% discount on your ticket. That means it'll cost you $28.75.
Max OK. Here's my student card…and my credit card.
Ticket clerk And here's your ticket.
Max Thanks. [4] _____.
Ticket clerk No, you don't. The bus goes straight through.
Max And [5] _____
Ticket clerk Yes, it gets to Boston at 2.20 p.m.
Max Thanks a lot.

3 SOCIAL ENGLISH

Complete the conversation with the words and phrases from the list.

either   I guess   It's obvious   Of course   ~~Stop it!~~
What if

A [1] *Stop it!* _____ You keep yawning. Everyone will think you're bored.
B Oh, sorry. [2] _____ I'm a bit tired.
A [3] _____ you're tired. You've had a long day.
B Well, I did get up at six o'clock this morning.
A Oh, come on. Let's go. [4] _____ you aren't enjoying the party.
B I'm sorry. I think I need to go to bed.
A I know. [5] _____ we go home and do something nice tomorrow?
B That sounds like a great idea. And I promise I won't yawn all day, [6] _____.
A Good!

 Go online to practise the Practical English phrases

1 GRAMMAR

Complete the sentences with the correct form of the verbs in brackets.

1 I _____ my girlfriend for three years. We met when we were at university. (know)

2 When I was a child, I _____ like big dogs – they frightened me. (used to)

3 I'm not sure, but I think that man _____ Susan's brother. (be)

4 If I lived in the city centre, I _____ to work instead of driving. (walk)

5 Jake's room is a mess, and he refuses _____ it. (tidy)

6 The police officer asked the man where he _____ the day before. (be)

2 VOCABULARY

Circle the word that is different.

1 duck   mussels   prawns   squid
2 colleague   couple   flatmate   partner
3 comedy   script   thriller   western
4 degree   head   pupils   students
5 attic   basement   gate   ground floor
6 apply for   be made redundant   resign   retire

3 PRONUNCIATION

Circle the word with a different sound.

⬆ up	1 **c**our**se** en**ou**gh l**u**cky t**o**ngue
horse	2 b**ough**t keyb**oar**d l**oa**n w**a**ll
ph**o**ne	3 alth**ough** r**ou**ter thr**ow** t**oe**s
b**oo**t	4 fl**oor** r**oo**f s**ui**t thr**ough**
cl**o**ck	5 c**ou**gh l**o**ss n**o**se w**a**tch

4 GRAMMAR & VOCABULARY

Read the article. Circle a, b, or c.

DANGEROUS DEVICES

Most of us would agree that computers and smartphones ¹____ made life easier for us. However, there are a ²____ people who might not think the same because they've ³____ injured by their electronic devices. Experts are becoming increasingly worried ⁴____ this problem. One of the ⁵____ dangerous devices appears to be phone chargers. You probably ⁶____ be injured if you use your original charger, but fake chargers are different. Fake chargers are sold at much lower prices than originals, and when customers choose ⁷____ them, they're often tempted to buy the cheaper of the two. They think they've found a ⁸____ because they've spent very little money ⁹____ it. It's thought that a Chinese woman died recently because of a fake charger. She had plugged ¹⁰____ the charger and attached her phone before she tried to make a phone call. Unfortunately, she received a massive electric shock from the charger, and she ¹¹____ killed instantly. Phone companies say that she ¹²____ have died if she hadn't used a fake charger.

1 a are   b had   c have
2 a few   b less   c little
3 a be   b been   c was
4 a about   b in   c of
5 a less   b more   c most
6 a don't   b not   c won't
7 a between   b from   c to
8 a bargain   b bill   c budget
9 a about   b in   c on
10 a in   b on   c out
11 a is   b was   c were
12 a didn't   b won't   c wouldn't

✓ **Go online** to check your progress

G relative clauses: defining and non-defining   **V** compound nouns   **P** word stress

1 GRAMMAR relative clauses

a Complete the sentences with a relative pronoun. Where two answers are possible, write both pronouns.

1 What's the name of the city *where* you can see the Ponte Vecchio?

2 Apple is the company *which / that* makes the iPhone.

3 Who's the actor _____ wife died in a skiing accident?

4 The thing _____ my son wants most for his birthday is a bike.

5 Helen Sharman was the first British woman _____ went into space.

6 That's the restaurant _____ we celebrated my dad's 80th birthday.

7 Alexander Graham Bell is the man _____ invented the telephone.

8 What's the name of your friend _____ parents have a huge house in the country?

9 Mountain View, California, is the city _____ Google is based.

10 Amazon is the company _____ has the largest number of online sales in the world.

b In which sentence in **a** can you leave out the relative pronoun?

c Cross out the extra word in each of the sentences.

1 Those are the students who ~~they~~ won the competition.

2 Isn't he the actor who he played the role of Sherlock Holmes?

3 Why don't we stay in the hotel where we stayed there last year?

4 I always use the supermarket which it is closest to where I live.

5 She's the woman whose her daughter went to the same school as me.

6 What's the name of the shop where you bought your jacket there?

7 That's the computer that it isn't working.

8 This is the series I was telling you about it.

9 These are the boots I bought them last Saturday.

10 That's the woman whose car we bought it.

d Complete the sentences with a relative pronoun and the phrases from the list. You will need to leave out one of the words in each of the phrases.

~~he plays the part of Jon Snow in *Game of Thrones*~~
it is in the Himalayas
her husband is a Spanish footballer
the *Mona Lisa* can be seen there
it was opened in China in 2011
she helped hundreds of slaves to escape

1 Kit Harington, *who plays the part of Jon Snow in* Game of Thrones, was born in London.

2 The Louvre, _____, is in the centre of Paris.

3 Mount Everest, _____, is the world's highest mountain.

4 Jiaozhou Bay Bridge, _____, is the longest bridge in the world.

5 Shakira, _____, is originally from Colombia.

6 Harriet Tubman, _____, has been chosen to appear on the $20 note.

2 VOCABULARY compound nouns

a Complete the compound nouns.

1 *website*

2 s_____ b_____

3 h_____

4 m_____ st_____

5 tr_____ j_____

6 gr_____ fl_____

7 f_____ p_____

8 cl_____

9 d_____ l_____

b Match a word from **A** to a word from **B** to make compound nouns. Then complete the sentences.

A boarding ~~cash~~ cycle flat rush science sound speed top training

B camera course fiction floor hour lane ~~machine~~ mate school track

1 I need to get some money out of the *cash machine* on the way to the theatre.
2 They live on the _____, so they've got a great view over the city.
3 I love the _____ of the latest *Star Wars* film – I listen to it all the time.
4 My brother has gone on a _____ to learn about health and safety.
5 Do you get on well with your _____ or do you argue about paying the bills?
6 Pupils at a _____ only see their families during the holidays.
7 Cyclists should use the _____ to keep away from traffic.
8 Commuters usually travel to work during the _____.
9 All the drivers are slowing down because there's a _____ up ahead.
10 I quite like fantasy films, but my favourite genre is _____.

c Complete the word puzzle and find the missing compound noun.

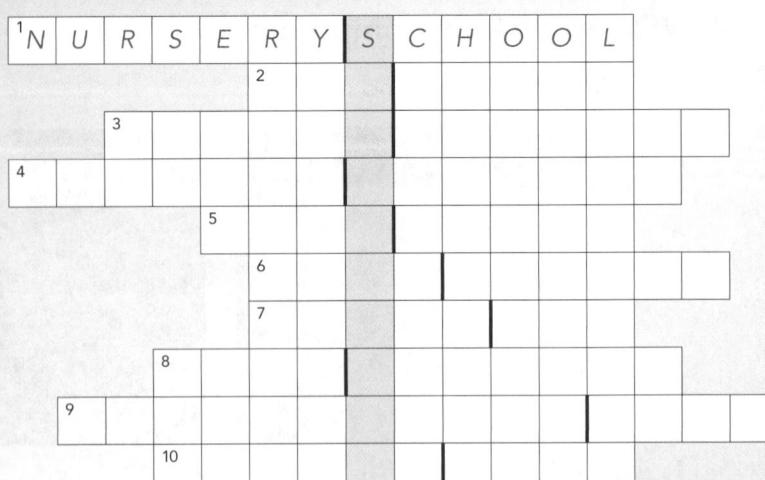

| ¹N | U | R | S | E | R | Y | | S | C | H | O | O | L |

(crossword grid with numbered clues 2–10)

1 A school for children aged from about two to five. (7, 6)

2 Water that comes through pipes and isn't sold in bottles. (3, 5)

3 A device for controlling equipment such as the TV from a distance. (6, 7)

4 Illusions created in a film by computer graphics, etc. (7, 7)

5 Repairs to streets and motorways. (4, 5)

6 The place where golf is played. (4, 6)

7 A product you can use for frying food or putting on salads. (5, 3)

8 You can send this to a friend if you don't want to call them. (4, 7)

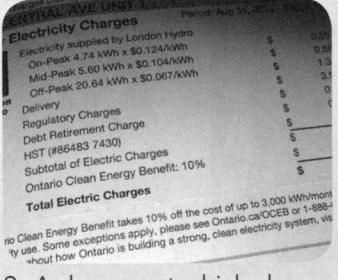

9 A document which shows how much you owe your energy company. (11, 4)

10 A place where people can play sports such a five-a-side football indoors. (6, 4)

3 PRONUNCIATION word stress

a Match 1–8 to the words in the list to make compound nouns.

board   court   fine   lights   ~~products~~   school   page   tone

1 clean|ing _products_
2 key _____
3 pro|file _____
4 par|king _____
5 ring _____
6 se|con|dary _____
7 te|nnis _____
8 tra|ffic _____

b 🔊10.1 Listen and check. Then listen again and repeat the words. Underline the stressed syllables.

Go online for more practice

G question tags **V** crime **P** intonation in question tags

1 VOCABULARY crime

a Order the letters to make words that complete the sentences.

1 A *murder* (urmrde) was committed last night.
2 _____ (tecesdetiv) are investigating the crime.
3 They're hoping to _____ (vesol) it as soon as possible.
4 The _____ (vticim) was the wife of a millionaire.
5 The main _____ (pecsusts) are the woman's husband, their son, and their driver.
6 _____ (neswitses) say they heard gun shots at around 10 p.m.
7 The police are convinced that the son is the _____ (dermurer).
8 They're currently looking for more _____ (denevice).
9 They need to be able to _____ (ovepr) that they've caught the right person.

b Complete the text with the words from **a**.

| NEWS | ENTERTAINMENT | TECH | LIFESTYLE | SPORT |

Murder investigation after body found next to country road

Police appeal after murder of man in Birmingham

¹*Detectives* are investigating a ²_____ in north Birmingham. The ³_____ was a 26-year-old man, whose body was found last night next to a country road. No ⁴_____ was found at the scene, and police are appealing to ⁵_____ who saw the man yesterday to help them with their enquiries. They believe that the ⁶_____ was someone known to the man. The main ⁷_____ are the man's flatmate, his girlfriend, and a neighbour. These people are currently being interviewed by police in an attempt to ⁸_____ the crime. A police spokesman said that they had a theory, but as yet they had been unable to ⁹_____ who had committed the crime.

2 GRAMMAR question tags

a (Circle) the correct words.

1 You live in Manchester, *(don't you) / aren't you*?
2 But you weren't born in Manchester, *weren't you / were you*?
3 You moved to Manchester when you were ten, *weren't you / didn't you*?
4 That means you've been living here for 20 years, *haven't you / have you*?
5 But you're emigrating to Canada next month, *won't you / aren't you*?
6 Your brother lives there, *doesn't he / does he*?
7 You've been in prison before, *aren't you / haven't you*?
8 I expect you'd like to call your lawyer now, *would you / wouldn't you*?

b Complete the question tags.

1 Adam's living with his parents, *isn't he*____?
2 You don't like dogs, _____?
3 It isn't difficult, _____?
4 Anthony works in London, _____?
5 They left yesterday, _____?
6 Kathy hasn't come home yet, _____?
7 I'm late, _____?
8 You'll see him tomorrow, _____?
9 I wouldn't like that film, _____?
10 You haven't had lunch yet, _____?

c Rewrite the sentences using question tags.

1 I think your sister's in my class.
   *Your sister's in my class, isn't she?*____
2 I'm sure you're younger than me.
   _____?
3 I have a feeling you don't like cheese.
   _____?
4 I heard your brother lives abroad.
   _____?
5 Is it right that you studied physics?
   _____?
6 I'm sure we've been here before.
   _____?
7 I'm sure you wouldn't do that.
   _____?
8 I'm hoping the flight won't be cancelled.
   _____?

3 PRONUNCIATION intonation in question tags

◉ 10.2 Listen and repeat the sentences. <u>C</u>opy the <u>rhythm</u>.

1 You **called** me **last night**, **didn't you**?
2 He's **older** than **you**, **isn't he**?
3 They **aren't coming tonight**, **are they**?
4 We've **missed** the last **bus**, **haven't we**?
5 She'll be **late**, **won't she**?
6 I **can't dance** very **well**, **can I**?
7 We **had** a **great holiday** in **Rio**, **didn't we**?
8 You've **never been** to the **opera before**, **have you**?
9 **That film** was **really boring**, **wasn't it**?

Go online for more practice   **Go online** to check your progress

6A

1 GRAMMAR

a 2 wrote
3 will be used
4 have been invited
5 are showing
6 is going to be dubbed
7 were filming
8 can be bought

b 2 has / 's been nominated
3 is / 's being filmed
4 had been transformed
5 were directed
6 was being built
7 will be / is going to be released
8 be shot

c 2 c, 3 b, 4 a, 5 c, 6 b, 7 b, 8 c, 9 b, 10 a

2 PRONUNCIATION

a 2 used, 3 waited, 4 written, 5 shot,
6 worn, 7 said, 8 won, 9 taken, 10 told

3 VOCABULARY

a 2 action film
3 science fiction film
4 drama
5 musical
6 thriller
7 historical film
8 horror film
9 war film
10 western
11 animation
12 rom-com

b 2 plot, 3 script, 4 audience, 5 review,
6 scene, 7 subtitles, 8 sequel,
9 soundtrack, 10 special effects,
11 extras, 12 cast, 13 critic, 14 set,
15 trailer

c 2 is set in
3 is based on
4 was shot
5 plays the part of
6 was dubbed into

6B

1 GRAMMAR

a 2 must, 3 might not, 4 could, 5 must,
6 can't

b 2 can't, 3 might, 4 must, 5 can't,
6 might not, 7 can't, 8 might

c 2 might have a meeting
3 can't be going to work today
4 might not like it
5 can't be tired already
6 must have an exam tomorrow
7 might not be working
8 might be driving home from work

2 VOCABULARY

a 2 neck, 3 back, 4 arms, 5 legs, 6 feet,
7 face, 8 nose, 9 chin, 10 stomach,
11 fingers, 12 knees

b 2 thumb, 3 tongue, 4 mouth, 5 lips,
6 hands, 7 teeth, 8 ears, 9 toes
The hidden word is 'shoulders'.

c 2 kick, 3 touch, 4 point, 5 smell, 6 smile,
7 nod, 8 clap, 9 bite, 10 whistle,
11 Throw, 12 taste

d 2 finger, 3 mouth, 4 tongue, 5 head,
6 eyes, 7 nose, 8 fingers / hand,
9 lips / mouth, 10 teeth, 11 hands

3 PRONUNCIATION

a 2 eyes, 3 tongue, 4 shoulders, 5 here,
6 fair

7A

1 VOCABULARY

a 2 geography
3 biology
4 literature
5 chemistry
6 history
7 information technology
8 mathematics

b 2 primary school
3 head
4 state school
5 degree
6 private school
7 term
8 boarding school
9 nursery school
10 students
11 secondary school

c 2 elementary school
3 grades
4 semesters
5 high school
6 twelfth grade
7 college

d 2 misbehaved
3 weren't allowed to
4 made
5 were punished
6 cheated
7 let
8 revised
9 took
10 passed
11 failed

2 PRONUNCIATION

a 2 pull, 3 cut, 4 subtitles

3 GRAMMAR

a 2 c, 3 b, 4 f, 5 a, 6 h, 7 d, 8 g

b 2 when, 3 before, 4 if, 5 after, 6 until

c 2 will / 'll be, hurry
3 will / 'll have, go out
4 won't wait, aren't
5 doesn't come, won't have
6 won't leave, finds
7 won't be able to, lend
8 gets, will / 'll call
9 won't start, is / 's
10 will / 'll play, practise

d Students' own answers

7B

1 GRAMMAR

a 2 g, 3 c, 4 a, 5 h, 6 b, 7 e, 8 f

b 2 would be, cleaned
3 wouldn't drive, didn't have
4 Would…carry on, won
5 would sleep, didn't drink
6 would lend, needed
7 wouldn't be, snowed
8 wasn't / weren't, could
9 Would…wake up, didn't set
10 had, wouldn't be

c 3 I'd call her
4 you don't hurry up
5 I'll tell him the news
6 he didn't love you
7 she'd be happier
8 they'll cancel the match
9 you didn't eat out every night
10 she doesn't feel better

2 PRONUNCIATION

a 2 grow, vegetables, garden
3 buy, cottage, had enough money
4 my house, wouldn't make, kitchen
bigger
5 wouldn't have, car, lived, city centre

c 3 D, 4 S, 5 S, 6 D, 7 S, 8 D

3 VOCABULARY

a 2 on, 3 on, 4 in, 5 on, 6 in

b Down: 2 top floor, 3 steps, 5 attic,
6 balcony, 7 entrance, 9 roof
Across: 2 terrace, 4 path, 6 basement,
8 ground floor, 10 gate, 11 chimney

c 2 b, 3 b, 4 c, 5 a, 6 a, 7 c, 8 b, 9 b, 10 b,
11 a, 12 a

Practical English

1 MAKING SUGGESTIONS

a 2 I'm not very keen on raw fish
3 That's a great idea
4 Why don't we try that new sushi
restaurant
5 What about having a Chinese
6 Where shall we go for lunch
7 We could get a cab to save time
8 How about going to an Italian
restaurant
9 Let's go there

b 2 Let's go there
3 How about going to an Italian
restaurant
4 Why don't we try that new sushi
restaurant
5 I'm not very keen on raw fish
6 what about having a Chinese
7 Why not
8 We could get a cab to save time
9 That's a great idea

2 VERB FORMS

2 watch, 3 meeting, 4 play, 5 going,
6 eat out

3 SOCIAL ENGLISH

2 why, 3 make, 4 off, 5 not, 6 word,
7 happen

Can you remember...? 1–7

1 GRAMMAR

1 's getting, 2 's been playing, 3 mustn't, 4 be able to, 5 have, 6 'd tell

2 VOCABULARY

1 sympathetic, 2 salary, 3 head, 4 coach, 5 plot, 6 shoulder

3 PRONUNCIATION

1 cinema, 2 cosy, 3 city, 4 stare, 5 fail

4 GRAMMAR & VOCABULARY

1 c, 2 a, 3 c, 4 b, 5 b, 6 a, 7 c, 8 b, 9 c, 10 b

8A

1 VOCABULARY

a 2 sacked, 3 resign, 4 applied, 5 shifts, 6 promoted, 7 redundant, 8 training course, 9 set up, 10 ran, 11 retire

b 2 at, part-time
3 in, temporary
4 in, full-time
5 for, unemployed
6 permanent, for
7 freelance, for

c 2 translator
3 employment
4 pharmacist
5 retirement
6 promotion
7 lawyer
8 scientist
9 resignation
10 application
11 farmer
12 qualifications

d 2 fired
3 work
4 run
5 fired
6 market
7 company
8 market
9 work
10 run

2 PRONUNCIATION

a 2 apply
3 employment
4 farmer
5 freelance
6 lawyer
7 musician
8 permanent
9 pharmacist
10 promotion
11 qualification
12 qualify
13 redundant
14 resignation
15 retire
16 retirement
17 scientist
18 temporary
19 translation
20 unemployed

3 GRAMMAR

a 2 a, 3 b, 4 c, 5 a, 6 b, 7 c, 8 a, 9 b, 10 a

b 3 asked me to wait
4 ✓
5 I promise not to laugh
6 ✓
7 went on studying
8 ✓
9 I don't mind staying in
10 ✓

c 2 talking
3 to tell
4 to turn off
5 not speaking
6 laugh
7 Being able to
8 not to charge

8B

1 GRAMMAR

a 2 it was
3 told me
4 she bought
5 might
6 if I could
7 had to
8 the dress suited me
9 I wanted
10 had forgotten

b 2 told, 3 said, 4 told, 5 told, 6 said

c 2 if I had / 'd seen his wallet, (that) I didn't know where it was
3 if her school shoes still fit her, me (that) they fit her perfectly
4 how much he had / 'd paid for his jacket, (that) it had been a bargain
5 where I was going the next day, her (that) I was meeting some friends
6 if he needed anything from the shop, (that) he wanted some chocolate
7 if we had / 'd enjoyed our stay, her (that) it had been very enjoyable
8 when I was going shopping, (that) I might go on Saturday

2 VOCABULARY

a 2 b, a, 3 a, b, 4 a, b, 5 b, a, 6 a, b, 7 b, a, 8 a, b

b 2 service
3 treatment
4 agreement
5 improvement
6 argument
7 valuation
8 achievement
9 choice
10 management
11 demonstration
12 sale
13 consideration
14 failure
15 temptation

c 2 payment
3 complaint
4 attachment
5 response
6 explanation
7 success
8 compensation

3 PRONUNCIATION

a 2 certain
3 said
4 railway
5 captain
6 brain

9A

1 GRAMMAR

a 2 would have
3 had
4 had
5 would / 've have
6 would / 'd have
7 had
8 had / 'd

b 2 would / 'd have arrived
3 hadn't booked
4 had / 'd checked
5 hadn't been
6 wouldn't have made
7 had / 'd known
8 wouldn't have invited
9 hadn't been
10 wouldn't have got

c 2 I hadn't passed my final exams
3 she would / 'd have got the job
4 we hadn't had lunch before we left
5 we would / 'd have played tennis
6 you had / 'd followed my directions
7 I would / 'd have won that game
8 he wouldn't have broken them

2 PRONUNCIATION

a 2 would have gone
3 would have bought
4 would have stayed
5 would have got
6 would have helped

3 VOCABULARY

a 3 fortunate, 4 unfortunate, 5 careful, 6 careless, 7 patient, 8 impatient, 9 lucky, 10 unlucky

b 2 impatiently, 3 carelessly, 4 Fortunately, 5 unlucky

c 3 possible, 4 impossible, 5, selfish, 6 unselfish, 7 useful, 8 useless, 9 suitable, 10 unsuitable, 13 possibly, 14 impossibly, 15 selfishly, 16 unselfishly, 17 usefully, 18 uselessly, 19 suitably, 20 unsuitably

d 2 selfishly, 3 useless, 4 successful, 5 unsuitably

e 2 impatient, 3 uncomfortable, 4 lucky, 5 desperately, 6 Unfortunately, 7 Luckily, 8 comfortable, 9 carefully

9B

1 VOCABULARY

a 2 printer, 3 speaker, 4 adaptor, 5 remote control, 6 socket, 7 charger, 8 switch, 9 plug, 10 USB cable, 11 memory stick, 11 router

b 2 memory stick, 3 charger, 4 printer, 5 USB cable, 6 keyboard, 7 remote

control, 8 adaptor, 9 speaker, 10 router,
11 plug, socket

c Down: 3 plug in, 4 switch off,
5 turn down, 6 update, 9 set
Across: 2 unplug, 4 switch on, 7 delete,
8 install

2 GRAMMAR

a 2 b, 3 b, c, 4 c, 5 a, b, c, 6 b, 7 b, 8 a,
9 c, 10 a, 11 a, 12 b

b 2 enough, too expensive / too much
3 a little, much
4 too many, enough
5 no, any
6 few, many

c 2 much money
3 any buses
4 very few people
5 old enough
6 very little / no work
7 too much / a lot of / lots of / loads of
furniture
8 no paper
9 a lot of / lots of / loads of traffic
10 too many / a lot of / lots of / loads of
children
11 a few / some phone calls
12 too small

3 PRONUNCIATION

a 2 updated it
3 turned it down
4 deleted it
5 plugged it in
6 switched it off
7 unplugged it
8 turned it up

c 2 although
3 through
4 laughed

Practical English

1 INDIRECT QUESTIONS

a 2 goes
3 I can
4 Lola is
5 comes
6 you're
7 the restaurant closes
8 you spoke to

b 2 what time it arrives
3 which stop the bus goes from
4 how much a one way ticket costs
5 if I need to change buses
6 how much discount I get with a
student card

c 2 Could you tell me how much a one
way ticket costs?
3 Can you tell me how much discount I
get with a student card?
4 I wonder if I need to change buses.
5 do you know what time it arrives?

3 SOCIAL ENGLISH

2 I guess, 3 Of course, 4 It's obvious,
5 What if, 6 either

Can you remember...? 1–9

1 GRAMMAR

1 have / 've known
2 didn't use to
3 might / may / could be
4 would / 'd walk
5 to tidy
6 had / 'd been

2 VOCABULARY

1 duck, 2 couple, 3 script, 4 degree, 5 gate,
6 apply for

3 PRONUNCIATION

1 course, 2 loan, 3 router, 4 floor, 5 nose

4 GRAMMAR & VOCABULARY

1 c, 2 a, 3 b, 4 a, 5 c, 6 c, 7 a, 8 a, 9 c, 10 a,
11 b, 12 c

10A

1 GRAMMAR

a 3 whose
4 that / which
5 who
6 where
7 who
8 whose
9 where
10 that / which

b sentence 4

c 2 he, 3 there, 4 it, 5 her, 6 there, 7 it,
8 it, 9 them, 10 it

d 2 where the *Mona Lisa* can be seen
3 which is in the Himalayas
4 which was opened in China in 2011
5 whose husband is a Spanish
footballer
6 who helped hundreds of slaves to
escape

2 VOCABULARY

a 2 seat belt
3 headphones
4 memory stick
5 traffic jam
6 ground floor
7 football pitch
8 classmates
9 desk lamp

b 2 top floor
3 soundtrack
4 training course
5 flatmate
6 boarding school
7 cycle lane
8 rush hour
9 speed camera
10 science fiction

c 2 tap water
3 remote control
4 special effects
5 road works
6 golf course
7 olive oil
8 text message
9 electricity bill
10 sports hall

The missing compound noun is
'speed limit'.

3 PRONUNCIATION

a 2 keyboard
3 profile page
4 parking fine
5 ringtone
6 secondary school
7 tennis court
8 traffic lights

b 1 <u>clea</u>ning, 2 <u>key</u>board, 3 <u>pro</u>file,
4 <u>par</u>king, 5 <u>ring</u>tone, 6 <u>sec</u>ondary,
7 <u>ten</u>nis, 8 <u>tra</u>ffic

10B

1 VOCABULARY

a 2 Detectives
3 solve
4 victim
5 suspects
6 Witnesses
7 murderer
8 evidence
9 prove

b 2 murder
3 victim
4 evidence
5 witnesses
6 murderer
7 suspects
8 solve
9 prove

2 GRAMMAR

a 2 were you
3 didn't you
4 haven't you
5 aren't you
6 doesn't he
7 haven't you
8 wouldn't you

b 2 do you, 3 is it, 4 doesn't he, 5 didn't
they, 6 has she, 7 aren't I, 8 won't you,
9 would I, 10 have you

c 2 You're younger than me, aren't you
3 You don't like cheese, do you
4 Your brother lives abroad, doesn't he
5 You studied physics, didn't you
6 We've been here before, haven't we
7 You wouldn't do that, would you
8 The flight won't be cancelled, will it

OXFORD
UNIVERSITY PRESS

Great Clarendon Street, Oxford, OX2 6DP,
United Kingdom

Oxford University Press is a department of the
University of Oxford. It furthers the University's
objective of excellence in research, scholarship,
and education by publishing worldwide. Oxford
is a registered trade mark of Oxford University
Press in the UK and in certain other countries

© Oxford University Press 2019

The moral rights of the author have been asserted

First published in 2019

2024

10 9 8 7 6 5

ISBN: 978 0 19 403575 0

Printed in China

This book is printed on paper from certified
and well-managed sources.

ACKNOWLEDGEMENTS

Back cover photograph: Oxford University Press building/David
Fisher

*The authors would like to thank all the teachers and students round the
world whose feedback has helped us to shape* English File.

The authors would also like to thank: all those at Oxford University
Press (both in Oxford and around the world) and the design
team who have contributed their skills and ideas to producing
this course.

*Finally very special thanks from Clive to Maria Angeles, Lucia, and Eric,
and from Christina to Cristina, for all their support and encouragement.
Christina would also like to thank her children Joaquin, Marco, and
Krysia for their constant inspiration.*

Student's Book

*The publisher and authors are very grateful to the following who have
provided personal stories and/or photographs*: Marianna Leivaditaki,
Jane Cadwallader, Dagmara Walkowicz, and Joe Kenyon.

*The publisher and authors would also like to thank the following for
their invaluable feedback on the materials*: Jane Hudson, Brian
Brennan, Isabel Orgillés Trol, Dolores Raventós, Paz Alonso,
Ana Ibáñez, Jose Requejo Sánchez, Philip Drury, Robert
Anderson, Maria Vanessa Ferroni, Cristina Cogollos, Lesley
Pouliaud, Abby Seddon, Magdalena Muszyńska, Dagmara Łata,
Sandy Millin, Sylwia Kossakowska-Pisarek, Ruth Valentová, Elif
Barbaros, Zahra Bilides, Polina Kuharenko, Gyula Kiss, Wagner
Roberto Silva dos Santos, Juliana Stucker, Sarah Giles, Wayne
Rimmer, Mowbray Bates

*The authors and publisher are grateful to those who have given
permission to reproduce the following extracts and adaptations of
copyright material*: p.130 'A Public Relations Disaster' adapted
from http://www.davecarrollmusic.com/songwriting/united-
breaks-guitars/. Reproduced by permission. p.86 Extract from
'A real Good Samaritan' 24 December 2010, www.bbc.co.uk/
news/magazine. p.93 Adapted from '25 Areas of Digital Clutter
to Minimize' by Joshua Becker, www.becomingminimalist.
com. Reproduced by permission of the author. p.80 Adapted
from 'Sales assistants: When 'Happy to help' becomes a
hindrance' by Jonathan Haynes, theguardian.com, 9 July 2010.
Copyright Guardian News & Media Ltd 2017. p.85 Adapted
from 'Look, but don't touch!', The Times, Body and Soul, 17
January 2009. The Times/News Syndication. Reproduced by
permission. p.70 '24 things you know if you still live with
your parents' by Vicky Chandler, originally published in
Metro: 10 February 2015. Reproduced by permission. p.91
Adapted from 'Help! I need a digital detox' by Anna Magee,
www.telegraph.co.uk, © Telegraph Media Group Limited,
2016. Reproduced by permission. p.72 Adapted from 'Welcome
to Handel & Hendrix in London', https://handelhendrix.org.
Reproduced by permission. p.82 Adapted from '11 of the
Best Customer Service Stories Ever' by Stacy Conradt, http://
mentalfloss.com. Reproduced by permission. p.112 Extract
from 'Who needs uni? How to be successful without a degree'
by Emily-Fleur Sizmur, www.express.co.uk. Reproduced by
permission of the author. p.130 Adapted from '24 Teary-
Eyed Stories You Must Read About the Touching Kindness of
Strangers' by Reader's Digest Editors, originally published
in RD.com. Copyright © 2016 by Trusted Media Brands, Inc.
Used by permission. All rights reserved. p.105 Adapted from
'The London Dungeon' www.thedungeons.com. Reproduced
by permission of Merlin Entertainments. p.88 Adapted from
'How to improve your luck and win the lottery twice (possibly)'
by Richard Wiseman, 2 April 2015, www.theguardian.com.
Copyright Guardian News & Media Ltd 2017. Reproduced by
permission. p.63 Adapted from 'I am not naturally magnetic':
can you learn how to be charismatic? by Colin Drury,
theguardian.com, 17 December 2016. Copyright Guardian
News & Media Ltd 2017. Reproduced by permission. p.102
'May and June' from *The Fever Tree and Other Stories* by Ruth
Rendell (© Ruth Rendell, 1993) published by Arrow is printed
by permission of United Agents (www.unitedagents.co.uk) on
behalf of Ruth Rendell and The Random House Group Limited
© 1982.

Sources: www.aol.com; www.bbc.co.uk;
www.dailymail.co.uk;www.devonlive.com;www.gradtouch.com;
www.huffingtonpost.co.uk; www.theguardian.com;
www.instagram.com; www.kenilworthweeklynews.co.uk;
http://mentalfloss.com; www.moneyadviceservice.org.uk;
www.pnas.org; www.reddit.com; www.thetimes.co.uk;
www.thewritersacademy.co.uk

*Although every effort has been made to trace and contact copyright
holders before publication, this has not been possible in some cases. We
apologize for any apparent infringement of copyright and if notified, the
publisher will be pleased to rectify any errors or omissions at the earliest
opportunity.*

Pronunciation chart artwork by: Ellis Nadler

Illustrations by: Peter Bull p.65; Sveta Dorosheva/Illustrationweb
pp.66, 88–89; Mark Duffin p.78; John Haslam pp.142, 143,
144, 145, 148, 150, 151; Joanna Kerr p.162; Laura Perez/Anna
Goodson p.76; Eva Tacheva/Anna Goodson p.92

Commissioned photography by: 87 (bread, paints), 109; Oxford
University Press video stills pp.63 (Style Doctors) 65,
83 (complaining), 85 (vox pops), 94, 95, 105 (vox pops)

*We would also like to thank the following for permission to
reproduce the following photographs*: 123RF pp.90 (7/Vyacheslav
Ryaschikov), (11/Jason Swalwell), (6/inbj), (13/scanrail); Aalto.
com p.99 (Aalto vase); Alamy pp.61 (girl on beach/James
Marchington/LatitudeStock), 68 (exam results/Chris Rout),
69 (Imagedoc), 70 (girl in river/Jacky Chapman/Photofusion
Picture Library), 72 (Jimi Hendrix/Pictorial Press Ltd), 86 (train/
John Morrison), 87 (biker/Jaen Stock/Westend61 GmbH),
90 (3/AKP Photos), 96 (Carrie Fisher/AF archive), 98 (Penguin
paperbacks/Granger, NYC./Granger Historical Picture Archive),
99 (St Paul's Cathedral/Keith Douglas), (Eames chair/V&A
Images), 101 (Walter Sickert/Paul Fearn), 102 (young girls/
Simon Robinson/Easy On The Eye), 110 (AF archive), 123 (Chris
Dorney), 160 (1/PBWPIX), (5/D.Hurst), 161 (Karen Spencer), (13/
Silas Manhood), (14/Lusoimages), (16/PhotoAlto), (17/Aflo Foto
Agency), 161 (Keith Morris), 162 (cottage/Elizabeth Whiting);
Image courtesy of Anglepoise p.98 (Angelepoise desk lamp);
Courtesy of Dr Jan Bondeson p.101 (Jan Bondeson), (Hendrik de
Jong; Camera Press p.98 (miniskirt/Mary Quant Collection.
Photo John Young); Dave Carroll, Singer-Songwriter and
Chief Storytelle, Big Break Break Enterprises Inc. p.83; Corbis
p.160 (4/13/Ocean); Getty Images pp.61 (3/Jam Media/CON), (4/
Stephen Maturen/AFP), 62 (B/Photodisc), 67 (Chinese teacher/
Asiaselects), (children/Photofusion/Universal Images Group),
68 (Jack Turner/Tom Werner/DigitalVision), 70 (washing up/
Peter Cade/Iconica), 71 (Marco/Ada Summer/Corbis/VCG/
Corbis), (Carlos/Juanmonino/E+), 78 (Deborah Meaden/David
M. Benett/Getty Images Entertainment), (Kelly Hoppen/
Tristan Fewings/Getty Images Entertainment), (Duncan
Bannatyne/Alex Moss/WireImage), (Peter Jones/Neale Haynes/
Contour By Getty Images), 85 (children/Alexander Manton),
96 (Prince/Kevin Winter), (Harper Lee/Chip Somodevilla/
Getty Images News), (Leonard Cohen/Jim Dyson/Getty Images
Entertainment), (Alan Rickman/Laura Cavanaugh/FilmMagic),
(Muhammad Ali/Allan Tannenbaum/Premium Archive), (David
Bowie/Terry O'Neill/Iconic Images), (Johan Cruyff/VI-Images/
Getty Images Sport), 98 (K2 phone box/track5), 99 (Captain
Scott/Hulton Deutsch/Corbis Historical), (Malala Yousafzai/
Jemal Countess/Getty Images Entertainment), 101 (Bruce
Robinson/Julian Broad/Contour by Getty Images), (Patricia
Cornwell/Heidi Gutman/Disney ABC Television Group),
(Michael Maybrick/Bob Thomas/Popperfoto), 102 (wedding/
George Marks), 103 (ring/Stanley K Patz), 107 (Ilan Omar/
Stephen Maturen/AFP), 110 (Kevin Winter), (Chip Somodevilla/
Getty Images News), (Jim Dyson/Getty Images Entertainment),
(Laura Cavanaugh/FilmMagic), (Allan Tannenbaum/Premium
Archive), (Terry O'Neill/Iconic Images), (VI-Images/Getty Images
Sport), 160 (2/Steve Wisbauer/Photodisc), (3/Jenna Woodward
Photography/Flickr Open), (6/Bill Varie/Corbis), (7/altrendo
images), (8/Philipp Nemenz/Lifesize), (10/Win Initiative), (15/
William Radcliffe/Science Faction), (19/Kris Timken/Digital
Vision), (20/The Image Bank), 162 (modern flat/Fotosearch);
Zoe Gower-Jones p.17; Copyright Guardian News & Media
Ltd 2017 pp.63 (Colin Drury and Danish Sheikh); Handel &
Hendrix in London p.73 (Justin Barton), 73 (Andy Paradise),
73 (Philip Reed); © Bernard Hare p.86; Paul Helm p.72 (Handel);
The London Dungeon p.105; Oxford University Press p.160 (9/
Masterfile), (11/BananaStock), (18/BananaStock); Cover of *The
Godfather* by Mario Puzo, published by William Heinemann.
Reproduced by permission of The Random House Group Ltd.
© 1969 p.99; Reuters Pictures p.56 (Nayak/Kamal Kishore),
(Lucy Nicholson); REX/Shutterstock pp.56 (Ripper Street set/
McPix Ltd), 60 (F/Dreamworks Animation/Kobal), 61 (1), 61 (2/
Imaginechina), 78 (Nick Jenkins/Jenny Goodall/Daily Mail),
96 (Zaha Hadid/Roger Askew), 100 (Jack the Ripper letter),
107 (Dominic McVey), 107 (Deshun Wang/Imaginechina), (Luz
Acosta/Lindsey Parnaby/Epa), 110 (Roger Askew), 121 (Von Der
Laage,Gladys Chai/action press), 159 (1/Birth 2004/New Line/
James Bridges), (2/The Sound of Music 1965/Twentieth Century
Fox), (3/Shrek 2001/Dreamworks LLC), (4/Apocalypse Now 1979/
Zoetrope/United Artists), (5/Blood Diamond 2006/Warner Bros./
Jaap Buitendijk), (6/Dracula Has Risen From the Grave 1968/
Hammer), (7/Paramount/Kobal), (8/Pale Rider 1985/Warner
Bros.), (9/Star Wars Episode V: The Empire Strikes Back 1980/
Lucasfilm/Twentieth Century Fox), (10/The Proposal 2009/
Touchstone Pictures), (11/Elizabeth:The Golden Age 2007/
Universal/Studio Canal/Working Title/Laurie Sparham), (12/I
Morgan Creek International J Farmer), (Florence Foster Jenkins/
Moviestore Collection); Shutterstock pp.59 (popcorn/Lepneva
Irina), 60 (A/Sergii Sobolevskyi), (B/blessings), (C/Ramon Espelt
Photography), (D/pixelheadphotodigitalskillet), (E/TorotheBull),
(G/Rawpixel.com), 62 (A/stockyimages), (C/ostill), 66 (exercise
book background/iunewind), 70 (man breakfast/SpeedKingz),
71 (Vivienne/Wayhome studio), (Andrea/auleena), 72 (sofa
icon/Farah Sadikhova), (cooker icon/Stock Vector), (bed icon/
vectorchef), 77 (hat/ekler), (stethoscope/VectorSun), 79 (dragon/
Elena Kazanskaya), 82 (iPad/r.nagy), 83 (guitar case/Chaiyapop
Bhumiwat), (United Airlines plane/Tupungato), 90 (1/Ruslan
Ivantsov), (8/Bohbeh), (2/Kelvin Wong), (9/Roman Arbuzov), (10/
Sonia Dubois), (4/vitec), (12/gorbelabda), (5/srzaitsev), 91 (phone
stacking/xtrekx), 98 (spring/neungpongsak), 99 (Apple logo/
mezzotint), 102 (torn paper/rangizzz), 120 (Florence/ariadna
de raadt), (Kusadasi/slava296), 160 (21/Denys Kurbatov), (22/
PachetoKZ); Emily-Fleur Sizmur p.68; Slappie Ltd p.78 (Slappie
watches); Tangle Teezer The Original p.78; © Anna Magee/
Telegraph Media Group Limited 2016 p.91 (Time to Log Off);
Trevellion Images p.100 (dark street); Courtesy of Dagmara
Walkowicz pp.58–59

Workbook

Alamy pp.44 (4/PBWPIX, 6/D. Hurst), 51 (flats/Isabelle
Plasschaert), 53 (Li Xin/Xinhua), 54 (mechanic/Image Source),
62 (river/Jeff Greenberg, alligator/James Schwabel), 63 (12),
66 (Robert Clayton), 68 (Kit Harington in *Game of Thrones*,
2012, *The Ghost of Harrenhal*/Photo 12, Shakira/dpa picture
alliance, Harriet Tubman/Science History Images), 70 (9/Jonny
White, 10/Russell Mills), 71 (police line/George Impey, field/
Newspix); Getty Images pp.40 (Steven Spielberg/Samir Hussein/
WireImage, poster/Jaws 1975/Universal History Archive/
UIG), 44 (3/William Radcliffe, 5/Juan Silva), 47 (corridor),
54 (retirement), 69 (7/Jason Hawkes); Oxford University Press
pp.44 (1, 7, 8, 9), 63 (1–11); Rex Shutterstock pp.42 (*The Revenant*
2015 poster/20th Century Fox/Regency Enterprises/Kobal,
The Revenant 2015 still/20th Century Fox/Regency Enterprises/
Kobal), 68 (Qingdao Jiaozhou Bay Bridge/KeystoneUSA-ZUMA);
Shutterstock pp.41, 44 (2), 45, 46, 47 (female student), 50 (all),
51 (cottage, house), 56, 57, 58, 59, 67, 68 (Louvre, Everest),
69 (1–6, 8, 9), 70 (1–8).

Illustrations by: John Haslam pp.43, 60, 61, 72; Roger Penwill
pp.48, 65; Laura Perez/Anna Goodson Illustration Agency p.44.